# On Gwendolyn Brooks

*Reliant Contemplation*

Edited by Stephen Caldwell Wright

*Ann Arbor*

THE UNIVERSITY OF MICHIGAN PRESS

for Henry and Nora

First paperback edition 2001
Copyright © by the University of Michigan 1996, 2001
All rights reserved
Published in the United States of America by
The University of Michigan Press
Manufactured in the United States of America
⊗ Printed on acid-free paper

2004   2003   2002   2001      4   3   2

*A CIP catalog record for this book is available from the British Library.*

Library of Congress Cataloging-in-Publication Data

On Gwendolyn Brooks : reliant contemplation / edited by Stephen
    Caldwell Wright.
        p.   cm.
    Includes bibliographical references (p.    ).
    ISBN 0-472-10423-3 (hard: alk. paper)
        1. Brooks, Gwendolyn, 1917-    .—Criticism and interpretation.
    2. Women and literature—United States—History—20th century.
    3. Afro-Americans in literature.
    PS3503.R7244Z78    1996
    811'.54—dc20                                              95-40036
                                                                   CIP

ISBN 0-472-08839-4 (pbk: alk. paper)

# Contents

# Preface

*On Gwendolyn Brooks* makes available selected reviews and essays on the works of the poet and novelist Gwendolyn Elizabeth Brooks, who received the Pulitzer Prize in 1950, became the poet laureate of Illinois in 1968, served as Consultant in Poetry to the Library of Congress 1985–86, and was selected by the National Endowment for the Humanities to deliver the 1994 Jefferson Lecture.

In the world of poetry, Gwendolyn Brooks is recognized as pioneer, teacher, benefactor, and hierophant and lauded for her intellectual prowess, her social consciousness, and her spiritual wealth. She knows the depth of the words of Langston Hughes, when he states, "We build our temples for tomorrow, strong as we know how, and we stand on top of the mountain, free within ourselves." This quote from "The Negro Artist and the Racial Mountain," printed in 1926, points to the resiliency and tenacity of Brooks who echoes, in her own words, "Do not be afraid of no."

The reviews and essays selected for *On Gwendolyn Brooks* begin to measure the literary life and the social, cultural, and political promptings in her work. As Brooks continues to assess the status of humanity, her achievements and her creativity continue to flourish; she, resisting encapsulation, continues her "blooming."

I wish to thank Gwendolyn Brooks, who entrusted to me this opportunity; Donald Hall, for his seasoned advice and probing insight; Kellie Taylor and Richard Young, the reference librarians at Seminole Community College, for their assistance; D. H. Melhem for her inspiration during the initial stages of this project and for writing *Gwendolyn Brooks: Poetry and the Heroic Voice,* which, like George E. Kent's *A Life of Gwendolyn Brooks,* served as an invaluable reference; Houston Baker, Henry Taylor, and Dan Jaffe for vital encouragement during critical stages of this undertaking; Shawna Cohen, James A. McFarley, Annye L. Refoe, Helen Tucker, Kitty Burnett, Princess Bowman, Diana S. Dillon, and Leslie Castle for their unfaltering support; LeAnn Fields for her spirited and sensitive prodding; and the staff at the University of Michigan Press for its assistance and expertise.

PART ONE   *Reviews*

PAUL ENGLE

# Chicago Can Take Pride in New, Young Voice in Poetry

The publication of *A Street in Bronzeville* is an exceptional event in the literary life of Chicago, for it is the first book of a solidly Chicago person. Miss Brooks attended Englewood High School and Wilson Junior College. I hope they know it and are proud. But it is also an event of national importance, for Miss Brooks is the first Negro poet to write wholly out of a deep and imaginative talent, without relying on the fact of color to draw sympathy and interest. Her poems would be finely lyrical and delightfully witty without the fact of color ever being mentioned. This is a remarkable thing which must be praised.

But the poems must be praised too, and in their own right. Here is the story of a day on the south side; it has the marvelous title of "The Sundays of Satin-Legs Smith," itself a poem. In it Miss Brooks shows that she has a vigorous mind of her own, and she uses it cunningly and with slow concentration of word. There are many poems about people, and they are all accurate, human, alert, moving. Miss Brooks goes through Chicago with her eyes wide open and the poems are wide open too, taking you right inside the reality observed. There are keen notes on our mortal frailty, such as the amorous gentleman who, seeing an attractive woman, "wonders as his stomach breaks up into fire and lights":

> How long it will be
> Before he can, with reasonably slight risk of rebuke,
> put his hand on her knee.

There are poems which bear the immediate sense of the personal life strongly lived out:

*Chicago Tribune Books*, 26 August 1945, 11. Permission granted by Hualing Nieh Engle.

It was quite a time for loving. It was midnight. It was May.
But in the crowding darkness not a word did they say.

There is the quick observation of the shame and sorrow behind the gay performance, as in "Queen of the Blues":

Mame was singing
At the Midnight club.
And the place was red
With blues.
She could shake her body
Across the floor.
For what did she have
To lose?

The biggest piece in the book is a sequence of poems about the soldier, called "Gay Chaps at the Bar." They are the most controlled, the most intense poems in the book. And finest of all, they can be read for what they are and not, as the publishers want us to believe, as Negro poems. For they should no more be called Negro poetry than the poems of Robert Frost should be called white poetry. They are handsome and real and genuine poems by a civilized American citizen. They are poems for all men who left warmth and a softness and quick hand and slow voice. They come out of the pages of the book, as Miss Brooks says in another connection, "like the tender struggle of a fan."

I hope that the people of Chicago, who generously support genuine midwestern writing, will find in Miss Brooks exactly the kind of young but permanent talent they are looking for. The finest praise that can be given the book is that it would be a superb volume of poetry in any year by any person of any color. This is the kind of writing we need in this time. I want to show you a final example from a poem in which a hunchback girl thinks of heaven:

My Father, it is surely a blue place
And straight. Right. Regular . . .
. . . . . . . . . . . . . . . . . . . . . .
I shall walk straightly through most proper halls
Proper myself, princess of properness.

This is the real thing. So is Miss Brooks.

# Review of *A Street in Bronzeville*

A first book by a young Negro who successfully crosses the vigorous folk poetry of her people with traditional forms. She writes with style, sincerity, and a minimum of sentimentality. Her city-folk poetry is particularly fresh.

*New Yorker,* 22 September 1945, 88.

J. SAUNDERS REDDING

# Cellini–Like Lyrics

If *A Street in Bronzeville* indicated that the author, Gwendolyn Brooks, possessed valuable poetic gifts, her second thin volume goes a long way towards proving them. *Annie Allen*—bad and detrusive title for such a book—is as artistically sure, as emotionally firm, and as esthetically complete as a silver figure by Cellini. Nor is the comparison so incongruous as it seems. The same liquid lyricism, momentarily held in delicate static poise, that informs a Cellini informs the pieces in Miss Brooks's new work.

No one can cavil at a poetic talent that expresses itself with intensity, with a richness and aptness of imagery and with glowing warmth.

> What shall I give my children? who are poor,
> Who are adjudged the leastwise of the land,
> Who are my sweetest lepers . . .

But when that talent devotes itself to setting forth an experience even more special and particularized than the usual poetic experience, then it puts itself under unnecessary strain. And this, I think, Miss Brooks has done in some of her pieces.

> Stand off, daughter of the dusk,
> And do not wince when bronzy lads
> Hurry to cream–yellow shining.
> It is plausible. The sun is a lode.
>
> True, there is silver under
> The veils of the darkness.
> But few care to dig in the night
> For the possible treasure of stars.

---

A review of *Annie Allen*, *Saturday Review of Literature*, 17 September 1949.

Who but another Negro can get the intimate feeling, the racially particular acceptance and rejection, and the oblique bitterness of this?

The question is whether Miss Brooks or any poet (now when so many people find modern poetry obscure and unrewarding) can afford to be a coterie poet. The question is, further, whether it is not this penchant for coterie stuff—the special allusions, the highly special feeling derived from an even more special experience—that has brought poetry from the most highly regarded form of communication to the least regarded. No one wants to read a psychological treatise or any treatise whatever, for that matter, in order to get at the true meaning of a poem.

It may be that I exaggerate this flaw in *Annie Allen*, for certainly it shows but seldom. But if I do, it is only by way of warning. I do not want to see Miss Brooks's fine talents dribble away in the obscure and the too oblique.

Though Miss Brooks's style seems naturally indirect, she is at her best when she assaults our senses directly. I wish there were room enough to quote the whole of "Manicure," for it is worth it (and so are others), but perhaps the last four lines will do:

> The glass eyes break. The red
> Fat moves and melts. Brows rise in lean surprise.
> Bosom awakes. Maybe, she says. She might.
> Well, possibly . . . Well, call at nine tonight.

When Miss Brooks succeeds as in "Manicure" and "The Anniad"—and she does more often succeed than fail—she is a glory to read and "a joy worth all thine enjoying."

ROLFE HUMPHRIES

# Verse Chronicle

*Annie Allen,* by Gwendolyn Brooks, both in form and content, in strength and weakness, resembles a good deal the author's first book, *A Street in Bronzeville.* Where the subject is the Negro people or the Negro person, Miss Brooks has gone considerably beyond some of the quaint and for-tourists-only self-consciousness that at times made one a little uncomfortable in reading her first book. Her weakness lies in streaks, as it were, of awkwardness, näiveté, when she seems to be carried away by the big word or the spectacular rhyme; when her ear, of a sudden, goes all to pieces. The first two sections of the present collection contain much more of this kind of work than does the third. Her strength consists of boldness, invention, a daring to experiment, a naturalness that does not scorn literature but absorbs it, exploits it, and through this absorption and exploitation comes out with a remark made in an entirely original way, not offhand so much as forthright. Miss Brooks, by now, must realize that the greatest danger to her progress lies in the risk of her being taken up; she needs to be both very inquisitive about and very remorseless to her weaker side.

This article is reprinted from *The Nation* magazine. 24 September 1949. Copyright 1949 The Nation Company, Inc.

# Still Remarkable

*A Street in Bronzeville,* published in 1945, announced Miss Brooks's insight into the Negro dilemma in the Northern urban milieu. She has allowed herself in this new volume a good deal of experimentation in language, not all of which comes off. Her sense of form, which is basic, is still remarkable, and she can pull a sonnet as tight as a bowstring—a loaded bowstring, at that.

Review of *Annie Allen, New Yorker,* 17 December 1949, 130.

STANLEY KUNITZ

# Bronze by Gold

One of the things that the eponymous heroine of Gwendolyn Brooks's collection of poems tries to tell her mother is how much "just a deep and human look" means to her. The work of this young Chicago poet never fails to be warmly and generously human. In a surly and distempered age one is genuinely grateful to Miss Brooks for the lively and attractive spirit that sallies forth from her poems. In contrast to most of her contemporaries, she is neither ridden by anxiety nor self-consumed with guilt. There is in her work a becoming modesty. Though the materials of her art are largely derived from the conditions of life in a Negro urban milieu, she uses these incendiary materials naturally for their intrinsic value without straining for shock or for depth without pretending to speak for a people. In reading this second volume by the author of *A Street in Bronzeville* I have been impressed by how little of the energy that should go into the building of the work has been diverted to the defense of the life.

Like many second books, this is an uneven one. In his first book, as a rule, the poet exults in his discovery that he can fly; in his second book he tests his speed and his range and possibly even begins his examination of the theory of flight. I should suppose that "the birth in a narrow room" represents Miss Brooks in her most characteristic vein, or at least in the vein where what one identifies as her personality seems to express itself authentically as the genius of the form, to be communicated as a configuration of the verse:

> Weeps out of western country something new.
> Blurred and stupendous. Wanted and unplanned.
> Winks. Twines, and weakly winks
> Upon the milk-glass fruit bowl, iron pot,
> The bashful china child tipping forever
> Yellow apron and spilling pretty cherries.

Review of *Annie Allen*, *Poetry*, April 1950:52–56. Copyright 1950 by The Modern Poetry Association. Reprinted by permission of the Editor of *Poetry*.

Now, weeks and years will go before she thinks
"How pinchy is my room! how can I breathe!
I am not anything and I have got
Not anything, or anything to do!"—
But prances nevertheless with gods and fairies
Blithely about the pump and then beneath
The elms and grapevines, then in darling endeavor
By privy foyer, where the screenings stand
And where the bugs buzz by in private cars
Across old peach cans and old jelly jars.

The effect here is one of technical assurance, combined with freshness and spontaneity. The imagery, recaptured out of the world of childhood, has a particularized intensity, an almost painful luminosity of individuation, which is enhanced by devices of syntax proper to a design of separatedness. In this context the wryly humorous adjective "pinchy" is a little masterpiece all by itself. At the same time the poem is deftly inwoven, as by the series of fruit images extending to the ironic artifice of the last line and, even more subtly, by the set of verbal dissolves (weeps, blurred, unplanned, winks . . . weakly winks, milk-glass) that anticipates and counterpoints the eventually achieved clarity of focus. My only dissatisfaction is with the awkward locution, "I have got not anything," and, in the thirteenth line, with the adjective "darling," which seems to me totally out of key.

In some of her poems Miss Brooks confuses simplicity with näiveté. Whenever she is self-consciously naive, as in her ballads, her sentimental lyrics of the "bronze girl," she writes badly. If there be virtues in the stereotypes of "my own sweet good" I am unable to say where:

"Not needing, really, my own sweet good,
To dimple you every day,
For knowing you roam like a gold half-god
And your golden promise was gay.

"Somewhere, you put on your overcoat,
And the others mind what you say
Ill-knowing your route rides to me, roundabout.
For promise so golden and gay . . ."

Furthermore, I do not believe that Miss Brooks should be encouraged to pursue her cultivation of early Millay inflection:

By all things planetary, sweet, I swear
Those hands may not possess these hands again
Until I get me gloves of ice to wear.
Because you are the headiest of men!

In other poems Miss Brooks apostrophizes, "Oh mad bacchana-
lian lass"; recommends taking "such rubies as ye list"; proclaims
"we two are worshippers of life," etc. The faults are not faults of
incapacity or pretension: what they demonstrate at this stage is an
uncertainty of taste and of direction. Another kind of uncertainty
appears in her poems that touch more or less directly on problems
of caste and prejudice, wherein one senses a contest between deco-
rum and indignation for the possession of her voice:

They get to Benvenuti's. There are booths
To hide in while observing tropical truths
About this—dusky folk, so clamorous!
So colorfully incorrect,
So amorous,
So flatly brave!
Boothed-in, one can detect,
Dissect.

Miss Brooks is particularly at home in the sonnet, where the
tightness of the form forces her to consolidate her energies and to
make a disciplined organization of her attitudes and feelings. In
the first of a sequence of five related sonnets entitled "the chil-
dren of the poor" she writes with mature authority:

People who have no children can be hard:
Attain a mail of ice and insolence:
Need not pause in the fire, and in no sense
Hesitate in the hurricane to guard.
And when wide world is bitten and bewarred
They perish purely, waving their spirits hence
Without a trace of grace or of offense
To laugh or fail, diffident, wonder-starred.
While through a throttling dark we others hear
The little lifting helplessness, the queer
Whimper-whine; whose unridiculous
Lost softness softly makes a trap for us.
And makes a curse. And makes a sugar of
The malocclusions, the inconditions of love.

One might question "wonder-starred," "whimper-whine," and the redundant "softly," but undeniably the poem as a whole has nobility and force with certain extraordinary developments as in the fifth and final lines.

And yet there is better still. If only a single poem could be saved out of this book, I should speak up for the one entitled (from a witty line by Edward Young) "pygmies are pygmies still, though percht on Alps":

> But can see better there, and laughing there
> Pity the giants wallowing on the plain.
> Giants who bleat and chafe in their small grass,
> Seldom to spread the palm; to spit; come clean.
>
> Pygmies expand in cold impossible air,
> Cry fie on giantshine, poor glory which
> Pounds breast-bone punily, screeches, and has
> Reached no Alps: or, knows no Alps to reach.

I should vote for this brief poem because of the exquisite rightness of its scale; because, knowing its own limits, it is cleanly and truly separated from the jungle of conception and sensibility that constitutes the not-poem; because the imagery is sharp, the rhythm supple, the word-choice and word-play agreeably inventive; because the small and sequent pleasures of the verse are continually linked and at the last resolved, made one, and magnified. The concluding line is obviously triumphant in its massive concentration; among the other details that please me are the effective manipulation of the off-rhyme, the wallowing and bleating of the giants, the teasing ambiguity of "come clean"; the magical connotations of "giantshine"; the explosive irony in context of the adverb "punily."

How right Gwendolyn Brooks can be, as in projecting the crystalline neatness of—"Pleasant custards sit behind / The white Venetian blind": or in arriving at the studied casualness of—"Chicken, she chided early, should not wait / Under the cranberries in after-sermon state. / Who had been beaking about the yard of late"; or in producing on occasion the flat, slapping image—"stupid, like a street / That beats into a dead end"; or in distilling her irony into—"We never did learn how / To find white in the Bible"; or in raising her voice without shrillness to the pitch of—"What shall I give my children? who are poor, / Who are adjudged the leastwise of the land, / Who are my sweetest lepers . . ."; or in achieving the beautiful and passionate rhetoric of the lines that close her book—"Rise. / Let us combine. There are no magics or elves / Or timely godmothers to guide us. We are lost, must / Wizard a track through our own screaming weed."

These are as many kinds of rightness, scattered though they be, as are tentatively possessed by any poet of her generation. To make the possession absolute and unique is the task that remains.

# From Poet to Novelist

Miss Brooks is a young Negro poet who won a Pulitzer Prize in 1949 [1950]. This book, her first try at fiction, is really not a novel but a series of sketches, each based on a significant moment or incident in the life of Maud Martha, a spunky, sophisticated Negro girl growing up in Chicago. It is through Maud Martha's eyes that we see her family and friends—among the latter a university student trying to act at ease with his new white companions, the Negro proprietress of a beauty shop blandly accepting the word "nigger" from a fat-headed saleswoman, and a little boy quietly taking care of himself while his mother is out at work all day. The author's impressionistic style—a hopeful piling up of small details to achieve a single effect—is adequate for dealing with a kind of conventional sensitivity, but while it seldom gets in the way, it is not quite sharp or firm enough to do justice to her remarkable gift for mimicry and her ability to turn unhappiness and anger into a joke.

Review of *Maud Martha*, *New Yorker*, 10 October 1953, 153.

HENRY F. WINSLOW

# Soft Meditations

There is every indication in *Maud Martha* that poetess Gwendo-
lyn Brooks is capable of well-rounded characterizations of which
her heroine Maud is a fine-spun, fractional specimen. For what
Miss Brooks presents in this slender volume are bright glimpses
of a world turning upon Maud's soft meditations, Writing with
the quiet charm and sparkling delicacy of tone which brought
Emily Dickinson's bird down the walk to drink a dew, Miss
Brooks has begat a kind of beauty upon ugliness by lighting up
the humanity of her creation against the background of a Chi-
cago slum area:

> . . . It was August, and Thirty-fourth Street was all in
> bloom. The blooms, in their undershirts, sun-dresses and dia-
> pers, were hanging over porches and fence stiles and strollers,
> and were even bringing chairs out to the rims of sidewalks.

Maud has not accepted herself with that unconscious assur-
ance which makes her male counterpart, Jesse Simple, so articu-
late in his easy living with hard conditions. She finds herself too
often wishing to be what her husband, Paul, absorbed as he is in
surface values, believes he wants her to be. For all practical pur-
poses, this is as it should be, for what the author is dealing with
from the inside of her creation are those very human hopes
which grasp straw values in reaching very hungrily for real ones.
In all this, Miss Brooks maintains a kind of subtle, close-lipped
control over her style which so heightens its rich suggestiveness
that one is led to believe he understands more for being told less.

But the glory of *Maud Martha* is that in it we meet people
whom we know (and whose problems we know too well): such
as David McKemster, who finds himself caught up in the signifi-
cance of Parrington's *Main Currents* before he has caught up with
the reading of it. True, Miss Brooks strokes her canvas lightly,
but simultaneously, she rings a bell every time, and quite clearly.

---

Review of *Maud Martha*, *The Crisis*, February 1954, 114. Copyright 1954.

NICK AARON FORD

# From "Battle of the Books"

There is one book of poems among this year's harvest, Gwen-
dolyn Brooks's *The Bean Eaters*. Although it does not seem
worthy of a Pulitzer Prize winner, several individual pieces
offer delight and intellectual stimulation. It is more akin to
*A Street in Bronzeville* than to *Annie Allen* and consequently
touches more chords that vibrate with sincerity and humanity
than is true of the latter. More than half of the thirty-six poems
deal with experiences that are characteristically Negro, and most
of the remainder are concerned with the poor and the underprivi-
leged of the urban community.

Some of the poems have long, strange titles such as "A
Bronzeville Mother Loiters in Mississippi. Meanwhile, a Missis-
sippi Mother Burns Bacon" and "For Clarice It Is Terrible Be-
cause with This He Takes Away All the Popular Songs and the
Moonlights and Still Night Hushes and the Movies with Star-
eyed Girls and Simpering Males," the latter poem consisting of
only eleven short lines. But, despite the titles, the pedantry and
obscurity which marred her prize-winning *Annie Allen* do not
appear. The title poem, "The Bean Eaters," is one of the best. It
pictures a very old couple:

> Two who have lived their day,
> But keep on putting on their clothes
> And putting things away.

In "Callie Ford" the retreat where two lovers go to be alone is
described in the following terms:

> We'll go where trees leap up out of hills
> And flowers are not planned.

Review of *The Bean Eaters, Phylon:* from"Battle of the Books: A Critical Survey
of Significant Books by and about Negroes Published in 1960," copyright 1961
by Clark Atlanta University, Atlanta, Georgia. Reprinted with permission.

Of a visit to a beach in Buffalo, the poet says,

> You said, "Now take your shoes off," while what played
> Was not the back-town boogie but a green
> Wet musicstuff, above the wide and clean
> Sand, and my hand laughed.
> Toes urged the slab to amber foam.
>
> And I was hurt by cider in the air
> And what the lake-wash did was dizzying.

In other poems she talks about the death of Emmett Till, the school situation in Little Rock, a Negro woman in domestic service, society ladies bringing charity to the slums, and the dilemma of a Negro man of the middle class.

To her credit, Miss Brooks has exhibited a strong sense of irony and paradox in these poems. Her imagery is usually fresh and striking, and she avoids every semblance of sentimentality. But there are shortcomings. If she was trying to exemplify T. S. Eliot's philosophy that poetry is an escape from emotions, she has succeeded admirably. There is little warmth in these verses, little that involves the reader by forcing upon him a compelling sense of concern for outcomes. In too many instances, the reader reaches the contrived end of dilemmas with no greater response than the relieved sigh: so what? There is too little that is deeply satisfying emotionally or intellectually. Possibly the lack of a greater concern for metered argument might account for part of this deficiency. But the most probable cause lies in the poet's philosophy of the nature and function of poetry for our time.

HARVEY CURTIS WEBSTER

# Pity the Giants

In times as troubled as ours what sensitive writer can avoid a certain obsession with contemporary ills that may be temporary? Gwendolyn Brooks, from her very good *A Street in Bronzeville,* through her nearly as good *Annie Allen,* to her better *The Bean Eaters,* has never denied her engagement in the contemporary situation or been overobsessed by it. In her engagement she resembles Langston Hughes, Countee Cullen and Margaret Walker, to name the other Negro poets I know best. In her ability to see through the temporal, she equals Richard Wright, James Baldwin and Ralph Ellison, writers of fiction who accept Negro-ness as prizeable differentiation and a dilemma, [and] include it to transcend it. Of course she writes of Emmett Till, of Little Rock, of Dorie Miller, of a white maid disgusted to see her child embrace the Negro maid. Of course, she uses (less frequently and less successfully than Langston Hughes) blues rhythms, writes of the blessing-curse, the accident of color. Like all good writers, she acknowledges Now by vivifying it, accepts it, accepts herself and the distinguishing background that is part of her distinction. But she refuses to let Negro-ness limit her humanity. She does not "marvel at this curious thing: / to make a poet black, and bid him sing." Gwendolyn Brooks accepts to transcend.

To me, now, her poems about the Negro dilemma today seem her best because they help me and others to identify as we must. Excluding the trivial verse that emphasizes Now or color too much ("patent leather" and "the battle" in her first volume; "downtown vaudeville" and "old laughter" in *Annie Allen;* "My Little 'Bout-town Gal" and "For Clarice . . ." in *The Bean Eaters*), her bitter and sympathetic poems make the Negro a problem in the heart of every American. Her best social poems yet are in *The Bean Eaters.* "A Bronzeville Mother Loiters in

---

Review of *The Bean Eaters, Annie Allen,* and *A Street in Bronzeville.* This article is reprinted from *The Nation* magazine, 1 September 1962. Copyright 1962, The Nation Company, Inc.

Mississippi. Meanwhile, a Mississippi Mother Burns Bacon" is notable because it is written from the point of view of the white woman married to a man who thinks with pride of the killing of Emmett Till. "Mrs. Smith," serious light verse about Mrs. Small's spilling of coffee on the white insurance collector, is as good. So are "The *Chicago Defender* Sends a Man to Little Rock," "The Ballad of Rudolph Reed" (perhaps her best in this mode) and "Bronzeville Woman in a Red Hat."

Yet these poems, necessary for Gwendolyn Brooks to write and for us to read, are not really the best. Negro-ness, the contemporary situation, Miss Brooks's individuality, mastered craft, and foreverness coalesce in her best poems. "Race" is then an accident; the contemporary situation a source of detail; craft the skilled accomplice of matter; Miss Brooks everywoman differentiated. Increasingly, in each of her books these poems have appeared.

From *A Street in Bronzeville:*

Surely you stay my certain own, you stay
My you. All honest, lofty as a cloud.
Surely I could come now and find you high,
As mine as you ever were; should not be awed.
Surely your word would pop as insolent
As always: "Why, of course I love you, dear."
Your gaze, surely, ungauzed as I could want.
Your touches, that never were careful, what they were.
Surely—But I am very off from that.
From surely. From indeed. From the decent arrow
That was my clean naïveté and my faith.
This morning men deliver wounds and death
They will deliver death and wounds tomorrow.
And I doubt all. You. Or a violet.

From *Annie Allen:*

"pygmies are pygmies still, though percht on Alps"
—Edward Young

But can see better there, and laughing there
Pity the giants wallowing on the plain.
Giants who bleat and chafe in their small grass,
Seldom to spread the palm; to spit; come clean.

Pygmies expand in cold impossible air,
Cry fie on giantshine, poor glory which
Pounds breast-bone punily, screeches and has
Reached no Alps: or, knows no Alps to reach.

From *The Bean Eaters:*

A LOVELY LOVE

Let it be alleys. Let it be a hall
Whose janitor javelins epithet and thought
To cheapen hyacinth darkness that we sought
And played we found, rot, make the petals fall.
Let it be stairways, and a splintery box
Where you have thrown me, scraped me with your kiss,
Have honed me, have released me after this
Cavern kindness, smiled away our shocks.
That is the birthright of our lovely love
In swaddling clothes. Not like that Other one.
Not lit by any fondling star above.
Not found by any wise men, either. Run.
People are coming. They must not catch us here
Definitionless in this strict atmosphere.

In these poems, and in others I would like to quote, the ice-
berg beauty depends on what is not said. (And note the mastery
of the half-rhyme sonnet in the first, of the skilled opening of
each line with trochees followed by a basic iambic rhythm in the
second. Space permitting, it would be a pleasure to show how
expertly Gwendolyn Brooks commands differing kinds of son-
nets, of terza rima, of couplets, quatrains, free verse, even a
variant rhyme royal in "The Anniad," a diffuse, inferior poem
despite its technical excellence. It would be pleasant, too, to
show the gradual development of freedom, of her own spontane-
ity disciplined, culminating in the frequent free verse that is used
almost as often as regular forms in *The Bean Eaters.*)

Though, like any poet, she continues to print bad or only
adequate poems, *The Bean Eaters* contains her best work. I have
mentioned the excellent social poems. The poems that may last
longer are more and better: "In Honor of David Anderson
Brooks, My Father," a dignified eloquent elegy; "Jessie Mitch-
ell's Mother," the always war of generations, with "race" a
happy accidental increment; "The Lovers of the Poor," bitter

irony about "loathe-love largess"; "A Sunset of the City," spare brilliance about aging; "The Crazy Woman," Yeats absorbed; "A Lovely Love," the Virgin Mary's conception and Lillian's contrasted; "Leftist Orator in Washington Park Pleasantly Punishes the Gropers," a fine hortatory poem for those who believe gradualism rights everything: "In Emmanuel's Nightmare: Another Coming of Christ," a poem about the flaw of everyman that deserves comparison with Marianne Moore's "In Distrust of Merits." She is a very good poet, the only superlative I dare use in our time of misusage; compared not to other Negro poets or other women poets but to the best of modern poets, she ranks high.

LOUIS SIMPSON

# Taking the Poem by the Horns

Gwendolyn Brooks's *Selected Poems* contains some lively pictures of Negro life. I am not sure it is possible for a Negro to write well without making us aware he is a Negro; on the other hand, if being a Negro is the only subject, the writing is not important. Unfortunately, Miss Brooks too often says the obvious in the easiest way:

> Oh, warm is the waiting for joys, my dears!
> And it cannot be too long.
> Oh, pity the little poor chocolate lips
> That carry the bubble of song!

Contrast with this, "Jessie Mitchell's Mother," where Miss Brooks takes a harder look at a more complex scene—one that could not be represented on television or in the newspapers—the confrontation of a rather intellectual, black-skinned young girl and her lighter-skinned mother, who was a beauty in her day and given to the joys of the flesh. This writing moves beyond jazz and sociology; it is poetry. Miss Brooks must have had a devil of a time trying to write poetry in the United States, where there has been practically no Negro poetry worth talking about. She deserves to be praised for her seriousness and to be criticized into writing more poems on the order of her *The Bean Eaters*.

---

*New York Herald Tribune Book Week,* 27 October 1963, 27. Mr. Simpson writes (1993): "I am glad to see my review of Gwendolyn Brooks's *Selected Poems* reprinted because this gives me an opportunity to set the record straight. When I published this review, Ms. Brooks wrote to me and thanked me for it. In later years the review was quoted in an anthology of black writing, in a law school examination, and in other places, I believe, as an example of racism. I had said in my review that black writing that concentrated on being black was of limited interest. I did not mean to suggest that black writers should not speak of their blackness—only that they could write about other things as well."

BRUCE CUTLER

# A Long Reach, Strong Speech

Gwendolyn Brooks does the thing that so few poets anywhere can do, and that is to take a really spoken language and make it work for her. Most everyone writes a "writing" language, but in her work, there are all the familiar cadences and sounds of speech, right down to the bonehard rhetoric of the 1960s:

> We real cool. We
> Left school. We
>
> Lurk late. We
> Strike straight.

The same kind of spontaneity is important in her building a structure of imagery and metaphor in "Big Bessie throws her son into the street": it leads to statement, but the words seem neither arbitrary nor arty.

She is also one of the few poets who do not shy away from taking on topical subject matter and handling it with real comprehension, as in "The *Chicago Defender* Sends a Man to Little Rock":

> In Little Rock is baseball; Barcarolle.
> That hotness in July . . . the uniformed figures raw and implacable
> And not intellectual,
> Batting the hotness or clawing the suffering dust . . .

and there is a restrained, but meaningful irony she draws out of the squeeze between the urgency to remedy injustice, the fact of human complexity, and the need for news. In "Strong Men, Riding Horses," she plays deftly with a set of associations in a man's mind ("Lester after the Western"), working slowly from fragments of visual imagery to "nicks, slams, buttonholes"— and the disorientation of a Negro in a culture rigidly organized to

Review of *Selected Poems*, Poetry 103 (March 1964): 388–89.

exclude minorities from a meaningful place in its literature is here pinned down beautifully.

She has a very wide range of techniques that are really useful to her, ranging from a scalpel-like ability with aphoristic rhyme in "the parents":

> Pleasant custards sit behind
> The white Venetian blind

to a handling of imagery that makes full use of the senses of people driven to use them, cut off from everything except their enjoyment, as in "The Sundays of Satin-Legs Smith":

> . . . wonder-suits in yellow and in wine,
> Sarcastic green and zebra-striped cobalt.

I say that her technique is really useful to her because in addition there is visible a whole person behind her poems, and you always feel that she "writes committed." She is one of the very best poets.

WILLIAM STAFFORD

# Books That Look Out, Books
# That Look In

Coming to Gwendolyn Brooks, we find a writer avowedly a
spokesman, and in this sense a writer who "looks in" to a group
more than any of the earlier writers. Indulging a fancy to make a
point, one could say that Gwendolyn Brooks writes in the confi-
dence and momentum of a tradition that *intends to be* established.
Put in this way: there is a language that goes with current city
events, or there are languages that attempt to hold that existence
in human perspective that is local, indigenous. In Gwendolyn
Brooks's writings there is this determination to see what is, not
to opt for any falsity, and not to abandon the risk of individual
judgment either. The result is a special kind of complexity. Some-
times the poems are confusingly local in reference; they shimmer
with strong feelings that surface abruptly. But throughout there
is implied a steady view, an insight. Portions of the book come
through strong:

A garbageman is dignified
as any diplomat.
Big Bessie's feet hurt like nobody's business,
but she stands—bigly—under the unruly scrutiny, stands in the wild weed.

In the wild weed
she is a citizen,
and is a moment of highest quality; admirable.

It is lonesome, yes. For we are the last of the loud.
Nevertheless, live.

Conduct your blooming in the noise and whip of the whirlwind.

Review of *In the Mecca, Poetry* 113 (March 1969): 424. Copyright 1969 by The
Modern Poetry Association. Reprinted by permission of the Editor of *Poetry*.

M. L. ROSENTHAL

# *In the Mecca*

The real interest of Gwendolyn Brooks's new collection lies in her title piece, a long, essentially grim narrative poem that dominates the few slight, mainly topical poems that follow it. This tale of the murder of a little black girl in the Chicago ghetto ought to have the unrelenting directness of Crabbe's "Peter Grimes" but is overwrought with effects—alliterations, internal rhymes, whimsical and arch observations—that distract from its horror almost as if to conceal the wound at its center.

Perhaps a certain backing off from her overpowering subject is the whole answer to the puzzle of Miss Brooks's baroque method here. An appropriately remorseless, driving style would not only be hard for any poet to sustain but also call for an absolute toughmindedness. The setting is a sprawling tenement, once a garishly posh apartment "palace" but now, seventy years or more after it was built, a microcosm of the world of the Negro poor.

Sallie Smith, who works as servant, returns home to get supper for her large, fatherless family:

> Now Mrs. Sallie
> confers her bird-hat to her kitchen table,
> and sees her kitchen. It is bad, is bad,
> her eyes say, and My soft antagonist,
> her eyes say, and My headlong tax and mote,
> her eyes say, and My maniac default,
> my least light.
> "But all my lights are little!"
> Her denunciation
> slaps savagely not only this sick kitchen but
> Her Lord's annulment of the main event.

Sallie discovers that tiny Pepita is missing and the hunt, which involves some indifferent policemen, begins. At last the poem

*New York Times Book Review,* 2 March 1969, 15–16. Copyright © 1969 by The New York Times Company. Reprinted by permission.

moves ahead of the searchers and shows us the murdered child hidden under the cot of "Jamaican Edward."

On the way we are given portraits of good, hardworking people and sinister ones, of old folk with crazed wits, of flamboyant girls and nobly or madly dreaming young men—while, in her desire to express her love and compassion and understanding, the poet indulges herself in the forced, occasionally grotesque effects I have noted. Except in isolated passages, we are held off from the pain at the center almost as if the author were an old-fashioned local colorist commenting from a distance. Meanwhile, the plot is left to make its own way by the sheer force of its intrinsic elements.

Incidentally, The Mecca is a real building, but we are nowhere told that the story of Pepita is based on an actual incident. We must in any case find the poem's meaning in its own structure, and it is interesting that its closing focus is on a *foreign* black man as the murderer. It is as though, despite the familiar squalor and violence and terror—the ambience of rats, roaches, and poisoned fantasies fermenting in thwarted American souls—it would be unbearable to point up a native son's literal guilt as well. The displacement at this crucial point is like the stylistic distortions.

Nevertheless, the poem has the power of its materials and holds the imagination fixed on the horrid predicament of real Americans whose everyday world haunts the nation's conscience intolerably. Miss Brooks herself puts the matter succinctly at the beginning of another poem in this collection, "The Blackstone Rangers" (about the well-publicized Chicago gang of that name):

> Black, raw, ready.
> Sores in the city
> that do not want to heal.

ADDISON GAYLE, JR.

# Making Beauty from Racial Anxiety

The gypsy cab moved rapidly through Harlem traffic. In the passenger seat, Gwendolyn Brooks, official Poet Laureate of the state of Illinois, now Distinguished Visiting Professor of the Arts at the City College of New York, and I debated the importance of the sonnet form to black literature and life. Suddenly the cab swerved to avoid a collision with another car, evoking a shout from the Afro-American driver: "You old squat!" Miss Brooks laughed, turned to me and noted, "Now that's a great line, a *great* line!"

Now aged fifty-five and the mother of two children, Miss Brooks, who began to write "at the age of seven," is one of an eminent group of Post-Harlem Renaissance poets—among them Robert Hayden, Melvin B. Tolson, Margaret Danner, and Margaret Walker. Although she was born in Topeka, Kansas, most of her life has been spent in Chicago, where she has received awards and recognition accorded few of her American contemporaries. Before the publication of her first volume of poetry, *A Street in Bronzeville,* in 1945, she had won four Midwestern Poetry Workshop awards. In 1946, she was awarded two Guggenheim Fellowships and an American Academy of Arts and Letters Grant in Literature.* Four years later, she won the Pulitzer Prize for *Annie Allen,* and in 1971, she received her most cherished award, a volume of poetry and prose, edited and compiled by Afro-Americans, *To Gwen, with Love.*

In her long journey to world renown as a poet, mastery of form and technique and versatility with the sonnet have been indispensable. Yet, in *The World of Gwendolyn Brooks,* an anthology of her works from 1945 to 1968, she has written: "Not the pet bird of poets, the sweetest sonnet / shall straddle the whirlwind." I recalled the skill with which both she and Claude

---

Review of *The World of Gwendolyn Brooks, New York Times Book Review,* 2 January 1972. Copyright © 1972 by The New York Times Company. Reprinted by permission.
*In actuality, Brooks received Guggenheim Fellowships in 1946 and 1947.

McKay had handled this most Western of art forms, had managed to inject the black idiom into it, and I argued for its relevancy.

Sudden, explosive, filled with the energy of angry and joyous folk expression, her response to the cab driver's outburst swung the argument in her favor. To contain and retain the symbolic fury of such an idiomatic expression, to capture its vibrancy of tone and meaning, mandated forms different from those handed down to the Western mind from Petrarch and Shakespeare; it mandated a poetry that, in the Pulitzer Prize winner's words, said something meaningful to black people about their lives, spoke to Afro-Americans on the street corners and in colleges as well.

"I went with the young poets to a bar," she related. "They read their poetry. The response was tremendous. I want to be able to do that." Although her movement in this direction is not complete, more recent volumes of her work (such as *In the Mecca, Riot* and *Family Pictures*) evidence continual progression towards poetry based upon the precepts of her younger contemporaries.

The mutual concern and affection between Miss Brooks and the young black poets—demonstrated in *Jump Bad,* an anthology of their works edited by her, and in *To Gwen, with Love*—are based upon the fact that they are determined to create poetry that is more meaningful to black people, poetry that speaks with the fire and determination of the first Afro-American poets, the creators of "Negro" spirituals. Those poets ("unknown bards," as James Weldon Johnson called them) were the first voices of the whirlwind, their compositions as spontaneous and remarkable as those of the moderns. They created beauty out of the anxiety and sometimes the joy of the lives about them. They searched for new and distinctive forms, founding a poetry in which "there breathes a hope—a faith in the ultimate justice of things."

That poetry, derived from unique racial experiences, was modified in the works of the more form-oriented poets who followed—Phillis Wheatley, Jupiter Hammon and George Moses Horton. These poets sought not to create new forms, but to adapt old ones, to accept the models bequeathed to them by those whose experiences were dissimilar to their own. The result was poetry that moved away from its moorings (the people), that became artificial and stereotyped. Only occasionally, as in the works of the poets of the Harlem Renaissance (Sterling Brown, Langston Hughes and Jean Toomer), was the vigor of Negro spirituals duplicated.

After the Harlem Renaissance, the choice for Afro-American poets was either to write "academic" poetry—to reflect the Afro-American world through artificial devices, insincere language, falsified images and clichéd metaphors and symbols—or to bring poetry back to the people, which requires new symbols, images and metaphors.

*The World of Gwendolyn Brooks* represents a return to the spirit of the old tradition. Her poetry reveals the ancient in the guise of the modern, the dedicated Afro-American of humane sensibility in the guise of the philosopher-poet. ("God gave Noah the rainbow sign, no mo' water, but fire next time" sang the ancients. "This is the urgency," writes Miss Brooks. "Live! / and have your blooming in the noise of the whirlwind.") The four volumes of poetry and the fictional work *Maud Martha,* included here, reveal a firm control of technique and form and reflect the growth of the poet's awareness.

In *A Street in Bronzeville* (1945), Miss Brooks displays a talent for creating symbols, images and metaphors, both meaningful and beautiful, from the storehouse of the black experience. Picture Matthew Cole, an old, alienated man, living upon remembrances of things past, who smiles only at "Say, thoughts of a little boy licorice-full / Without a nickel for Sunday School." Share the experience of Satin-Legs Smith upon awakening to face a new day: "He sheds, with his pajamas, shabby days. / And his desertedness, his intricate fear, the / Postponed resentments and the prim precautions."

The same skill is seen in such poems as "Gay Chaps at the Bar," "when Mrs. Martin's Booker T," "kitchenette building" and "the mother"; sentiment is expressed with a technical virtuousity that comes close to excellence in such poems as "love note II: flags"; "I pull you down my foxhole, Do you mind? / You burn in bits of saucy color then. / I let you flutter out against the pained. / Volleys. / Against my power crumpled and wan."

There are poems devoted to the chaos and noise of the whirlwind: "Negro Hero," "The Ballad of Pearl May Lee" and "the white troops had their orders but the Negroes looked like men." In such poems the poet is concerned with the confusion which results when men are forced to accept images contrary to their actual experiences. "Negro Hero" relates the story of Dorie Miller, the black sailor-hero of the battle of Pearl Harbor, who "had to kick their law into their teeth in order to save them." "Their white gowned democracy was my fair lady. / With her knife lying cold, straight, in the softness of her sweet-flowing sleeve. / But for the sake of the dear smiling mouth and the stuttered promise I toyed with my life. / I threw back! / I would not remember / Entirely the knife."

The strength of this first volume lay in the poet's determination to point out the duplicity of the old images and symbols, to substitute new ones, to make the historically unimportant important, to give grandeur and humanity to the wretched of the earth: "He was born in Alabama. / He was bred in Illinois. / He was nothing but a / Plain black boy. / Swing low swing low sweet sweet chariot. / Nothing but a plain black boy."

The concern with creating new forms continues in the Pulitzer Prize-winning volume, *Annie Allen*. This collection of poems, though not grouped around a common theme, is, nevertheless, a commentary on the lives of those "whom the higher Gods forgot. / Whom the lower Gods berate." Such poems as "beauty shoppe," "Men of careful turns," "do not be afraid of no" and the sonnet series, "Children of the Poor," are models for the younger poets, metaphors of their strivings as concrete as that of the new birth in the opening lines of "the birth in a narrow room": "Weeps out of western country something new. / Blurred and stupendous. Wanted and unplanned."

In *Annie Allen,* the poet digs beneath the superficial, exploring deeper facets of the human soul: "True, there is silver under / The veils of the darkness. / But few care to dig in the night. / For the possible treasure of stars."

The form of *The World of Gwendolyn Brooks* is not marred by the inclusion of the fictional work, *Maud Martha,* for this novella—episodic in form, plotted around vignettes in the life of Maud, the heroine—is a narrative poem disguised as fiction, one in which poetic and fictional technique combine to present a portrait of a woman who, despite domestic conflict and tragedy, has one desire: "What she wanted was to donate to the world a good Maud Martha. That was the offering, the bit of art, that could not come from any other."

*A Street in Bronzeville, Annie Allen,* and *Maud Martha* are testimonials to a remarkable career, books in which the poet displays a control of language equalled by few of her contemporaries. In *The Bean Eaters* (1960) and *In the Mecca* (1968), another aspect of the poet's work however, emerges, and the words of Lerone Bennet become significant: "Gwendolyn Brooks was there—she heard the screams, felt the pains, saw the blood, laughed the laughs." She was there in the role of the passionate observer recording the historic trials and tribulations of a race and enriching them with her own deep-felt humanity.

When she portrays the wife of a child-murderer (in "A Bronzeville Mother Loiters in Mississippi. Meanwhile, a Mississippi Mother Burns Bacon") as one who loathes both the act of murder and her husband, or when she has the reporter in "The *Chicago Defender* Sends a Man to Little Rock" comment that "They are like people everywhere," or when she is only slightly satirical instead of meanly cutting in describing the self-important liberals who pose as "The Lovers of the Poor," she is writing, not out of näivité, but out of a highly refined and restrained sensibility.

Of all the poems from *The Bean Eaters,* "The Ballad of Rudolph Reed" is the most compelling. Here is the creation of a new folk hero, one who moves beyond the old stereotype, who chooses human life over property values. Rudolph Reed, who made his application for a home "in a street of bitter white," is moved to action only after one of the rocks "big as two fists" draws blood from Mabel, his wife: "He ran like a mad thing into the night. And the words in his mouth were stinking. / By the time he had hurt his first white man / He was no longer thinking."

The keen eye of the poet is equally penetrating in *In the Mecca.* In such poems as "The Wall" (the series dealing with "The Blackstone Rangers") and "The Second Sermon on the Warpland," her kinship with the poets of the tradition of the spirituals and their successors is evident. The title poem, "In the Mecca," provides the unifying theme for the anthology's two disparate sections, and serves as a metaphor for the poet's concern with the life of black people, which is revealed more explicitly in such subsequent volumes as *Riot* and *Family Pictures.* The characters in "In the Mecca" comprise a nation spiritually and physically locked behind doors of "yelling oak / or pine—many flowers start, choke, reach up, / want help, get it, do not get it, rally, bloom, or die on the wasting vine."

*The World of Gwendolyn Brooks* is not flawless; there are defects in each of the works included in this volume that are endemic to a poet who harbors an almost child-like fascination for words. Often Miss Brooks twists words into obscure and abstract patterns and is hypnotized by sound, and the rich, colorful images produced by word clusters. All too often, as in the case of Jean Toomer, her fascination leads her to break the unwritten pact between writer and reader—that at some point, the words must communicate; symbols, myths, and metaphors should not be obscured beyond all relationship to the reader's life and experiences. In some of the poems in this anthology—passages from "The Anniad," "Children of the Poor" or, for instance, from "A Lovely Love": "Let it be alleys. Let it be a hall / Whose janitor javelins epithet and thought / To cheapen hyacinth darkness that we sought / And played we found, rot, makes the petals fall"— there is a tendency towards obscurity and abstraction.

Such poems are few; the majority contain the muscular tone and energy that characterized the nuance of expression of those whose poetry first told "of Death and suffering and unvoiced longing towards a truer world, of misty wanderings and hidden ways." A modern equivalent of the artistic creations of the first black poets and a documentation of the hopes, aspirations and dreams of black people, *The World of Gwendolyn Brooks* is a tremendous achievement, one which reaffirms Gwendolyn Brooks's works as classics in our times.

ROBERT FARNSWORTH

# The World of Gwendolyn Brooks

Gwendolyn Brooks is a poet-reporter. She has a quick eye for the people and events of a black urban world pushed inward by white repression. It is a world of poverty, loyalty, violence, feverish glitter, but ultimately of strong prideful persistent humanity; such persistent humanity, in fact, that it is often an oppressive indifference of that other world which surrounds and threatens it.

But the poetry presents not just a world, but a world seen, a world seen by an articulate, strong, proud woman. *A Street in Bronzeville* opens with "the old-marrieds," a Millet-like portrait of an elderly couple sitting in silence "in the crowding darkness" at midnight, "a time for loving." It is austerely simple, but broodingly powerful. It matches the strong clear photograph of Gwendolyn Brooks on the back of the paper jacket.

Such austerity, however, is only one tone. Bronzeville is also a gaudy vibrant world seen with arch irony, but understanding, in "The Sundays of Satin-Legs Smith."

Events are given the resonance and depth of folk experience in "The Ballad of Pearl May Lee." And two sonnet sequences, "Gay Chaps at the Bar" and "the children of the poor," demonstrate extraordinary technical facility.

*A Street in Bronzeville* is the first of four books of poems along with the novel, *Maud Martha,* collected in *The World of Gwendolyn Brooks*. The poems span a period from 1945–1968, a period of remarkable change in mood and self-consciousness within the Afro-American world. The poems report and reflect this change.

The returning black World War II veteran and his frustration and disillusion with American racism play a strong part in the first book. *Annie Allen* focuses more personally on the life of black women. *The Bean Eaters* reflects the 1950s and the civil rights movement. And *In the Mecca* reflects the emerging black nationalism of the 1960s. But characteristically the timely themes

Review of *The World of Gwendolyn Brooks*, Johnson County Library *Bookmark* (Winter 1971–72): 5–8. With permission of the author.

and events are incorporated into poems which demonstrate that a stern respect for craft is a means of chastening the meaning of a poem, "The boiling of an egg is heavy."

Yet, there are poems in which good lines fail to redeem flaccid overgeneralization. "A Man of the Middle Class," for example, is a much too easy put-down. Since the narrator is a man of the middle class and we never move outside his world we expect a much more penetrating comment on that world than we get. And the more interesting, "The *Chicago Defender* Sends a Man to Little Rock," contains a similar but lesser fault. The biggest news from Little Rock—which can't be reported—is that the whites of Little Rock, "are like people everywhere." This sets the stage for a description of the violence of white racists and the concluding irony "The loveliest lynchee was our Lord." The narrator's attempt to represent and understand the ordinariness of white life in Little Rock leads to unconvincing generalization even as a preparation for the final sweeping irony.

On the other hand the poet does a devastating job with a similar situation in "A Bronzeville Mother Loiters in Mississippi. Meanwhile, a Mississippi Mother Burns Bacon." Here Gwendolyn Brooks enters into the white world with understanding and power. The indictment against that world becomes all the more compelling for the intimacy with which she deals with it.

When Miss Brooks gives herself to fiction the results are frequently dazzling. Her novel, *Maud Martha,* surprisingly enough, belongs with these four books of poems. The chapters of the novel are characteristically brief, the language and sense of incident is generally very spare and quick. Consider, for instance, the opening paragraph of a chapter nicely titled, *brotherly love:*

> Maud Martha was fighting with a chicken. The nasty, nasty mess. It had been given a bitter slit with the bread knife and the bread knife had been biting in that vomit-looking interior for almost five minutes without being able to detach certain resolute parts from the walls. The bread knife had it all to do, as Maud Martha had no intention of putting her hand in there. Another hack—another hack—STUFF! Splat in her eye. She leaped at the faucet.

David Ray once wrote of Gwendolyn Brooks, "She writes with the empty eye Keats commended; accepting life's flatness and rejecting its phony miracles, finding real ones where they are neglected and despised." I do not know whether Ray had in mind the long titled "For Clarice It Is Terrible Because with This He Takes Away All the Popular Songs and the Moonlights and Still Night Hushes and the Movies with Star-eyed Girls and Simpering Males," but it fits and will testify to the extraordinary vision this woman has:

> They were going to have so much fun in the summer.
> But winter has come to the edges of his regard.
> Not the lace-ice, but the bleak steep sorrow.
> Not the shy snow, not the impermanent icicles but the hard
> The cruel pack and snarl of the unloved cold.
>
> There is nowhere for her to go.
> There is no tenderness on whom she may frankly cry.
> There is no way to unlatch her face
> And show the gray shudder
> Of this hurt hour
> And the desert death of tomorrow.

ANNYE L. REFOE

# *Children Coming Home:*
# A Tribute to Survival

Gwendolyn Brooks celebrates survival in her latest poetry vol-
ume *Children Coming Home*. In it, she emphasizes the lack of
attention focused on children who endure the gross circum-
stances of their lives, oftentimes anonymously and without fan-
fare, but who survive. *Children Coming Home* focuses on the real-
life dilemmas that some children face on a day-to-day basis.
Brooks juxtaposes school lessons intended to give a child a wider
view of life with everyday lessons that prioritize survival over
well-roundedness. She initiates this juxtaposition with her pre-
lude "After School" in which she says: "Not all of the children
come home to cookies and cocoa." Through this verse, she pro-
vides the reader with the givens of various situations that are so
heinous many choose not to consider them. Brooks reminds the
readers to, in the words of Mari Evans, "speak the truth to the
people."

To emphasize her view of the overwhelming forces of every-
day life and to bring humanity to these situations, Brooks con-
nects situations to names. This technique rids Brooks's point of
view of the subjectivity that could cause readers to ignore these
poems with the pronouncements of the children—strong pro-
nouncements that cause the thinking reader to wince. As one
reads the problems of the children, the matter-of-fact manner
with which "they" tell their stories emphasizes the poignancy of
their experiences.

The uniqueness of this volume lies in the tone that each poem
assumes. The inhibitions that accompany adults are usually ab-
sent in children; therefore, what is stated and attributed to the
children is exactly what is on "their" minds without embellish-
ment or self-pity. Tinsel Marie, in "The Coora Flower," is able
to distinguish between what is real and necessary for survival

Review of *Children Coming Home*, *Revelry* 5 (Spring 1992): 17–21, by permission
of the author. Copyright 1992.

and what is unreal to her world. She states calmly that "My mother will be screaming in an almost dirty dress. The crack is gone." Tinsel Marie does not moan and groan about the unfairness of it all. She states the situation, and mentions, as if in passing, that a strange man will be at her house, and she must be careful. The image of a child having to think logically about illogical circumstances in order to survive is ludicrous, yet Tinsel Marie states it with a calm acceptance, a tone that becomes Brooks's signature within this volume.

Merle, in "Uncle Seagram," echoes this tone when he discusses his uncle, and the vile things his uncle has done to him. The power in this poem is present in the idea that before Merle's uncle is finished, he will have abused him sexually, and Merle will probably absorb that fear and pain in the same way he has absorbed the "foreplay" to the crime. Brooks uses the poem as a metaphor for the inability of a child to associate events, compile that knowledge, and make the correlation between the actions and the personal danger that threaten him. The very construction of "Uncle Seagram" mirrors the mental process of a five-year-old.

While Mary Frances in "Questions" and Sala in "In East Africa Sala Means Gentleness" seem to be dealing with different situations, essentially, each is trying to cope with the ugliness of her life through escaping. Each poem indicates that its child sees things very differently from the way things really are. Mary Frances calmly mentions her Mother's beatings in the same breath with the dirty dishes while Sala trips up on the daily grind of living. Both girls close their eyes to what is actually in front of them: and, instead, embrace a mental attitude that allows them to survive their circumstances. Mary Frances has been exposed to the abuse for such a long time that she associates it with the everyday occurrences of life, thus robbing it of its destructive power. Sala, on the other hand, can survive the catastrophic occurrences because it is the everyday living that causes her to need a means to escape.

As with the other children, Ulysses, who owns "Religion" and lives in a home with two parents and a daily and nightly ritual of "turning to God in prayer," denies the actual occurrences in his life. He pretends that everything is fine and that the religious fervor of his family's daily activities is the realness of his life. However, it is the in-between times that shout the moral and educational bankruptcy led by the lifestyles of the parents. Ulysses accepts his parents' behavior (i.e., adultery, homosexuality) seemingly very calmly; however, the parents' hypocritical stance is mimicked by Ulysses and his siblings.

That they carry weapons to school, consort with "the man who's cool at the playground gate," and reject the education that they need so desperately is clearly emulation of their parents' dishonest and inappropriate behavior. At the end of the day, Ulysses, his brothers, and sisters return home to assume the mask of prayer and singing "hallelujah." Again, Brooks uses the structure of her poem to illustrate the behavior of the subjects of the poem. The prayer stanzas contain the actions between, yet the prayers do not affect the actions nor do the actions affect the prayers.

Calvert, in "My Brothers Greet Me Every Afternoon," reiterates the need for men to be independent. His mother "gives" this independence to his brothers. Brooks allows us a glimpse into the chagrin men feel at having to be taken care of by someone for whom they should be caring. Calvert's brothers realize that their lives are not the way they planned, so they admonish their younger brother. With any luck at all, he will not "decorate the corner," but will, instead, become self-sufficient. This mention of his brothers on the corner captures the plight of many Black men—captures it in a way that stamps it with history and pain.

Fleur, in "Our White Mother Says We Are Black But Not Very," echoes, unintentionally and, probably, unknowingly, the historical view of Blackness—the idea that light skin, "good hair," and lots of money are the ideals of most successful Black people. Brooks implies through the listing of physical, social and economic characteristics that some believe that to be a good, acceptable Black person one must exhibit qualities that are close to appearing, behaving, and living as a middle-class white would. She does this in the lines: "We are black, but we have creamy skin"; "But at Home we'll wait for High Tea"; and "We live in the biggest house on our street / and will move Very Soon to a Special Neighborhood." Fleur's Mother has brainwashed her children into believing that they are "nice," whereas other children who do not look like them or act like them are not. Quietly, the children admit that they do not have many friends and that they do not like things from the real world. Again, Brooks softly points out that the myths about color, hair texture, houses, and choice of neighborhoods are meaningless in light of that which really matters—"children with dull hurt eyes."

Unlike Fleur, Novelle in "My Grandmother Is Waiting For Me To Come Home" presents a poignant portrait of finding the unexpected. She lives with her grandmother. Having very little materially, they live above a liquor store. Their diet is woefully inadequate, but they have each other, and that is a gracious plenty. Novelle appreciates her grandmother and her home, a realization seldom seen in small children. The love that Novelle receives there is long lasting, and the atmosphere fostered by the grandmother is happy. Brooks quietly informs the reader of Novelle's nurturing environment: "She is warm wide and long. / She laughs and she lingers." Simultaneously, Brooks, through Novelle's understated, positive assessment of her Grandmother, is careful not to overwhelm the reader with sentimentality while making a strong statement for the reader to realize that Novelle and her grandmother symbolize the significant aspects of living—aspects that should not be overlooked when assessing the positive sides of life.

Through Nora in "I'll Stay," Brooks salutes those people who remain in the neighborhoods given over to crime and poverty. She gently chides those who leave the city not trying to effect change and uses positive, stable (i.e., "Confident things stand and stay") images to convey the wonder and necessity that accompany staying in the urban cities and not abandoning them—not abandoning the children. All of the poems graphically describe situations that need to be resolved, and, through this last poem, Brooks gives hope that something can be done.

The children of *Children Coming Home* are not protagonists of the fictional Cleaver family. These children do not always have doting parents to greet them when they return from school, nor do they have the traditional family situation. To her credit, Brooks does not harp on the single-parent family or the treachery of life in the "ghetto." She is an equal opportunity poet; she clearly sees that neglect and abuse are alive and well in every economic, educational, and social stratum. Brooks's assessment of the burdens of childhood include family problems, neighborhood surroundings, physical and emotional need, and moral dilemmas. That the children come from varied and numerous cultural backgrounds is an added strength. Insuring balance, Brooks includes poems on love and nurturing, creativity, and personal value systems.

If there is a weakness in this volume it would have to be Gladys's poem "In The Persian Gulf." It does not have the clear message that the other poems of *Children Coming Home* have. Instead, its ambiguity surfaces and the message recedes. Its last line, "Then the Other Killers came," does not indicate that

Gladys's information comes from the teacher. That part of the construction is strong with Gladys's voice, but the end seems to be Brooks talking. The continuity that is so strong throughout the rest of the volume is less noticeable in this poem.

Brooks's arrangement of poems in *Children Coming Home* predisposes the reader to anticipate one gut-shattering, heart-wrenching tale after another. The reader may flinch in anticipation of the awful story about to accost some or all of his or her senses. This experience seemingly echoes the lack of hope to which many of the children of *Children Coming Home* could fall prey but do not. Instead, the novel love poems (i.e., "My Grandmother Is Waiting for Me to Come Home," and "I'll Stay") that reflect positive lives in spite of less than ideal circumstances, mirror the hope that whispers from the children. As in most of her poems, Brooks uses the construction and arrangement of the volume as imagery. She insists that her readers see and feel the truth—even if at their own pace.

PART TWO  *Essays*

JAMES N. JOHNSON

# Blacklisting Poets

No one pretends anymore—despite the street renaissance of the Beats and the Beatles, Bob Dylan and the Flower Children—that poetry can have any genuine popularity. Poetry in our time has become a cult art practiced and appreciated mainly in the academy, and its estrangement from the average educated man is now so complete that Randall Jarrell did not exaggerate much when he called the poet "a condemned man for whom the State will not even buy breakfast." But for some poets, the public dereliction goes even deeper—about the depth, as a matter of fact, of skin color.

Poet-critic Louis Simpson recently discovered, after reading the new collection of black poetry, *I Am the Darker Brother,* that there are Negro poets plainly superior to "the white poets who are much anthologized." Yet he also admits that until he picked up the book for review, he had "never read half the poets in it." This is understandable; there is almost nowhere he *could* have read them. The college paperback market of casebook studies abounds with second-string white writers, but you will thumb the pages in vain for a black name. The apartheid is yet more stinging in anthologies of American verse, which have of late become the quasi-official social registers for the status of poet.

Mr. Simpson explains all this by saying that there has not been a conspiracy to keep the black man out of poetry in America; there has been, rather, an indifference to him. This kind of distinction may seem clearsighted from a university office window, but on the ground it is merely gibberish and about as useful as saying that West Oakland's ghetto exists because of indifference, not design. Sooner or later we are going to have to act on the knowledge that wrongdoing in the arts is as real as wrongdoing in our social structure: In point of fact, nothing but the racism our media bosses and curriculum-makers are now scurrying to correct at this twelfth hour has prevented even those who

*Ramparts* 7, no. 9 (1968): 53–56.

know what a poem is from reading Paul Vesey, Robert Hayden, Langston Hughes, and most emphatically, Gwendolyn Brooks.

One cannot help but dwell on this inequity in light of Gwendolyn Brooks's new collection of poems, *In the Mecca*. No white poet of her quality is so undervalued, so unpardonably unread. She ought to be widely appreciated, at least as one of our most remarkable woman poets—certainly as important as the much-made-of Leonie Adams, Elizabeth Bishop or Denise Levertov—and possibly as an artist of higher caliber.

*In the Mecca* is Brooks's best collection since *A Street in Bronzeville*. Elegant and stringent, it asks more of itself than her *Annie Allen,* which won a Pulitzer Prize in 1950 (and which guaranteed her about as much lasting attention as the Academy Award did Jane Darwell). None of her surest qualities has diminished; she still, as Phyllis McGinley said, induces "almost unbearable excitement" through her uniquely detached compassion.

Auden said pleasure is not an infallible critical guide, but it is nonetheless the least fallible. And the poems of Miss Brooks give that outmoded, quenching pleasure that can make you read her again in place of poets you think more clever and ambitious. It is difficult these days to say simply that she moves the affections, stirs the heart. Instead, we use "scientific" language like "psychic tension" and "restored equilibrium." In an age when poetry is plunged into a cryptic absorption with the self, the large and simple emotions which Miss Brooks arouses seem almost beside the point. But they are still the means of implicating us in our own humanity, and this she does brilliantly. The most obvious reason is that she writes about people. It may not be alarmingly apparent yet, but most contemporary poets cannot do this. Regrettably, modern poetry as it exists in the official anthologies does not typically touch the workaday vein of human sympathy.

But to say this much may imply a kind of swooning tenderheartedness that does not exist in Gwendolyn Brooks's poems. She is very tough indeed, and to say that she finds at the core of a specific destitution the ordinary humanness common to all men does not mean she sells out. The ill-chosen selections from her work which appear in the few black anthologies do not suggest the fierce truth she has written about madams, whores, haters, broken children, fathers driven to murder, the solemn hungers and hellish silences of the ghetto. But her toughness goes further. It takes courage to claw up out of the self those costly insights most of us—black or white—spend our lives avoiding. It takes even greater courage to shape them into art.

It is her restraint which enables Miss Brooks to put a living character before you. She has written, for instance, the only successful poem on abortion I've read ("The Mother"). Its power as a poem is that it's neither tendentiously nor mawkishly "about" destruction of foetal life; rather, it is "about" a woman whose bare recollection of waste is also the measure of her life:

> Abortions will not let you forget.
> You remember the children you got that you did not get,
> The damp small pulps with a little or with no hair,
> The singers and workers that never handled the air.
> You will never neglect or beat
> Them, or silence or buy with a sweet.

Her "Sundays of Satin-Legs Smith" (of the major poems that rank below the best few, surely one of the most potent and skillfully wrought of our time, but one that has appeared in no major anthology) takes us through the desolate, vibrant Sunday of a stud. In its patience with the ignorance of the white, it is as severe and uncompromising as the savage revolutionary vision of LeRoi Jones. Another early poem, "Negro Hero," written before the end of World War II, recreates in one Dorie Miller's mind the dizzying, scathing ambivalence of what it means to become a black hero by saving the lives of your white enemies.

Miss Brooks has real range, but she writes mostly about the ghetto, the strident street of the 1960s in which violence—that is to say, murder—has become our society's way of demonstrating how it feels about itself. The long title poem of *In the Mecca* sets the brutal slaying of a child against the vast, indifferent misery of others trapped in Mayor Daley's slums. She does not excoriate; she simply observes, with quiet and merciless accuracy. If anything, her subject matter has become more "public" since the 1940s, the irony more edged. This new book has some sharply beautiful poems on the Blackstone Rangers, on civil rights leaders from H. Rap Brown to Martin Luther King, and a memorial to Medgar Evers, who "annoyed confetti and assorted / brands of businessmen's eyes."

But it is impossible through skimpy quotation to evoke the sinewy, tensile impact of her lines, for they achieve their effect in an essentially dramatic whole. She does not write what Dylan Thomas called "knock-me-down" lines, but she has one of the finest ears in contemporary verse. One can think of few poets who have so gracefully wrung out of the slow pacings of ordinary speech the intensity of authentic poetry. She keeps the inner ear alive in the plainest and fewest words, and I can imagine a poet like Roethke prizing this from *In the Mecca:*

> Mary is
> a rose in a whiskey glass.

For me this annealed balance of simplicity and sophistication is unique. It may have misled Miss Brooks's readers as it did those of a spiritual ancestor, Emily Dickinson. Like her, Gwendolyn Brooks sometimes walks on the edge of the ruefully sentimental, the merely womanish, but she gains a rich tension from not losing her footing, as in this marvelously complete lyric, "Old Mary":

> My last defense
> Is the present tense.
>
> It little hurts me now to know
> I shall not go
>
> Cathedral-hunting in Spain
> Nor cherrying in Michigan or Maine.

We speak of writers achieving "universality," but I'm not sure we understand very clearly what this term means. I'm certain that reviewers don't when they say—speaking of black authors—that so-and-so has "transcended" his Negritude, as if he had climbed out of his skin into a sacrosanct social club, assimilating white standards the way a ghetto dweller might put on a business suit. If "universality" has any meaning as applied to writers, it is that an experience—while being true to itself—must also be large enough to allow our entire humanity to enter it.

The excellence of Gwendolyn Brooks is that she is able to tell it like it is while speaking to the basic humanness in us. The loveliest poem in her book does just this. It is an austere, plain elegy to Malcolm X:

> He had the hawk-man's eyes.
> We gasped. We saw the maleness.
> The maleness raking out and making guttural the air
> and pushing us to walls.

And in a soft and fundamental hour
a sorcery devout and vertical
beguiled the world.

He opened us—
who was a key,

who was a man.

DAN JAFFE

# Gwendolyn Brooks: An Appreciation from the White Suburbs

Not long ago Gwendolyn Brooks appeared as part of an Afro-American week program at a small Midwestern university. She began her poetry reading by briefly discussing "black poetry." Her metaphors were earthy and appropriate. They suited the tone of the occasion, an occasion aimed at, among other things, infiltrating the academic atmosphere too long dominated by overtones of ivory rather than ebony.

Miss Brooks observed that we call the juice of oranges "orange juice" and the sauce from apples "apple sauce." It follows she said that we should call the poetry from black poets "black poetry."

Gwendolyn Brooks has dealt with the question of racial as well as personal identity from the start. She turned what for many was a psychological and practical liability, her blackness, into an asset. But she wrote about black Americans not only because she was one. Some black writers like Frank Yerby and Willard Motley have generally avoided confronting specifically black characters and situations in their work. Gwendolyn Brooks has never practiced this kind of aesthetic sublimation.

Nor has she practiced that other out so often opted for by writers with social conscience. She has not denied the demands of the Muse for the demands of the Cause. Her work reveals her dedication to craft, to the business of making. This is the test of any poet. American culture has tried for years to still the disquieting voice of the poet by insinuating that what he does has no real value. The culture seeks to undermine his faith in himself and thereby make him powerless. The black poet must find his position particularly difficult. Many of the militant voices that demand changes in the society curiously still regard the poet as a

From *The Black American Writer: volume 2 Poetry/Drama,* ed. C. W. E. Bigsby (Deland, Fla.: Everett/Edwards, 1969), 89–98. Reprinted with permission of the author.

dangerous inessential. Better to have men who will man barricades rather than typewriters. The best the writer can do is utilize his talents to help the cause. The attitude is essentially the same as the establishment's. The individual, non-predictable voice is distrusted. The man sincerely concerned with the social good may feel compelled to quit his personal vocation so that he may contribute to the movement. To do so would be to deny the significance of poetry. It would really be a surrender to the establishment point of view in another guise.

Gwendolyn Brooks has managed to balance these two weights magnificently. She has dealt with black experience honestly and expansively without becoming a sort of poetic pamphleteer. The designation "black poetry" seems to me an unfortunate one to attach to her work. The label veils her considerable achievement. I suspect the implications of the term are erroneous. The effects of such a term if widely accepted may be damaging. It may make it more difficult for other black poets to equal or improve upon Gwen Brooks's example.

True, the term "black poetry" may please those who seek to encourage black pride. Poetry is the oldest literary form, but somehow most people, even those who rarely read it, continue to regard it as the most cultivated as well as the most subversive, the most difficult as well as the most expressive, and the most sophisticated as well as the most basic form of linguistic expression. The label "black poetry" therefore calls attention to the achievement of black men.

There is of course a less insidious explanation for the label. Gwen Brooks may have had in mind the notion that poetry is the heightened expression of the personality. The poems of black poets one might presume would register the particularly "black" experiences of the poets. They would therefore be different from poems by white poets. Pride in the label "black poetry" probably implies that one of the obligations of black poets is to register those peculiar experiences that set them apart from whites.

On the surface the assumptions behind such leveling seem clearly justifiable, perhaps so self-evident they hardly require discussion. But they seem to me only dubious.

The designation "black poetry" arbitrarily ignores the nature of the creative act and the creative personality and the enormous difficulty of assessing either with certainty. It also ignores what I do not mean to be merely a facetious observation: The minority of poets is smaller and in some ways (certainly not all) more cohesive than the minority of blacks. It may be that LeRoi Jones and Robert Creeley have more in common than LeRoi Jones and Malcolm X. Nor will any protestations to the contrary by Jones alter this real possibility.

The label "black poetry" suggests that the body of poetry by black poets has certain common characteristics and that these characteristics give the poetry its literary value. If it has no *literary* value we can hardly consider it poetry. Nor can we anticipate that it will have any other lasting value.

Poets of any kind are linked by common concerns despite their differences. Foremost is the concern with language and rhythm. In addition even the most subjective poet must have imagination. This is really the capacity to put oneself into situations not actual, into skins not his own, into circumstances created and defined by emotions generated in the world of form rather than in the world of flesh. The real world is his raw material. He remakes it in his own image.

The language the poet develops emanates from the self as well as the world. It expresses his uniqueness and his magical ability to perceive in a way different from all others. The paradox is that poets are committed to step outside of themselves in order to find the special within themselves. The label "Black poetry" ignores Gwen Brooks's ability to speak as a hunchbacked girl, a male preacher, a white spokesman, in varying voices all clearly her own. It ignores Robert Frost's suggestion that the purpose of any poem is to be as different from any other poem as possible. And it forgets that though Gwen Brooks learns from Langston Hughes, she also learns from T. S. Eliot; and that she must be more than a replica of either or both.

Certainly ghetto experience has influenced the character of Gwen Brooks's poems. Some will certainly propose that she writes as a black spokesman. But this is half truth. How she sees and responds reflects her training as a poet as well as the circumstances of her life. When she functions as a poet she changes things. She must see differently not only from whites but from blacks, and especially from other black poets.

If what she presents seems to many of us heightened reality, it is because it is artifice, the real fashioned and shaped to poetry. It is both larger and smaller than that outside reality so inadequately reported on in the press. It is larger because Gwen Brooks heightens our awareness of its multiplicity, textures, and significances. It is smaller because the totality of the world of flux has too many instances and variables for any human to fully record or comprehend.

What I've said thus far is really a defense of any black poet to be himself first. The label "black poetry" cheapens the achievement of Gwendolyn Brooks. It recommends that race matters more than artistic vocation or individual voice. It would lessen achievements by blacks by supporting a notion of caricature.

It suggests to me also that some hierarchy of blacks might best judge the merits of black poets. I'm sure that such a committee would finally distinguish between "black poetry" and "Negro poetry." Eventually a poet, no matter what his pigmentation, who did not deal with social problems in an approved way would very likely be read out of his skin. I don't suspect Gwen Brooks of such inclinations. I only object to "black poetry" as a useful appellation, as much as I might object to "white poetry" or "yellow poetry." The whole point of a poem is to avoid such easy categorizations, all of which are dangerous.

Gwen Brooks is a wise woman. It may be that her remarks were motivated by her realization of the dangers of a programmatic appearance to poetry. Maybe she meant only to affirm her identity as a black while retaining her individuality as an artist.

As a poet and novelist Gwen Brooks never seems to have wondered who she was. She announced herself to the world as a person, as a woman, as a poet, and as black. We may honor her for her courage to be herself in the face of so many obstacles that inhibit blacks. It may seem to some more fashionable to announce one's blackness now. It may even seem more safe. But we should remember that to announce the self, no matter what the time or the social pressures, is always to become vulnerable. It may be less difficult to make a public pronouncement of blackness now, but to be oneself is as difficult as ever, perhaps more so. Gwen Brooks has done both.

It's too soon to say anything definitive about the work of Gwendolyn Brooks. Perhaps she hasn't yet written the poems that will stand out a hundred years from now as her major ones. But she has already written some that will undoubtedly be read so long as man cares about language and his fellows.

There have been no drastic changes in the tactics and subjects she has dealt with over the years. It's doubtful if future critics will talk about the early and the late Brooks, not unless she strikes out into much different territory after 1969. What one observes is a steady development of themes and types.

Her poetry is marked by a number of central concerns: black experience; the nature of greatness; the way in which man expresses his needs, makes do, or lashes out. Ordinarily the view is one of delicate balance, that of a passionate observer. The poems strike one as distinctly those of a woman but always muscled and precise, written from the pelvis rather than the biceps. It seems only natural that a lost child should figure so importantly in "In the Mecca," the long title poem of Miss Brooks' most recent book.

In *A Street in Bronzeville,* her first book, one finds poem after poem in which the lyric voice is subordinated to a dramatic intention. It's as if she were intent on singing somebody else's blues. We get what I would call vivid snapshots, except the label snapshots is far too casual. A poem like "kitchenette building" is more than an ashcan school vignette although it contains "fried potatoes" and "garbage ripening in the hall." The subdued conclusion is more than clever though it generally evokes delighted laughter from audiences. The poem recounts the difficulty of aspiring while breathing in the onion fumes of reality. It concludes with the dramatic voice anticipating a lukewarm bath now that Number Five is out of the bathroom. It's a little anticipation substituting for a big dream symbolized by an earlier reference to an aria. The last line of the poem, "We think of lukewarm water, hope to get in it" has delicacy and thrust. The simplicity of the language, the caesura before "hope," which makes us savor with the kitchenette occupant the small pleasure waiting, the idiomatic insistency of "get in it" with its alliterative tickle, all make one feel like a renter down the hall. But what is really important remains unsaid, the enormous pathos generated by the dramatic voice's capacity to find joy in such surroundings, surroundings that provide such limited opportunities.

It's not the sociological observations that make this poem and many others such successes. It is the quiet way in which the poems invade the spirit, the technical dexterity that makes the poems into experiences rather than just ideas.

There may be some who will maintain that only a black can judge the validity of Gwen Brooks's poems, or those of any other black poet. The real judgment they may insist is not to be made by white readers and critics. It has already been made affirmatively by the black artists who fashioned the mural communicating black dignity on the wall of a Chicago slum building at 43rd and Langley, a mural that includes Gwen Brooks.

But the real question is not what Gwen Brooks has to say to those who have shared her experiences, who already know some of what she has to say. The real question is whether or not she can make the alien feel. The purpose of art is always to communicate to the uninitiated, to make contact across seemingly insurmountable barriers. Can the poet make the white feel black; the healthy, sick; the defeated, hopeful? One of the measures of a black poet's work is whether he can make a comfortable white (who has not had his sense of language and humanity thoroughly shattered) respond. This is not to say that Gwen Brooks's poetry will have no value for black readers. They may well find their own surprises.

There are a number of short folk pieces in her first book, poems like "the vacant lot," "the independent man," "when I die," and "patent leather," which unabashedly present pictures of ghetto life. This was ground mined by Langston Hughes. Like Hughes, Miss Brooks does not merely reproduce ghetto language. Neither are dialect poets. But both are attuned to the differences between black speech and white speech. They make use of the special quality of black speech when it suits their purposes. More often than not Miss Brooks suggests with just a phrase. The final lines of "the battle" illustrates this capacity. After mentioning the whipping Moe Belle Jackson got from her husband and commenting on how differently she would have responded, the dramatic voice says sarcastically of Moe Belle:

> Most like, she shed a tear,
> And this mornin' it was probably
> "More grits, Dear?"

Like Robert Frost and William Carlos Williams, Gwen Brooks is attuned to the voicebox of the people. Far too many readers underestimate the blues and folk poetry of many black poets because they miss the special intonations that enrich the poems. It may well be that "the battle" is about the special flavor of that last line, in which the alliteration functions to help produce a voice that is both cajoling and foredefeated.

Gwen Brooks poetry is not of one texture. *A Street in Bronzeville* concludes with a sequence of remarkable sonnets, "Gay Chaps at the Bar." They don't have the characteristic literary feeling of the sonnet, the feeling that encouraged Robert Bly to comment that "The sonnet is the place where old professors go to die." In a poem like "the white troops had their orders but the Negroes looked like men" Gwen Brooks demonstrates how attitudes can change, even white attitudes. The tone of the poem changes subtly as the poem progresses, moving from overtones of stiffness and artificiality to a more natural ease.

> They had supposed their formula was fixed.
> They had obeyed instructions to devise
> A type of cold, a type of hooded gaze.
> . . . . . . . . . . . . . . . . . . . . . . . .
>     Who really gave two figs?
> Neither the earth nor heaven ever trembled.
> And there was nothing startling in the weather.

Although these sonnets incorporate a more formal language, different from the folk pieces, they provide a sense of rising black expectations. The last sonnet, "The progress," foreshadows later poems such as "Riders to the Blood-Red Wrath."

> For even if we come out standing up
> How shall we smile, congratulate: and how
> Settle in chairs? Listen, listen. The step
> Of iron feet again. And again wild.

It is curious that a gentle woman should have written this sequence of war poems. They are poems of dignity, skill, and empathy. If white soldiers return to civilian life strangers, black soldiers return doubly so. What we get here is the painful awakening of men to the threats of war and the threats as well as the hopes of peace, to a new idealism and a heightened cynicism. These poems may tell us as much about the time of the Vietnam debacle as they do about World War II.

Other poems in *A Street in Bronzeville* show the range of Gwen Brooks' language. "The Sundays of Satin-Legs Smith" opens with a couplet reminiscent of Wallace Stevens:

> Inamoratas, with an approbation,
> Bestowed his title. Blessed his inclination.

The tone of this opening establishes a sense of ironic contrast between the royal inclinations of the dude and the grossness of so much ghetto life. One can't help suspect that the bravura of such opulence of language and attire is a gauntlet in the face of poverty.

Gwendolyn Brooks has fashioned a style that reflects the shifting quality of the American Dream. She fuses the flavor of black dialect with rhetorical formality. She can stir the grits or stroke the rococo. Her style deals with the contradictions of American life, contradictions most apparent to blacks who must suffer through them.

When *Annie Allen* won the Pulitzer Prize for Gwendolyn Brooks in 1950, many critics and unwary readers must have been startled. Rumor has it that the telegram announcing the prize arrived at a house without electricity. *Annie Allen* makes apparent that Gwen Brooks is a student of poetry. "The Anniad" with its echoes of Robert Browning, T. S. Eliot, and W. H. Auden illustrates her technical dexterity. Unfortunately, some readers are more conscious of the language of the poem than its substance. The rhymes seem more important than the character. The often ornate diction shadows the psychological journey. But the promise of *A Street in Bronzeville* is more than amplified elsewhere. The section entitled "The Womanhood" includes some of the best poems by any contemporary American poet. I find it strange that those makers of taste, the anthologists, have seen fit to ignore poems like "the children of the poor" and "Beverly Hills, Chicago."

Both poems are rich brews of language. "The children of the poor" is a poem of statement, often startlingly direct, full of images and direct references to the ordinary stuff of the world, at the same time incorporating with extraordinary daring and precision the most elevated diction. "Beverly Hills, Chicago" is essentially dramatic. It plays rhetorical elegance, associated with the wealthy, against colloquial speech patterns, associated with the outsiders motoring through the rich suburbs. Social, emotional, and linguistic range—Gwendolyn Brooks exhibits them all. She yokes compassion and toughness, teaching by example the most important lesson, how to keep the sensitivity alive in a world that so often brutalizes or destroys.

Her next book, *The Bean Eaters,* makes one feel the whole personality trying to pull together the fragments of an often deceptive, often confusing, often unjust world. It is a world of possible and impossible dreams, personal loss, insecurity, arrogant and measured responses; a world which justifies the silken lyric, the detached and ironic observation, and the scathing file of satire. *The Bean Eaters* includes deft examples of all these types.

The opposite face of Gwen Brooks's compassion must be her hatred of hypocrisy especially that hypocritical sensitivity exhibited by the "Ladies from the Ladies Betterment League" in "The Lovers of the Poor." She describes them so:

Keeping their scented bodies in the center
Of the hall as they walk down the hysterical hall,
They allow their lovely skirts to graze no wall,
Are off at what they manage of a canter,
And, resuming all the clues of what they were,
Try to avoid inhaling the laden air.

Although Gwendolyn Brooks never seems hysterical, neurotic or lost, although she does not seem much like a modern anti-heroine in search of her own identity, she regularly identifies, in both senses of the word. In the final poems of her *Selected Poems* and *In the Mecca* one finds portraits and biographies, moments of life and summarizations of lives, the unknowns and the famous of the world. She looks at Robert Frost ("some specialness within), Langston Hughes ("helmsman, hatchet, headlight") and Malcolm X ("the maleness"), as well as the Blackstone Rangers. She provides us with her sense of their essentials, a clarification of their substance and meaning.

"In the Mecca," the long title poem of her most recent book, accomplishes much of the same sort of thing. Along the corridors of the decaying apartment building once a "showplace of Chicago," in a search for a lost child whose body is finally found "in dust with roaches" under a bed, we meet the contradictory faces and gestures of the ghetto. Along the way we hear songs of feeling, learn of terror and self abuse, feel ourselves in the place where "silence is a place to scream." Gwendolyn Brooks seems to be trying to pull it all together, to feel for them all at once, for the bold and the fearful, the deranged and the evasive, the fashionable and the bleak. And although "In the Mecca" may at times seem more like a collection of items than a well-paced narrative in an environment of enormous pressures, it is a major attempt at synthesis.

The history of American literature it has been said is the history of a search for a definition of *American*. It seems to me that the question of race, as it is called, is at the center of that larger question. Gwen Brooks leads us to a sense of the ghetto and the black man. She leads us also to a sense of the American dilemma, one hopes towards some resolution. She has fashioned a style, developed a virtuosity, that makes it possible for her to grab big chunks of the American reality, moments of its hopefulness, portions of its resentments, and give them cohesiveness and shape.

She writes in "The Second Sermon on the Warpland,"

> This is the urgency: Live!
> and have your blooming in the noise of the whirlwind.

This is no death wish but a prideful stance reminiscent of the Old Testament it alludes to. It may stir the hearts of black militants. These words might well have been uttered at Valley Forge.

## ELEANOR HOLMES NORTON

# For Sadie and Maud

Some subjects are so complex, so unyielding of facile insight, that it will not do to think about them in the ordinary way. Black women—their lot and their future—is for me such a subject. Thus, the new crop of literature concerning women—attuned to the peculiar relationship between white women and white men in America—has inspired me much, but less than the poetry of the great black poet, Gwendolyn Brooks, who writes for me and about me. Take, for example Miss Brooks's poem "Sadie and Maud,"[1] a sad ballad which in a few stanzas touches in some intimate respect all of us who are black women:

> Maud went to college.
> Sadie stayed at home.
> Sadie scraped life
> With a fine-tooth comb.
>
> She didn't leave a tangle in.
> Her comb found every strand.
> Sadie was one of the livingest chits
> In all the land.
>
> Sadie bore two babies
> Under her maiden name.
> Maud and Ma and Papa
> Nearly died of shame.
>
> When Sadie said her last so-long
> Her girls struck out from home.
> (Sadie had left as heritage
> Her fine-tooth comb.)

From *Sisterhood Is Powerful: An Anthology of Writings from the Women's Liberation Movement*, ed. Robin Morgan (New York: Random House, 1970), 353–59. Copyright © 1970 by Eleanor Holmes Norton.

Maud, who went to college,
Is a thin brown mouse.
She is living all alone
In this old house.

Sadie and Maud are blood sisters, each in her own way living the unrequited life of the black woman. Sadie has two children out of wedlock, but the Sadies of this world also include black women who have been married but have lost their husbands in America's wars against the black family. Maud "went to college"—or wherever black women have gone over the years to escape the perils of living the nearly predestined half-life of the black woman in this country. Maud, the "thin brown mouse," lives alone rather than incur Sadie's risks or risk Sadie's pleasures.

The difference in the lives of these two women cannot conceal the overriding problem they share—loneliness, a life lacking in the chance to develop a relationship with a man or satisfactory family relationships. The complexities of the problem facing black women begin to unfold. Not only must we work out an unoppressive relationship with our men; we must—we can at last—establish a relationship with them *de novo*.

In this respect, we conceive our mission in terms which are often different from the expressed goals of many white women revolutionaries. To be sure, our goals and theirs in their general outlines are the same, but black women confront a task that is as delicate as it is revolutionary. For black women are part of a preeminent struggle whose time has come—the fight for black liberation. If women were suddenly to achieve equality with men tomorrow, black women would continue to carry the entire array of utterly oppressive handicaps associated with race. Racial oppression of black people in America has done what neither class oppression nor sexual oppression, with all their perniciousness, has ever done: destroyed an entire people and their culture. The difference is between exploitation and slavery. Slavery partakes of all the worst excesses of exploitation—and more—but exploitation does not always sink people to the miserable depths of slavery.

Yet, black women cannot—must not—avoid the truth about their special subservience. They are women with all that that implies. If some have been forced into roles as providers or, out of the insecurity associated with being a black woman alone, have dared not develop independence, the result is not that black women are today liberated women. For they have been "liberated" only from love, from family life, from meaningful work, and just as often from the basic comforts and necessities of an ordinary existence. There is neither power nor satisfaction in such a "matriarchy." There is only the bitter knowledge that one is a victim.

Still, the stereotypic image of matriarchy has basic appeal to some black men who in their frustration may not see immediately the counter-revolutionary nature of such a battle cry. To allow the white oppressor to share the burden of his responsibility with the black woman is madness. It is comparable to black people blaming Puerto Ricans for competing with them for jobs, thus relieving the government of the pressures it must have to fulfill its duty to provide full employment. Surely, after hundreds of years, black men realize that imprecision in detecting the enemy is an inexcusable fault in a revolutionary.

But our problems only *begin* with the reconstruction of the black family. As black men begin to find dignified work after so many generations, what roles will their women seek? Are black people to reject so many of white society's values only to accept its view of woman and of the family? At the moment when the white family is caught in a maze of neurotic contradictions and white women are supremely frustrated with their roles, are black women to take up such troubled models? Shall black women exchange their ancient insecurity for the white woman's familial cocoon? Can it serve us any better than it has served them? And how will it serve black men?

There is no reason to repeat bad history. There is no reason to envy the white woman who is sinking in a sea of close-quartered affluence, where one's world is one's house, one's peers [are] one's children, and one's employer [is] one's husband. Black women shall not have gained if Sadie and Maud exchange the "fine-tooth comb" and the "old house" for the empty treasures white women are today trying to turn in.

We who are black have a chance for something better. Europeans who came to this country struggled to be accepted by it and succeeded. Occasionally, they changed America—for the better and for the worse—but mostly they took it as it was, hoping it would change them. Black people imitated this process pitifully, generation after generation, but were just so much oil on all that melting-pot water. Today we are close to being true outsiders, no longer desiring to get in on any terms and at any cost. Racial exclusion has borne ironic fruit. We are perhaps the only group that has come to these shores who has ever acquired the chance to consciously avoid total Americanization with its inherent, its rank, faults. On the road to equality there is no better place for blacks to detour around American values than in forgoing its example in the treatment of its women and the organization of its family life.

With black family life so clearly undermined in the American environment, blacks must remake the family unit, not imitate it. Indeed, this task is central to black liberation. The black male will not be returned to his historic strength—the foremost task of the black struggle today—if we do not recreate the strong family unit that was a part of our African heritage before it was dismembered by the slave-owning class in America. But it will be impossible to reconstruct the black family if its central characters are to be crepe-paper copies acting out the old white family melodrama. In that failing production, the characters seem set upon a course precisely opposite to ours. White men, in search of endless financial security, have sold their spirits to that goal and begun a steady emasculation in which the fiscal needs of wife and family determine life's values and goals. Their now ungrateful wives have begun to see the fraud of this way of life, even while eagerly devouring its fruits. Their even more ungrateful children are in bitter rejection of all that this sort of life signifies and produces. White family life in America today is less than a poor model for blacks. White family life is disintegrating at the moment when we must reforge the black family unit. The whole business of the white family—its softened men, its frustrated women, its angry children—is in a state of great mess.

But it would be naive to think that the temptatious aspects of this sort of life are incapable of luring black people into a disastrous mockery. The ingredients are all there. We are a people in search of what for us has been the interminably elusive goal of economic security. Wretchedly poor for three-hundred-fifty years in a country where most groups have fattened, we could come to see the pain of much of white family life as bearable when measured against the tortures we have borne. Our men, deliberately emasculated as the only way to enforce their servile status, might easily be tempted by a family structure which, by making them the financial head of the household, seemed to make them its actual head. In our desperation to escape so many suffering decades, we might trip down the worn path taken by so many in America before us.

If we are to avoid this disaster, the best, perhaps the only, place to begin is in our conception of the black woman. After all, the immediate tasks of the black man are laid out for him. It is the future role of the black woman that is problematical. And what she is allowed to become—or relegated to—will shape not simply her future but that of the black family and the fate of its members.

If she is forced into the current white model, she is doomed to the fate of "The Empty Woman" about whom Miss Brooks has also written:

> The empty woman had hats
> To show. With feathers. Wore combs
> In polished waves. Wooed cats

If so, she will be unfit for the onerous responsibilities she must meet if the struggle for black freedom is to bring us out of our ancient bondage into a truly new and liberated condition.

In any case, it is too late for any group to consciously revert to old familial patterns of male dominance and female servility. Those roles have their roots in conditions of life that are rapidly disappearing, and especially so in this country. If the woman's place has historically been at home, it was at least in part because there was much work to be done there and, as the natural custodian of the children, it seemed logical for her to do it. But today there is neither so much work to be done there nor so many children. Do-it-all appliances and technology are making housework a part-time job, freeing millions of women to do something else. An increasing array of birth preventatives has released women from the unwanted multiples of children it was difficult to avoid in the past. The effect on the family of these work-and child-liberating phenomena will reverberate in ways we still cannot foresee.

Yet it is certain that the institution of the family will undergo radical alteration largely through the new roles women will have to seek. With birth preventatives and with world overpopulation, many couples will rethink whether it is wise to have children at all. And even though most may choose to have children, it is doubtful that it will any longer be prestigious or wise to have very many. With children no longer the universally accepted reason for marriage, marriages are going to have to exist on their own merits. Marriages are going to have to exist because they possess inherent qualities which make them worthy of existing, a plane to which the institution has never before been elevated. For marriage to develop such inherent qualities, the woman partner, heretofore oriented toward fulfilling now outmoded functions, will have to seek new functions. Whether black or white, if American women are to find themselves, they must begin looking outside the home. This will undoubtedly lead them into doing and thinking about matters now pretty much reserved for men. Inevitably, women are going to acquire new goals and a new status.

We who are black are taking up the long delayed work of family-building at a historic moment in history. We embark upon this goal at a time when the family institution in America is in a state of great and undecided flux. This is fortunate happenstance, for had we been about this task in the years immediately following World War II, we might have fallen into the mold which today traps white families, and especially white women. As it is, we have a chance to pioneer in forging new relationships between men and women. We have a chance to make family life a liberating experience instead of the confining experience it more often has been. We have a chance to free woman and, with her, the rest of us.

NOTE

1. Gwendolyn Brooks, *Selected Poems* (New York: Harper and Row, 1963).

GEORGE E. KENT

# The Poetry of Gwendolyn Brooks

Gwendolyn Brooks shares with Langston Hughes the achieve-
ment of being most responsive to turbulent changes in the Black
community's vision of itself and to the changing forms of its
vibrations during decades of rapid change. The depth of her
responsiveness and her range of poetic resources make her one of
the most distinguished poets to appear in America during the
twentieth century.

She shares with Margaret Walker the achievement of sum-
ming up the Black mood of the 1940s: Margaret Walker in her
famous poem, "For My People"; and Gwendolyn Brooks in
"Negro Hero," whose memorable image is that of a Black am-
bivalent man laying his life on the line for the sake of a "white-
gowned democracy" with a dagger for his heart's blood up her
sleeves. "Riders to the Blood-Red Wrath" (*Selected Poems,* 1963)
more than any other poem renders the Black mood of the 1950s
and early 1960s. It dramatizes the inner attitudes, from which
Blacks expended great spiritual resources under the leadership of
Martin Luther King, Jr.

During the 1960s, the deepest poem to portray the deadened
hopelessness of urban Blacks which exploded in the city rebellions
was (and is) "In the Mecca" which appeared in the book by that
title in 1968. It portrays the misery, beauty, and frustration of
Black occupants of a once existing huge apartment building in
Chicago, in which were jammed roughly 2,000 people. The
book, *In the Mecca,* also contains dramatic poems and portraits
reflecting the poet's absorption of the tensions implying revolu-
tionary change and nationhood which arose during the late 1960s.
Surrounding such peaks are simply poems which probe at great
depth the daily dues-paying lives of "ordinary" people, who must
act out the ultimates of their existence bereft of grand stages or the
grand lines provided by a set script. Perhaps the publication of
Miss Brooks's collected poetry (with the exception of the poign-

From *Black World,* September 1971, 30–43. Copyright 1971. Reprinted with
permission of Johnson Publishing Company, Inc.

ant children's poems, *Bronzeville Boys and Girls,* 1956) in September 1971, will place her poetic contributions in commanding perspective, and reveal that underneath the poet's restless changes and responses is an unchanging steel of commitment.

It was this unchanging steel of commitment which provided the basis for the mutual shock of recognition between Miss Brooks and the new young radical Black poets. She was inspired by the raw, new, and bold expression of the young poets—by their seeming to be what Margaret Walker had called for in 1940: "Let a new race of men now rise and take control." They saw in her an inspiration, an example of brilliant writing long-committed to the community, a foundation, a bridge. As evidenced by the new wide range of reference to her poetry in *To Gwen, with Love* (1971), which contains poems and other works in tribute to her influence and achievement, Black poets of radical and other persuasions had experienced an impact from her that was wide and deep. As Hoyt W. Fuller points out in the foreword to the tributes, the response was nationwide, and "it is fair to assume that none paid her homage merely on the basis of her great public fame" but either to the dedicated woman, mother, artist, community worker, known particularly to Chicagoans, or as a person who had deeply touched them in one way or another. Variations of this touch had been experienced by the national community of Black poets.

Thus Miss Brooks's current way with the expression of Black tensions must be seen as a natural organic progression and growth. Although the poet gained an inspiration during the 1960s which provided further extension of herself and her vision, and approach to community, the experience was not that sudden hot conversion on the road to Damascus so absolutely required by the inner weather of St. Paul.[1] Blacks who see in her writing a sudden "homecoming" are often celebrating a return trip of their own. White critics who bemoan the loss of the "pure poet of the 'human condition' " reveal that they have not understood the depths of the body of her work, nor the source of her genuine universality. Despite the erratic approach of many white critics (one which really began with the publication of *The Bean Eaters,* 1960), Miss Brooks continues to receive the universal recognition which the quality of her poetry demands.

For the rest of this essay my concern will be with matters of form, sensibility, and the light upon the poet's achievement provided by poems selected from the body of her work. I begin with form.

## II

But here I must be careful to identify Miss Brooks's way with form and technique and to avoid the common garden variety of connotations which they evoke. For example, she has pointed out repeatedly that she is neither form-conscious nor an intellectual, and that she writes from the heart and without making conscious decisions about form.[2] A partial exception to her usual practice was the decision which she made prior to writing the sonnet series concerning the dilemma of soldiers at war, "Gay Chaps at the Bar" (included in *A Street in Bronzeville* and *Selected Poems*). Before writing the first sonnet (with no thought of creating a series), she did decide that it would be written in "off-rhyme" because she felt that her subject, the consciousness of soldiers at war, was an "off-rhyme" situation.[3] That is, soldiers-at-war is not an experience that is necessarily to be celebrated by the full harmonic sound that conventional rhyme delivers, but by the edginess (sometimes, dis-harmony or dissonance) which deliberately chosen "imperfect" rhymes can render.

Thus, although in conventional rhyme the rhyming words have the same sounds in "their stressed vowels and all sounds following, but unlike sounds *preceding* the stressed vowels," Miss Brooks, in the opening sonnet of "Gay Chaps at the Bar," rhymes "dash" and "lush," with stressed vowels "u" and "a" unlike in sound. Deciding later to write a series of sonnets on the war situation, she created additional sonnets in conformity with the off-rhyme pattern.

> I said, there are other things to say about what's going on at the front [Second World War] and all, and I'll write more poems, some of them based on the stuff of letters that I was getting from several soldiers, and I felt it would be good to have them all in the same form, because it would serve my purpose throughout.[4]

Miss Brooks's usual practice is to lean upon an intuitive sense of the form appropriate to her subject. Thus in an interview with George Stavros, managing editor of *Contemporary Review,* Miss Brooks could confess uncertainty as to why she used a modified form of the Chaucerian rhyme royal stanza for "The Anniad" (*Annie Allen*), but then suggest the intuitive basis for her choice: "but I imagine I finished one stanza, then decided that the rest of them would be just like that."[5]

I should add here that by "intuitive sense" of appropriate form, I mean a discovery concerning form and fitness and *discoveries* (often not consciously articulated) concerning fit techniques made *during* the moment of creation. I mean a *feeling sense* of such matters—and *not* a Chairman of the Board type of decision.

It is well to stress the above principles on the basis of "The Anniad," since it is the most consciously developed poem among Miss Brooks's creations. She, herself, points out that it is a "labored poem," "a poem that's very interested in the mysteries and magic of technique." Though not trying to do something new, she "was just very conscious of every word; I wanted every phrase to be beautiful, and yet to contribute sanely to the whole, to the whole effect." The poem is thus closely and carefully textured in every stanza: "every one [stanza] was worked on and revised, tenderly cared for, more than anything else I've written, and it is not a wild success; some of it just doesn't come off. But it was enjoyable."

The comments reveal Miss Brooks's love for the creative moment: "What a pleasure it was to write that poem!" But also revealed are the roles of revision and devoted work. She acknowledges that conscious shaping of form and selections among techniques occur during the process of revision. "The Anniad," though an extreme case, thus highlights approaches that are, in different degrees, intrinsic to the total body of her published poetry. Her comments finally reflect a stern self-criticism, and, above all, a reverence for the magic inherent in words to which the poet must do justice.

It should also be noted that Miss Brooks's intuition is one educated by years of workshop struggle and by saturation in progressive twentieth-century poetry and aspects of the nineteenth century. In an interview with Ida Lewis, former editor of *Essence,* she speaks of her early exposure to Paul Laurence Dunbar, a family idol, and important communication with James Weldon Johnson and Langston Hughes.[6] Through Countee Cullen's *Caroling Dusk,* an anthology of Black poetry, she became acquainted with Black writers of whom she had not heard before. One reading experience helped to define an approach to life which has become a hallmark of her work: "I read Langston Hughes's *Weary Blues,* for example, and got very excited about what he was doing. I realized that writing about the ordinary aspects of Black life was important."[7] (Earlier, her subjects had been nature, love, death, flowers, and the sky, with a fascinated fixation upon the beauty of clouds.) As everybody who has had casual contact with Gwendolyn Brooks's poetry knows, the devotion to "the ordinary aspects of Black life" is the hallmark of her poetry.

Her intuition is educated by contact with a variety of poets and writers. In Herbert Hill's *Soon One Morning,* she listed as her "admirations" Chekhov, Emily Dickinson, John Crowe Ransom, Langston Hughes, and the Joyce of a group of short stories, *Dubliners.*[8] She also acknowledges the T. S. Eliot of such poems as "Portrait of a Lady," "The Love Song of J. Alfred Prufrock," "The Hollow Men," and "The Waste Land"; and Merrill Moore, a member of a Southern-based group of poets called The Fugitives, who composed thousands of sonnets in colloquial and conversational idiom devoted largely to the "ordinary" aspects of life. Miss Brooks has a respect, though not a liking, for Ezra Pound as a master of language. Others could probably be mentioned, since she is very widely read.

In her first volume of poetry, *A Street in Bronzeville,* a favorite of Blacks, Miss Brooks reflects, it seems to me, the predominant influence of Langston Hughes and other Black writers, although the influence of other modernist poets is evident. I would suggest that Hughes's influence is apparent in such poems as "when Mrs. Martin's Booker T.," "a song in the front yard," "patent leather," the series of "Hattie Scott" poems, and "Queen of the Blues," although Miss Brooks frequently manages a distance of perspective and a gentle satire and humor which have their source in her own sensibility and values. This distance also derives from wide knowledge of such modernist techniques as irony; unusual conjunctions of words to evoke a complex sense of reality (Satin-Legs Smith rising "in a clear delirium"); sudden contrasts (say, from diction of formal eloquence to that of the common speech); squeezing the utmost from an image ("Negro Hero"—democracy as his "fair lady, / With her knife lying cold, straight, in the softness of her sweet-flowing sleeve); agility with mind-bending figurative language; sensitivity to the music of the phrase, instead of imprisonment in traditional line beats and meter; experimentation with the possibilities of *free verse* and various devices for sudden emphasis and verbal surprise; and authoritative management of tone and wide-ranging lyricism.

The education of Miss Brooks's formal intuition in the broad storehouse of modernist techniques and the implications of forms was suddenly widened in July 1941, when Inez Stark Boulton, a wealthy woman committed to the arts, began a poetry workshop for Blacks at the South Side Community Art Center,

Chicago, which continued for almost two years. Miss Brooks has stated that it was in the workshop that she learned "more about modern poetry—from one who had an excellent understanding of it," and also a good deal about technique.[9] The text was Robert Hillyer's *First Principles of Verse*. The Pulitzer Prize-winning traditionalist poet gives emphasis to the importance of traditional technique, and thus supplements the workshop's exposure to principles of modern poetry. Miss Brooks no longer feels, however, that *First Principles* is a good text for the young or beginning poet.[10]

Miss Brooks revealed in her first book considerable technical resources, a manipulation of folk forms, a growing sense of how traditional forms must be dealt with if the power of the Black voice is to come through with integrity. *A Street in Bronzeville* (1945) committed its author to a restless experimentation with an elaborate range of artistic approaches. Although there are particular peaks in Miss Brooks's experimental approaches, such as those commonly recognized in *Annie Allen* (1949), her experimental ways have continued throughout her career. Since the late 1960s, she has been committed to the creation of a simplicity from which the man who pauses reflectively at his glass in the tavern may gain a sense of the depth and meaning of Black lives. To get the specific feeling of this simplicity, in comparison with an earlier sonnet whose message is similar, one might turn from a reading of Sonnet II of "the children of the poor" (*Annie Allen*) to "Women in Love—II" (*Family Pictures*, 1970). The comparison will reveal that the second poem achieves its simplicity by the stark directness of its trajectory, not by an evasion of the complexity of experience, whereas the first carries a considerable load of explanation and carefully projected nuance as sources of complexity and depth. Each poem, of course, is a fine example of its type. The second poem, addressed primarily to a Black audience, can assume that the audience will supply many of the nuances that in the first poem had to be either stated explicitly or skillfully suggested.

But a final comment on what I have called Miss Brooks's educated intuitional approach to discovery of appropriate form: I have stated that usually her way involves a discovery of appropriate form while in the process of composition, and further shaping in the revision process.

It seems to me that her method of composition provided her with certain rewards and protections as she moved among forms heavy with the vibrations of tradition. An intimate knowledge of traditional forms, for example, can provide an understanding also of their limitations, and thus offer the artist encouragement, assurance, and a further defined ground for experimentation. Such possibilities would certainly offer themselves to a poet with a "feeling sense" for form. A form which invites experimentation is the ballad, since it is essentially at the furthest distance from the literary forms of very artificial traditions. In the many variations that Miss Brooks plays upon ballad form, she takes advantage of its flexibility, as can be seen by comparing such pieces as "Sadie and Maud," "The ballad of chocolate Mabbie," and "southeast corner" (*A Street in Bronzeville*). Also "of De Witt Williams on his way to Lincoln Cemetery" or (in *The Bean Eaters*) "The Ballad of Rudolph Reed." Miss Brooks's freedom with the ballad form may here be described in general terms: movement in different poems between the poles of the literary and traditional folk ballads, with some forays into aspects of the Black folk ballad ("Queen of the Blues," *A Street in Bronzeville*); a deliberate evoking of the tone of the sixteenth-century ballad, by means of one of its standard rhythms and the use of some of its set phrases; a movement of the form closer to the immediacy of contemporary life, by means of devices for subtle nuances and varied pacing.

Another form which does not necessarily impose the connotations and nuances of a set tradition upon the Black writer is *free verse,* since it is without either a set number of beats to the line or a requirement to rhyme. Mainly, the signature which Walt Whitman placed upon its use served to place it in the public domain for further modifications by subsequent writers. Miss Brooks, it must suffice to say here, has over a long period developed a highly economical free verse line, varying in length to suit the music of the phrase and voice tones, and accommodating itself to rhymes placed here and there for special emphasis.

It will be seen that one can get a wide sampling of Miss Brooks's command over a well disciplined free verse through the long poem, "In the Mecca," and her latest book, *Family Pictures.*

The obvious flexibility of such forms as the ballad and free verse suggests that where forms are not saturated with commanding connotations from Euro-American tradition the Black writer can make easy-going alliances with them. But there are others which are more self-consciously literary and so evocative of European tradition that they threaten to cancel out a sense of immediacy of the Black experience. All artists portraying unconventional experience face the threat to a degree, but for a Black writer it assumes a peculiar degree of intensity. The problem is further intensified by writers who place such an indelible signature upon a particular form that it seems completely exhausted by them. The sonnet (which Miss Brooks frequently used) is an obvious example. And critics have both marveled and coughed nervously in confronting Phillis Wheatley's use of the heroic couplet in conformity with the style of Alexander Pope, an eighteenth-century Englishman representative of (and therefore bearing its connotation) a highly ordered and sophisticated upper class society.

The outcome of such uses can be that the Black writer, while making interesting comments about the Black experience, seems to be taking care of somebody else's business. Thus Countee Cullen, in trying for the sensuous style of John Keats—the nineteenth-century Romantic—seems, at times, to be taking care of Keats's business. Claude McKay, more often than it is comfortable to experience, seems, in part, to be taking care of the business of Byron and Shelley.

It is, I think, Miss Brooks's intuitional approach to form which usually enables her to render the illusion of taking care of nobody's business but her own, although one can hear muted echoes of other poets. The situation may be here briefly illustrated through her use of the sonnet—a form bearing the commanding signature of such masters as Shakespeare, Milton, and William Wordsworth. In reading her sonnets, one may notice that, possibly with an assist from the example of the already mentioned Merrill Moore, she won a freedom from its traditional rigidity and formal eloquence. She attacked the sonnet's rigidity by breaking up the traditional sentence syntax into punctuated phrases, by emphasizing the colloquial, and by the pressure of her contemporary realism. In winning a freedom from traditional formal eloquence, however, she won also a freedom to use at will her own style of formal eloquence without being constricted by tradition. As a matter of fact, some of her best sonnets are in a formal eloquence and a somewhat traditional syntax, as evidenced by Sonnet II of "the children of the poor."

The result of Miss Brooks's way with form and technique is usually a *legitimate* universalism. That is, her poems tend not to represent a reach for some preexisting Western universal to be arrived at by reducing the tensions inherent in the Black experience. Their universalism derives, instead, from complete projection of a situation or experience's *space* and *vibrations* (going down deep, not transcending). Even where a pre-existing universal may be paraphrasable, the true roots of the poet's universalism are in her power of enforcing the illusion that the vibrations from the space her imagination has encircled are captured and focused with all the power and significance which the raw materials afforded. As evidence for the foregoing judgments, one could cite at random such short poems as "kitchenette building," "southeast corner," selected sonnets from *A Street in Bronzeville;* "Do Not Be Afraid of No," selected sonnets from "The Womanhood" series and "Clogged and Soft and Sloppy Eyes" (*Annie Allen*); "Big Bessie throws her Son into the street" (*Selected Poems*); "Medgar Evers" (*In the Mecca*); and "To Don at Salaam" (*Family Pictures*). Among the longer poems, one thinks immediately of portions of "*The Anniad,*" "Riders to the Blood-Red Wrath," and "In the Mecca."

What I have suggested so far argues for and points to a tough and finely tuned sensibility (characteristic emotional, psychic, and intellectual response to existence).

On the basis of Miss Brooks's well-known devotion for her fellow man and the values informing her poetry, I would say that one source of her sensibility is a religious consciousness, from which dogma has been ground away. What remains is a muscular religious reflex, guided, to paraphrase a line from one of her poems, by eyes which retain the light that bites and terrifies.

On the basis of Miss Brooks's testimony concerning the qualities of the lives of her parents, it is possible to assume that her reflex has its roots in what her father and mother offered from the deepest level of traditional Black religious response. Not the level which Blacks unacquainted with the depth of their folk tradition understand within the flat categories of "narcotic" or "escapism."[11] And not the simple category of Jesus as the white folks' eternal Superstar—an instrument for consoling whites and making right their strange and bloody deeds while calling Blacks and other breeds without the law only apparently to "God," but really to the ways, service, and brainwashing machine of white men.

No.

But Black religious response on the still deeper level described by Paul Radin, the anthropologist, in his "Foreword" to *God Struck Me Dead,* a collection of post–Civil War conversion experiences edited by Clifton H. Johnson.[12] Basing his judgment upon a close study of Black religious testimonials, Radin saw the great depths of Black religious experience as a turning away from disintegration, an achievement of a status which the Black, himself, had ordained from within, a striving for some form of harmony, and a rebirth as cosmic man. Accordingly, Radin points out, "Any ordered framework would have done. That of Christianity happened to be at hand." In Radin's version, the pre–Civil War Black was not converted to God, but converted God to himself. This was done because he "needed a fixed point, for both within and outside of himself he could see only vacillation and endless shifting." The result of the religious experience, at such a depth, was a "unified personality" which, because of the hard realism of a people set upon and crowded by outrageous life, did not become *mystic* but committed itself to life.

Perhaps we may quarrel with Radin's idea that any "ordered framework would have done," and modify the statement to read, "Any ordered framework which could deal with the root uncertainty (Radin's "vacillation and endless shifting") at the base of the center of being." As Professor Charles Long, of the Divinity School, University of Chicago, points out, the probability is that Blacks were attracted to the Old Testament, not simply because the Hebrews were enslaved like themselves, but also because the stories of the Old Testament powerfully acknowledge the root uncertainties of existence (what philosophers call radical contingency) which they, themselves, were experiencing.[13]

The upshot of all this is that as late as the World War I period, which saw Miss Brooks's birth and her subsequent early childhood, people of the stripe of her parents, David and Keziah Brooks, had available a religion which enabled them to make simple but heroic decisions concerning the ordering of life and the commanding of whatever social space they could occupy. Thus, despite the fact that Mr. Brooks, who had aspired to become a doctor and had taken the first year of a premedical course at Fisk, was crowded into a corner by poverty and spent his life as a janitor, he could make the decision to create a kind and ordered life for his children, and could contribute to their cultural development. In the poem, "In Honor of David Anderson Brooks, My Father," Miss Brooks was able to speak of him as "He who was Goodness, Gentleness, and Dignity . . . ."

As to her mother, who had been an elementary school teacher in Kansas, one gets from Miss Brooks's remarks that she is a person of will, duty, and religious certainty. As in the case of Claude McKay, Miss Brooks's talent for poetry was a home discovery: McKay's by his brother; Miss Brooks's by her mother, who persuaded Gwendolyn to believe that her vocation was poetry and told her that she was to become the female Paul Laurence Dunbar. As to her mother's religion, Miss Brooks gives its depth and simplicity in a single sentence: "She feels firmly that you must pray, and that only good can come of it."[14]

In the interview with Ida Lewis, Miss Brooks gives a very simple and direct picture of her own religious sensibility of the 1940s and 1950s:[15] here she explains that she had believed that, "All we had to do was keep on appealing to the whites to help us and they would. . . . Because I believed in Christianity. People were really good, I thought; there was some good even in people who seemed to be evil." The evidence of the poetry, however, ranges from gentle questioning to skepticism. In her first volume, for example, the sonnet "God works in a mysterious way" demands that God take care of the world's business. "Or we assume a sovereignty ourselves." In "The Anniad," the young Black woman is she "Whom the higher gods forgot, / Whom the lower gods berate . . ." In the third sonnet of "The Womanhood" (*Annie Allen*), those who believe in the religious simplicities are "metaphysical mules" (stubborn), and the Black mother, in her compassion, stands ready to sew up the children's assaulted beliefs, "Holding the bandage ready for your eyes." Interestingly, this image of the merciful blindfold appears in her first volume of poetry (*A Street in Bronzeville,* 1945) in "the funeral," and in the same volume the women in "Satin Legs Smith" wend their way home from "service," with "Temperate holiness arranged ably on asking faces . . ."

It is true that Miss Brooks ended the over-anthologized poem, "The *Chicago Defender* Sends a Man to Little Rock," with the line "The loveliest lynchee was our Lord" (*The Bean Eaters*), but she now rejects the line, and feels that Blacks are the true figures on the Cross. It is also true that she wrote a poem on the second coming of Christ, "In Emanuel's Nightmare: Another Coming of Christ," but here Christ is more of a cultural fact than a passionate commitment. Christ is present largely to project a man's pitiful commitment to the dirtiness of war. Other poems might be cited. But perhaps the foregoing will suffice to suggest that, whereas Miss Brooks evidences a very deep religious consciousness, her commitment over the years to the idea of Christianity has been neither simple nor unquestioning.

The same judgment applies to the simplicity of Miss Brooks's statement that she had believed persistent appeals to whites for help would gain meaningful responses. Like many people, Miss Brooks has probably had periods of euphoric confidence in the

effectiveness of "education" in race relations, shored up by individ-
ual interracial friendships, but also periods and intervals of gnaw-
ing doubt and teeth-gritting frustration out of which her present
sense of the implacability of institutionalized racism grew. I have
already referred to the stern ambivalence of "Negro Hero" (1945).
"The Sundays of Satin-Legs Smith" reflects both a compassionate
and a skeptical attitude toward the white "you" whom she is
addressing. "I love those little booths at Benvenuti's" (*Annie Al-
len*) and "The Lovers of the Poor" (*The Bean Eaters*) range in tone
from cool signifying to sustained and slashing attack. In other
poems published prior to 1968, there are also an in-between mild-
ness and a variety of modulations.

At any rate, whites repeatedly called her bitter and asked
whether she didn't think things were changing. Many hated *The
Bean Eaters*. Miss Brooks, in the Stavros interview, refers to their
dislike of "Lovers of the Poor" and of so mild a poem as "The
*Chicago Defender* Sends a Man to Little Rock: Fall, 1957."[16]

On both issues of religion and race, Professor Arthur P. Davis
felt that, "She doesn't seem to have much faith in either the
American Dream or a Just God."[17]

Phyl Garland's passages on the childhood and growing up
years of Miss Brooks give further insight into her sensibility.[18]
On the one hand, she is the dreamy child who, by the age of
seven, was finding happiness in reading and writing. Her great-
est happiness came as she stood upon the neat patch of physical,
cultural, and spiritual ground won by the quiet but determined
devotion of her parents, and gazed upon the changeful beauty of
the clouds—a daydream analogy of the beauty she desired for
her future. Miss Garland points out that the adventure with
clouds meant seeing beyond the "grimy, tottering back stairs of a
row of tenements" facing the Brooks's backyard. On the other
hand, between the ages of thirteen and twenty, Miss Brooks had
published two neighborhood newspapers, *The Champlain Weekly
News* and the *News Review,* a fact which evidences an intense
interest in people and their doings.[19] When combined, her activi-
ties seem to predict her fascination with the people's vitality,
beauty, horror, pathos, and inchoate yearnings, reflected in her
published poetry, and her strong commitment to neighborhood
and community.

One notices the number of poems which are derived and
transformed from specific real life situations: "the vacant lot,"
"Matthew Cole," "the murder," "obituary for a living lady,"
"a song in the front yard" (autobiographically based), the World

War II poems, "Gay Chaps at the Bar," parts of *Annie Allen,* the situation and certain characters of "In the Mecca," friends and historical figures in *In the Mecca* and *Family Pictures.*[20] To these might be added in poetry carefully observed types such as Satin Legs Smith, and in fiction, the partly autobiographical novel, *Maud Martha.* Miss Brooks kept a notebook and, at one time, jotted down observations in restaurants and other public places.[21] The total situation highlights the fact that her poetry is people-centered, and that she makes very strong cases for them.

One other aspect of sensibility stemming from childhood seems inescapable: her experience of an unwanted awkwardness and separateness from other children, Black and white (outside her neighborhood), caused by shyness, lack of the usual childhood skills, intra- and interracial prejudice, and her unusual interests. Her sense of at-homeness in her neighborhood and her imaginative sympathies were a partial compensation. But the more formal social barriers in school set her apart. Thus, the issue of intra-racial prejudice crops up in her poetry sufficiently to rival, in quantity, her preoccupation with interracial prejudice. On the intra-racial level, her experience with prejudice against a black skin and preference for the light skin began in grammar school, as can be seen in the poem, "the ballad of chocolate Mabbie,"[22] and in a section of her novel, *Maude Martha.* On the interracial situation, she could say that at Hyde Park Branch High School, "I wasn't so much injured, just left alone. I realized that they were a society apart, and they really made you feel it. None of them [whites] would have anything to do with you, aside from some white boy if he fell in love with you."[23]

Miss Brooks's sensibility then comprises powerful negatives and positives. In the poetry we find them yoked and coordinated—a source of deep compassion and empathy reflected both in the strength of the cases she makes for her people and the sudden appearances of the author's own voice, as in this part from "The Sundays of Satin-Legs Smith":

> People are so in need, in need of help.
> People want so much that they do not know.
>
> Below the tinkling trade of little coins
> The gold impulse not possible to show
> Or spend. Promise piled over and betrayed.

This voice surges forward wherever misery and frustration challenge beauty and vitality and can be heard powerfully in such a poem as "In the Mecca." It also comes forth, at times, in incisive critical and slashing attacks.

It is this powerful sensibility which has caused the poet to invest her energies in assistance to her community and in a poetry which has resulted in formal recognitions which would require several pages to list. Her community activities are in such categories as financing and awarding numerous prizes in poetry and the arts; sponsorships of contests and workshops on all school levels and in the community; direct assistance to artists; teaching and lecturing; and editing a magazine soon to appear under the title, *Black Position Papers*.[24]

She has won an elaborate array of prizes for poetry within the state of Illinois, regionally, and nationally, being Illinois poet laureate and holder of the Pulitzer Prize for *Annie Allen*. From academic areas, there are two Guggenheim awards and a dozen academic honorary degrees. In September 1971, supplementing other academic posts, is her appointment as Visiting Professor at the College of the City of New York. From the Black community, there are the formal and public testimonials of 1969 in Chicago and a book of poems written by younger and mature Black authors in tribute to her personality and works entitled, *To Gwen, with Love*, 1971.

What should be clear so far is that her sensibility produces a unified confrontation with life and art, and that, in rendering the Black experience she can be said to be out real far on its perilous seas and in real deep.

NOTES

1. The impact of the radical movement can be seen in her poetry, and in the following descriptions: Phyl Garland, "Gwendolyn Brooks: Poet Laureate," *Ebony* 23 (July 1968): 48, 49, passim; Ida Lewis, "Conversation," *Essence*, April 1971, 27; George Stavros, "An Interview with Gwendolyn Brooks," *Contemporary Literature* 11 (Winter 1970): 5–7; *We Asked Gwendolyn Brooks*, n.d., Illinois Bell Telephone, passim.

2. See Stavros, for example, pp. 10–11, passim. (Also stated to me in Interview.)

3. Stavros, p. 10.

4. Ibid.

5. Stavros, p. 12. Other quotations on the page also from Stavros.

6. Lewis, p. 28.

7. Ibid.

8. Herbert Hill, *Soon One Morning* (New York: Random House, 1963), p. 326. The book contains also the first version of the piece, "The Life of Lincoln West," now with slight changes to heighten poetic effect reprinted in *Family Pictures*.

9. Glenda Estelle Clyde, *An Oral Interpreter's Approach to the Poetry of Gwendolyn Brooks*, unpublished dissertation (1966), p. 21.

10. Interview.

11. Garland, passim.

12. Clifton H. Johnson, ed., *God Struck Me Dead* (Philadelphia: Pilgrim Press, 1969), pp. vii–xiii. Also helpful: Close reading of folk sermons.

13. Conversations.

14. Stavros, p. 15.

15. Lewis, p. 29.

16. Stavros, pp. 18–19.

17. Arthur P. Davis, "Gwendolyn Brooks: A Poet of the Unheroic," CLA Journal 8 (December 1963): 25.

18. Garland, pp. 49–52, and passim.

19. Ibid. (I saw a copy of the News Review), courtesy of Miss Brooks.

20. The genesis of several poems is mentioned in Stavros, especially on pp. 7–8. I have also made deductions here and there.

21. Conversation with Miss Brooks.

22. Lewis, p. 28.

23. Ibid.

24. Conversations with Brooks and Don L. Lee.

HAKI R. MADHUBUTI

# Gwendolyn Brooks:
# Beyond the Wordmaker—
# The Making of an African Poet

"There is indeed a new black today. He is different from any the world has known. He's a tall-walker. Almost firm. By many of his own *brothers* he is not understood. And he is understood by *no* white. Not the wise white; not the schooled white; not the kind white. Your *least* pre-requisite toward an understanding of the new black is an exceptional Doctorate which can be conferred only upon those with the proper properties of bitter birth and intrinsic sorrow. I know this is infuriating, especially to those professional Negro-understanders, some of them *very* kind, with special portfolio, special savvy. But I cannot say anything other, because nothing other is the truth." These words, this precise utterance is Gwendolyn Brooks 1972, is Gwendolyn Brooks post-1967, a quiet force cutting through the real dirt with new and energetic words of uncompromising richness that are to many people unexpected, but welcomed by millions.

When you view Gwendolyn Brooks's work in the pre-1967 period, you see a poet, a black poet in the actual, (though still actively searching for her own definitions of blackness) on the roadway to becoming a conscious African poet or better yet a conscious African woman in America who chose poetry as her major craft. However, Gwendolyn Brooks describes her poetry prior to 1967 as "work that was conditioned to the times and the people." In other words, poetry that leaped from the pages bringing forth ideas, definitions, images, reflections, forms, colors, etc., that were molded over a distance of many years—her poetry notebook started at the age of eleven—as a result of and as a reaction to the American reality. And for black people, regardless of the level of their perception of the world, the American reality has always been a battle, a real alley fight.

From Gwendolyn Brooks, *Report from Part One* (Detroit: Broadside Press, 1973), 13–30. Reprinted with permission.

The early years reaped with self-awareness—there is no deny-
ing this—even though at times the force of her poetic song is
strained in iambic pentameter, European sonnets and English
ballads. Conditioned! There is a stronger sense of self-awareness
than most of her contemporaries with the possible exception of
Margaret Walker. She was able to pull through the old leftism of
the 1930s and 1940s and concentrate on herself, her people and
most of all her "writing." Conditioned! Her definitions of the
world as represented in the early poetry are often limited to
accommodating her work and her person to definitions that
were imposed on her from the outside; and she becomes the
reactor rather than the actor. She is being defined by her sur-
roundings and by the environment that has been built around
her, but the definitions and poetic direction from the Euro-
American world are also much a part of her make-up. As early as
1945 in the book *A Street in Bronzeville,* we see images of woman-
hood, manhood, justice and race worked into memorable lines:
"Abortions will not let you forget. / You remember the children
you got that you did not get"; and "Men hep, and cats, or corny
to the jive. / Being seen Everywhere (Keeping Alive), /
Rhumboogie (and the joint is jumpin', Joe, / Brass Rail, Key-
hole, De Lisa, Cabin Inn. / And all the other garbage cans."; and
"I had to kick their law into their teeth in order to save them.";
and "He was born in Alabama. / He was bred in Illinois. / He
was nothing but a / Plain black boy"; and "Mae Belle Jackson's
husband / Whipped her good last night. / Her landlady told my
ma they had / A knock-down-drag-out fight."; and "Mama was
singing / At the midnight Club. / And the place was red / With
blues. / She could shake her body / Across the floor / For what
did she have / To lose?"; and "you paid for your dinner, Sammy
boy, / And you didn't pay with money. / You paid with your
hide and my heart, Sammy boy, / For your taste of pink and
white honey." As the quoted lines indicate Gwendolyn Brooks is
deeply involved with black life, black pain and black spirits. To
seek white honey was natural; to seek anything white in those
early years was only keeping within the expected, within the
encouraged. However, this thing of doing the expected cannot
be fully applied to Gwendolyn Brooks because the medium she
worked in was that of the unexpected—"Negroes 'just don't
write, especially not poetry.' " Her movement into poetry is a
profound comment on her self-confidence and speaks to the
poetic-vision she possessed. The fact that she chose to be a poet

denotes that her view of the "whirlwind" was serious and challenging—yet conditioned.

Her growth and development partially depended upon the climate of the time. Those critical years of the 1930s and 1940s left deep scars of hunger and poverty, but because of a strong and closely knit family, she survived. She has always had unusual encouragement from her mother, who to this day is still quite active in "watching over" her daughter's output. Other major influences varied from Europe's war number two (known as World War II) to the work of Langston Hughes and Richard Wright; the South Side of Chicago where she lived and still lives today, Inez Cunningham Stark at the Southside Community Art Center (Gwendolyn Brooks walked off with four poetry prizes between 1943 and 1945 at Midwestern Writers' Conferences at Northwestern University), the appearance of poems in the *Chicago Defender* and *Poetry* magazine, working with the NAACP's young people's group, appearance in *Mademoiselle* magazine as one of the "Ten Women of the Year" in 1945, grants from the American Academy of Arts and Letters and Guggenheim Fellowships and other publishing in major magazines that published "American" poetry. Gwendolyn Brooks at this time, the late 1940s, was concerned with the "universal fact."

Her work like that of the late Langston Hughes has always touched at some level on the problems of blacks in America. Even allowing that, she was often singled out as the "exception" and proclaimed as an "artist"—a poet of the first rank—a poet who happens to be black; not that Gwendolyn Brooks readily accepted these nebulous titles. There was little she could do about it. We must note that she received major encouragement from *all* quarters to accept, participate and to be grateful for whatever recognition she received. After all, this was what everybody was working for, wasn't it? To go unnoticed is bad enough, but to go unnoticed and not eat is not a stimulus for creativity. By 1945 she had not only married, but had a son. Her family shared most of the time that was normally used for writing and these few literary "breaks" were not only needed, but well received and actively sought after.

If *A Street in Bronzeville* paved the way, *Annie Allen* opened the door. *Annie Allen* (1949) *ran* away with the Pulitzer Prize—the first black person to be so "honored." After winning the Pulitzer, she *now belonged to everybody*. In the eyes of white poetry lovers and white book promoters, the publicity was to read "she is a poet who happens to be black"; in other words, we can't completely forget her "negroness," so let's make it secondary. Her winning the Pulitzer Prize in 1950 is significant for a number of reasons other than her being the first person of African descent to do so. One unstated fact is obvious; *she was the best poet, black or white, writing in the country at the time*. Also in winning the Pulitzer she became internationally known and achieved a following from her own people whereas normally she would not have had access to them. She attracted those "negro" blacks who didn't believe that one is legitimate unless one is sanctioned by whites first. The Pulitzer did this. It also aided her in the pursuit of other avenues of expression and gave her a foothold into earning desperately needed money by writing reviews and articles for major white publications.

In her continuing frame of reference, the confusion over social responsibility and "art for art's sake" intensified. Even though she didn't actually see herself in the context of Euro-American poetry, she was being defined in that context. She was always the American poet who happened to be Negro—the definition was always from the *negative* to the *positive*. Again a Euro-American definition; again conditioned to accept the contradictory and the dangerous. If you cannot definitely and positively define yourself in accordance with your historical and cultural traditions, how in the world can you be consciously consistent in the direction your person and your work must take in accordance with that which is ultimately best and natural for you? At this time Gwendolyn Brooks didn't think of herself as an African or as an African-American. At best she was a "new negro" becoming black. Her view of history and struggle was that of the traditional American history and had not been challenged by anyone of black substance. In her next book the focus was not on history or tradition, but poetic style.

*Annie Allen* (1949), important? Yes. Read by blacks? No. *Annie Allen* more so than *A Street in Bronzeville* seems to have been written for whites. For instance, "The Anniad" requires unusual concentrated study. She invents the sonnet-ballad in part 3 of the poem "Appendix to the Anniad, leaves from a loose-leaf war diary." This poem is probably earth-shaking to some, but leaves me completely dry. The poem is characterized by fourteen lines with a three part alternating rhyme scheme and couplet at the last two lines. Only when she talks of "the children of the poor" do we begin to sense the feel of home again: "What shall I give my children? who are poor / Who are adjudged the leastwise of the land" or "First fight. Then fiddle" or "Not that success, for him, is sure, infallible. / But never has he been afraid to reach. / His lesions are legion." In the poem "Truth" we sense that *that* is what she is about: "And if sun comes / How shall we greet him? / Shall we not dread him, / Shall we not fear him / After so lengthy a / Session with shade? . . . Sweet is it, sweet is it / To sleep in the coolness / Of snug unawareness. / The dark hangs heavily / Over the eyes." The book has a very heavy moral tone, a pleading tone and "God's actual" in one way or another is prevalent throughout. The poems range from the ridiculous such as "old laughter" (written when she was nineteen years old) but included in the book:

> The men and women long ago
> In Africa, in Africa,
> Knew all there was of joy to know.
> In sunny Africa
> The spices flew from tree to tree.
> The spices trifled in the air
> That carelessly
> Fondled the twisted hair.

> The men and women richly sang
> In land of gold and green and red.
> The bells of merriment richly rang.

> But richness is long dead,
> Old laughter chilled, old music done
> In bright, bewildered Africa.

> The bamboo and the cinnamon
> Are sad in Africa.

to the careful profundity of "intermission" part 3:

> Stand off, daughter of the dusk,
> And do not wince when the bronzy lads
> Hurry to cream-yellow shining.
> It is plausible. The sun is a lode.

True, there is silver under
The veils of the darkness.
But few care to dig in the night
For the possible treasure of stars.

But for me there is too much "Grant me that I am human, that I
hurt, that I can cry." There is an overabundance of the special
appeal to the intelligence of the world-runners, even though para-
doxically in part 15 of "the children of the poor," she accurately
notes that their special appeal to the "intelligence" has been the
argument given to us ever since they raped us from Africa: "What
we are to hope is that intelligence / Can sugar up our prejudice
with politeness. / Politeness will take care of what needs caring."
Yet, Gwendolyn Brooks knows that politeness is not possessed by
the enemies of the sun, politeness does not *seek* to control the
world; and their intelligence is as misguided as their need to ma-
nipulate every living element that they come in contact with.
*Annie Allen* is an important book. Gwendolyn Brooks's ability to
use their language while using their ground rules explicitly shows
that she far surpasses the best European-Americans had to offer.
There is no doubt here. But in doing so, she suffers by not commu-
nicating with the masses of black people.

Her work in the late 1950s and early 1960s like that of James
Baldwin and Ralph Ellison appealed to a wide cross-section. The
mood of the land was integration. Come melt with us in the
wind at that time. Some of us are still recovering from the burns.
LeRoi Jones (now Imamu Amiri Baraka), William Melvin Kelly,
John O. Killens, Conrad Kent Rivers, Mari Evans and Melvin B.
Tolson's tone of persuasion was projected toward the conscience
of America. They wrote as if America (or the rulers of America)
had a conscience or a higher God that it answered to. They felt
that America had a moral obligation to its other inhabitants,
those who were not *fortunate* enough to be born white and Protes-
tant. However, a close reading of Indian history in America or
their own history in America would have wiped those illusions
out completely. But, even then the "I'm a writer, not a black
writer" madness was in the air and along with it existed other
distortions and temptations that forever kept the writers from
dealing with their African or African-American perspective.
They all produced important works and all, with the possible
exception of Ralph Ellison (Melvin B. Tolson and Conrad Kent
Rivers are deceased) had their hands on the stop sign and were
getting ready to cross the continent into the 1960s. The 1960s for

Gwendolyn Brooks was to be an entrance into a new life; however it didn't start with *The Bean Eaters*.

*The Bean Eaters* (1960) was the major appeal, the quiet confirmation of the "Negro" as an equal. She failed to question the measuring rod. Equal to what? The poems that come alive are the very personal, such as, "In Honor of David Anderson Brooks, My Father" and the title poem "The Bean Eaters." There is much black womanness in this book. Gwendolyn Brooks is careful to give black women their due, long before the women liberationists of the 1970s. Those poems that stick out are, "A Bronzeville Mother Loiters in Mississippi. Meanwhile, a Mississippi Mother Burns Bacon," "The Last Quatrain of the Ballad of Emmett Till," "Mrs. Small," "Jessie Mitchell's Mother," "Bronzeville Woman in a Red Hat" and "Callie Ford."

The power poem is "We Real Cool," of which she says "the ending WE's in 'We Real Cool' are tiny, wispy, weakly argumentative 'Kilroy-is-here' announcements. The boys have no accented sense of themselves, yet they are aware of a semi-defined personal importance. Say the 'we' softly."

The poem "The *Chicago Defender* Sends a Man to Little Rock" is structurally tight and was socially ahead of its time, but in the final analysis again its major appeal is to morality. The last line weakens the poem with "The loveliest lynchee was our Lord." In "A Man of the Middle Class" she shows accurate vision; her criticism of the middle class may be due to the fact that she, in her personal life, refused to become a part of make-up and costumery and insists that those who take part in it are "ineffectual." She also adds, "Moreover, the 'eminent' ones, the eminent successes of the society, whose rules and styles he imitated, seem no more in possession of the answers than he; excellent examples of dimness, moral softness and confusion, they are shooting themselves and jumping out of windows." "The Ballad of Rudolph Reed" is the excursion of a black man and his family into an all-white neighborhood. By moving in he jeopardizes the life of himself (which he loses) and that of his family. The poem shows the black man's will to "better" himself regardless of the sacrifices.

Yet, that type of sacrifice is senseless and unforgivable, and could have been avoided if blacks at that time accurately assessed their enemies. *The Bean Eaters* is to be the last book of this type. There won't be any completely new book of poetry published until *In the Mecca,* and *In the Mecca* "blacked" its way out of the National Book Award in 1968.

"I—who have 'gone the gamut' from an almost angry rejection

of my dark skin by some of my brainwashed brothers and sisters to a surprised queenhood in the new black sun—am qualified to enter at least the kindergarten of new consciousness now. New consciousness and trudge-toward-progress." With these words Gwendolyn Brooks begins to actively seek and express a new awareness, a black consciousness. She gives greater insight into her newness when she says: "It frightens me to realize that, if I had died before the age of fifty, I would have died a 'Negro' fraction." This is the beginning of defining from one's own perspective; this perspective is what Gwendolyn Brooks would wrestle with between *The Bean Eaters* and the publication of *In the Mecca.*

Her major associations during this period of redefinition were the young and the "Black" writing that was part of their make-up. She, at first hand, witnessed a resurgence of what has been termed the Black Arts Movement. In every aspect of the creative act, young brothers and sisters began to call their own images, from drama to poetry, from fiction to nonfiction, from plastic arts to film, and so on. In every area of creativity black poets cleaned house and carved their own statues into what they wanted themselves to be, regardless of who was watching and with even less regard for what critics, white and black, said. She felt the deep void when Medgar Evers and Malcolm X left us.

She conducted writers' workshops with the Blackstone Rangers and other young people. She took part in neighborhood cultural events like the dedication of the Organization of Black American Culture's Wall of Respect. She lived through the rebellion in Chicago after King's death while listening with disbelief to Mayor Daley's "Shoot to Kill" orders. She lives four blocks from the Black People's Topographical Center in Chicago, the first in the nation. The murder of Mark Clark and Fred Hampton and of other blacks continued to raise questions in her mind. And the major questions were: 'What part do I play?,' 'Where do I fit in?,' 'What can I do?' Her first and most important contribution was to be the redirecting of her voice to her people—*first and foremost.* This is what is evident in *In the Mecca, Riot,* and *Family Pictures.* She becomes "new music screaming in the sun."

Gwendolyn Brooks's post-1967 poetry is fat-less. Her new work resembles a man getting off meat, turning to a vegetarian diet. What one immediately notices is that all the excess weight is quickly lost. Her work becomes extremely streamlined and to the point. There are still a few excesses with language in *In the Mecca,* but she begins to experiment more with free and blank verse, yet her hand still controlled and timed. *In the Mecca* is about black life in an old Chicago landmark. This was to be her epic of black humanity. She wanted to exhibit all its murders, loves, loneliness, hates, jealousies. "Hope occurred, and charity, sainthood, glory, shame, despair, fear, altruism. Theft, material and moral." She included all the tools of her trade, blank verse, prose verse, off-rhyme, random rhyme, long-swinging free verse, the couplet, the sonnet and the ballad. She succeeds admirably with glimpses of greatness. Let's look at "Way-out Morgan":

> Way-out Morgan is collecting guns
> in a tiny fourth-floor room.
> He is not hungry, ever, though sinfully lean.
> He flourishes, ever, on porridge or pat of bean
> pudding or wiener soup—fills fearsomely
> on visions of Death-to-the-Hordes-of-the-White-Men!
> Death!
> (This is the Maxim painted in big black
> above a bed bought at a Champlain rummage sale.)
> Remembering three local-and-legal beatings, he
> rubs his hands in glee,
> does Way-out Morgan. Remembering his Sister
> mob-raped in Mississippi, Way-out Morgan
> smacks sweet his lips and adds another gun
> and listens to Blackness stern and blunt and beautiful,
> organ-rich Blackness telling a terrible story.
> Way-out Morgan
> predicts the Day of Debt-pay shall begin,
> the Day of Demon-diamond,
> of blood in mouths and body-mouths,
> of flesh-rip in the Forum of Justice at last!
> Remembering mates in the Mississippi River,
> mates with black bodies once majestic, Way-out
> postpones a yellow woman in his bed, postpones
> wetnesses and little cries and stomachings—
> to consider Ruin.

And there is compassion in "a little woman lies in dust with roaches. / She never went to kindergarten. / She never learned that black is not beloved." In "After Mecca" her power continues with the ultimate in manhood as in "Malcolm X":

> Original.
> Ragged-round.
> Rich-robust.

He had the hawk-man's eyes.
We gasped. We saw the maleness.
The maleness raking out and making guttural the air
and pushing us to walls.

The section on the Blackstone Rangers is outstanding. Look at "As Seen by Disciplines." "There they are. / Thirty at the corner. / Black, raw, ready. / Sores in the city / that do not want to heal." Gwendolyn Brooks knew in her new sense of sophistication and black association that it was difficult for the sores to heal because of the lukewarm medication. In "The Leaders" she said that "their country is a Nation on no map," and challenged, in "The Sermon on the Warpland," "My people, black and black, revile the River. / Say that the River turns, and turn the River." In "The Second Sermon on the Warpland," she commands, "Live and go out. / Define and / medicate the whirlwind." She ends the book with "Big Bessie":

The time
cracks into furious flower. Lifts its face
all unashamed. And sways in wicked grace.
Whose half-black hands assemble oranges
is tom-tom hearted
(goes in bearing oranges and boom).
And there are bells for orphans—
and red and shriek and sheen.
A garbageman is dignified
as any diplomat.
Big Bessie's feet hurt like nobody's business,
but she stands—bigly—under the unruly scrutiny, stands in the
        wild weed.

In the wild weed
she is a citizen,
and in a moment of highest quality; admirable.

It is lonesome, yes. For we are the last of the loud.
Nevertheless, live.

Conduct your blooming in the noise and whip of the whirlwind.

The books *Riot* (1969) and *Family Pictures* (1970) are important for a number of reasons other than the obvious. With the publication of *Riot* Gwendolyn Brooks began her association with one of the newest and most significant black publishing companies in the world, Broadside Press, under the quiet and strong editorship of Dudley Randall. As the poems in *Riot* and *Family Pictures* will testify, Gwendolyn Brooks was not only asking critical questions, but seeking substantive answers. She was very conscious of the contradictions in her own personal life, and as best as possible—living in a contradictory situation in America—began to systematically deal with those contradictions.

A major problem was that of Harper and Row publishers, a company she had been with for twenty-six years. Naturally, she had a certain affection and dedication to Harper and Row, even though Harper's never, and I mean that literally, pushed the work of Gwendolyn Brooks. But the decision that was to be made in regard to Harper's was not either/or, but: what is best for black people. And, when people begin to put their lives in a perspective of black people as a body and not as we've traditionally done—black people as individuals—the power and influence that we seek will come about because, in the final analysis, the *only* thing that an individual can do individually is *die*. Nobody ever built anything individually.

Thus, Gwendolyn Brooks's movement to Broadside Press was in keeping with what she said in *Family Pictures:* "Blackness / is a going to essences and to unifyings." She became the doer and not just the sayer. She ended her association with Harper and Row with the publication of *The World of Gwendolyn Brooks* and sought out after new boundaries of growth, institution building and black collective association. Before she could enjoy her new comradeship with Broadside Press, other young black writers began leaving Broadside Press and going to large white publishing companies proclaiming—loud and clear—that the "Black Arts Movement was dead" and they had to look after themselves.

Here Gwendolyn Brooks was in her fifties leaving a major white publishing company (and she never accumulated any money or security; she always shared her "wealth") because of her principles and commitment and the new young whom she so admired and patterned herself after were reversing themselves going to where she had just left. This was difficult for her to understand. This would be the black integrity of Gwendolyn Brooks and would lead to her final affirmation of self.

The "death" of the Black Arts Movement as seen by some writers was, of course, only a rationale for their own sick actions, was actually an excuse for the new young "stars" to move from the collective of "we, us and our" to the individuality of "my, me and I," was the excuse used so as not to be held accountable for the madness to come. Let's examine a little closer. The division that resulted is of an elementary nature and is fundamentally important to the writer if he is to remain true to himself and to his work.

The cutting factor was again in the area of definition. How does a black poet (or any black person working creatively) define himself and his work: is he a poet who happens to be black or is he a black man or woman who happens to write? The black and white "art for art's sake" enthusiasts embraced the former and the black nationalists expanded in the latter adding that he is an African in America who expresses himself, his blackness with the written word and that the creativity that he possesses is a gift that should be shared with his people and developed to the highest level humanly possible. And that this "art" form in some way should be used in the liberation of his people.

Gwendolyn Brooks had worked with this same question for about ten years now and had, in her own mind, resolved it. Yet, for the young in whom she had put faith and trust, to reverse themselves made her, too, begin to reexamine her conclusions.

This is the issue. To be able to define one's self from a historically and culturally accurate base and to follow through in your work; keeping the best interest of your history and culture in mind is to—actually—give direction to the coming generations. If one defines one's self as a Russian poet, immediately we know that things that are Russian are important to him and to acknowledge this is not to *leave out the rest of the world* or to limit the poet's range and possibilities in any way.

If a poet defines himself as Chinese we know that that designation carries with it a certain life style which will include Chinese language, dress, cultural mores, feelings, spirituality, music, foods, dance, literature, drama, politics, and so forth. If one is an Indian from India, one is first identified with a *land base;* is identified with a race of people; is identified with all the cultural, religious, and political advantages or disadvantages that are associated with that people whether the "poet" accepts them or not. *This must be understood.* To define one's self is to give direction and this goes without saying, that that direction could either be *positive* or *negative.* When one speaks of a Yasunari Kawabata or a

Yukio Mishima, one first through name association links them with Asia (specifically Japan) whether they reside in Asia or not. To speak of Ayi Kwei Armah, Wole Soyinka or David Diop is first to speak of Africa and then the world.

When seeking universality, one always starts with the local and brings to the universal world that which is particularly Russian, Asian, European, Indian, Spanish, African or whatever. If, in 1972, this is not clear I will concede that the "Black Arts Movement" is dead. But the overwhelming evidence shows us that by and large the majority of black "artists" at some level understand their commitment and are educating themselves to the realities of the world more and more: if we don't look after each other, nobody else is supposed to. The black "artist" understands this.

Gwendolyn Brooks is an African poet living and writing in America whose work for the most part has been "conditioned" by her experiences in America. By acknowledging her Africanness, her blackness, she reverses the trend of being defined by the negative to her own definition in the positive. She, in effect, gives direction in her new definition which, if it does nothing else, *forces* her reader to question that definition.

Why does she call herself African? To question our existence in this world critically is the beginning of understanding the world we live in. To begin to understand that we, Africans, in this country constitute the *largest* congregation of African people outside of Africa is important. To understand that black people in this country, who number thirty million upwards, will have to question why we don't have any say-so over domestic policy in reference to ourselves, to question *why* we have no say-so over foreign policy in relationship to Africa, to question why we exist as other people's door mats is important.

To question is the beginning of empowerment. Why does Gwendolyn Brooks call herself an African? Almost for the same reason that Europeans call themselves Europeans, that Chinese call themselves Chinese, that Russians call themselves Russian, that Americans call themselves Americans—people find a sense of *being,* a sense of worth and substance with being associated with *land.* Associations with final roots gives us not only a history (which did not start and will not end in this country), but proclaims us heirs to a future and it is best when we, while young, find ourselves talking, acting, living and reflecting in accordance with that future which is best understood in the context of the past.

The vision of Gwendolyn Brooks can be seen in lines like:

> Say to them,
> say to the down-keepers,
> the sun-slappers,
> the self-soilers,
> the harmony-hushers,
> "Even if you are not ready for day
> it cannot always be night."
> You will be right.
> For that is the hard home-run.
>
> Live not for Battles Won.
> Live not for The-End-of-the-Song.
> Live in the along.

The direction Gwendolyn Brooks gives to "Young Afrikans" is calm, well thought out and serious:

> If there are flowers, flowers
> must come out to the road. Rowdy!—
> knowing where wheels and people are,
> knowing where whips and screams are,
> knowing where deaths are, where the kind kills are.

Chester Hines said that "one of the sad things in America is that they try to control the Black people with creativity." And, to control your own creativity is the prerequisite to any kind of freedom or liberation, because if you tell the truth, you don't worry about offending. You just go ahead and cut the ugly away, while building for tomorrow.

We can see in the work of Gwendolyn Brooks of 1972 positive movement from that of the sayer to the doer, where she recognizes that *writing is not enough* for a people in a life and death struggle. For so few black writers to reflect the aspirations and needs of so many (there are about three hundred black writers who are published with any kind of regularity) is a responsibility that should not be taken lightly. Every word has to be considered and worked with so as to use it to its fullest potential. We know that her association with the young had a great effect upon her present work.

Also, her trip to East Africa in 1971 helped to crystallize and finalize her current African association. To understand that Jews' association with Israel is not only cultural, historical and financial, but is necessary for their own survival is to begin to deal with the real world. To understand why the Irish in Chicago sent $25,000 plus to Northern Ireland in 1972 is to associate people with *land* and survival. Gwendolyn Brooks by her dealings with the young poets, Broadside Press and other institutions is only "in keeping" with what other, "European" artists have always done to aid their own. By institutionalizing her thoughts and actions, she is thinking and acting in accordance with a future which will be built by nobody but the people themselves. As in her latest poem, her advice is not confused, clouded, or overly simple, but is the message of tomorrow:

> And, boys, in all your Turnings and your Churnings,
> remember Afrika.
> You have to call your singing and your bringing,
> your pulse, your ultimate booming in
> the not-so-narrow temples of your Power—
> you have to call all that, that is your Poem, AFRIKA.
> Although you know
> so little of that long leaplanguid land,
> our tiny union
> is the dwarfmagnificent.
> Is the busysimple thing.
>
> See, say, salvage.
> Legislate.
> Enact our inward law.

Characteristically she has said that

> My aim, in my next future, is to write poems that will some-how successfully "call" (see Imamu Baraka's "SOS") all black people: black people in taverns, black people in alleys, black people in gutters, schools, offices, factories, prisons, the con-sulate; I wish to reach black people in pulpits, black people in mines, on farms, on thrones; *Not* always to "teach"—I shall wish often to entertain, to illumine. My newish voice will not be an imitation of the contemporary young black voice, which I so admire, but an extending adaptation of today's Gwendolyn Brooks' voice.

Gwendolyn Brooks is the example for us all, a consistent monument in the real, unaware of the beauty and strength she has radiated. Above all, she is the continuing storm that walks with the English language as lions walk with Africa. Her pressure is above boiling, cooking new food for our children to grow on.

ARTHUR P. DAVIS

# Gwendolyn Brooks

Never a simple poet, Gwendolyn Brooks has grown more difficult with the years. Like Tolson, she changed her style as well as her viewpoint in midcareer. When she first published in 1945, most Negro writers were literary integrationists, and she definitely held this position. In her last two poetical collections, however, she has abandoned that attitude and gone "black." With the new blackness has come an increase in the obscurity of much of her verse.

Gwendolyn Brooks was born in Topeka, Kansas, and reared in Chicago. She began writing poetry when she was seven years old, and had her first poem published when thirteen. In the same year she published a mimeographed community newspaper called the *Champlain Weekly News*. Miss Brooks graduated from Englewood High School (Chicago) in 1934 and Wilson Junior College in 1936. Married in 1939 to Henry Blakely, she has a son, born in 1940, and a daughter, born in 1951. Her poetry has appeared in *Harper's, Poetry, Common Ground, Yale Review, Saturday Review of Literature, Negro Story,* and other magazines. Her first volume of poetry, *A Street in Bronzeville* (1945), won the Merit Award of *Mademoiselle* magazine. She received a $1,000 prize from the Academy of Arts and Letters in 1946 and two Guggenheim fellowships for study, in 1946 and 1947. Her second volume of poetry, *Annie Allen* (1949), won *Poetry's* Eunice Tietjens Memorial Award, and then the Pulitzer Prize for poetry in 1950. Miss Brooks has won the Poetry Workshop Award, given by the Midwestern Writers' Conference, three times (1943–1945). In 1964 she won the Friends Literature Award for Poetry and the Thormond Monsen Award for Literature. In 1969 she announced through the *Negro Digest* that she would award two prizes of $250 each to the best poem and best short story published by a black writer each year.

She has taught creative writing and poetry at Columbia,

From *From the Dark Tower: Afro-American Writers 1900–1960*. Copyright © 1974 by Arthur P. Davis. Reprinted by permission of Howard University Press.

Elmhurst, and Northeastern Illinois State College, all in Chicago; and at the University of Wisconsin. She is a member of the advisory boards of the Institute for International Education, the Society for Midland Authors, and the Illinois Art Council.

The bulk of Miss Brooks's work is found in the following publications: *A Street in Bronzeville* (1945); *Annie Allen* (1949), which won her the Pulitzer Prize in poetry for 1950; *The Bean Eaters* (1960); *In the Mecca* (1968); and *Riot* (1969). In addition, she has published one children's book, *Bronzeville Boys and Girls* (1956); a superb collection of poems entitled *Selected Poems* (1963); and one short work of fiction, *Maud Martha* (1953).

In her first three volumes of poetry, considered here as a unit, Miss Brooks wrote principally about life in the drab Bronzevilles of America (the black ghettos of our Northern cities); and she wrote with a great understanding of and a vast compassion for the unfortunates who lived in these places. Although she saw them as victims of America's vicious racial pattern, there is very little bitterness or hatred in the poems found in these first three works. On the contrary, she seems to imply that prejudice is a terrible but all-too-human weakness. The poem which best typifies this position is "The *Chicago Defender* Sends a Man to Little Rock." The reporter finds that, in spite of the violence that occurred there, he cannot write a story that his editor will accept. He discovers that the people in Little Rock "are like people everywhere"—small, petty, weak, and to be pitied rather than hated. After all, "The loveliest lynchee was our Lord."

Much of the poetry in Gwendolyn Brooks's first three works, like most Negro verse, falls into the protest category. But, again, one finds that Miss Brooks's protest poems tend to be subtly ironic or quietly humorous rather than strident or rhetorical or bitter. For example, in "Beverly Hills, Chicago" she relates the reaction of a group of Negroes driving through this upper-class white section:

> Nobody is furious. Nobody hates these people.
> At least, nobody driving by in this car.
> It is only natural, however, that it should occur to us
> How much more fortunate they are than we are.[1]

In "The Lovers of the Poor" she describes a group of well-meaning but obtuse whites from the Betterment League being confronted with the actual conditions among the Bronzeville poor:

> Keeping their scented bodies in the center
> Of the hall as they walk down the hysterical hall,
> They allow their lovely skirts to graze no wall,
> Are off at what they manage of a canter[2]

One of Miss Brooks's finest protest poems, "of DeWitt Williams on his way to Lincoln Cemetery," has no word of protest in it. Consisting of simple factual statements, it suggests a strong indictment of all that race means in our land:

> He was born in Alabama.
> He was bred in Illinois.
> He was nothing but a
> Plain black boy.
>
> Swing low swing low sweet sweet chariot.
> Nothing but a plain black boy.[3]

Note the effective repetition of the phrase "plain black boy."

Although generally restrained and relatively objective in most of her earlier work, Miss Brooks speaks sharply on the theme of color prejudice within the Negro group, particularly as it applies to the dark-skinned woman. This theme occurs often in her works. There are two very strong poems on this subject in *A Street in Bronzeville:* "The Ballad of Chocolate Mabbie" and "Ballad of Pearl May Lee." The first deals with the heartache a black child encounters. The second, a very bitter poem, deals with a situation often found in earlier Negro protest poetry: the story of a black man who gets involved with a white woman and is lynched. In the earlier poems the Negro is usually an innocent victim of circumstances, but here the victim neglects his dark girl for the white because he has a fatal taste for "pink and white honey."

This theme of the difficulties that arise between a "sweet and chocolate girl" and a "man of tan" occurs in "The Anniad," and plays a crucial part in the lives of the two lovers. There is also an especially bitter poem in *The Bean Eaters* on the theme; entitled "Jessie Mitchell's Mother." It concerns the unnatural hatred between a dark-skinned daughter and her light-skinned mother. In fact, even though her last two publications abandoned many themes found in the first three, Miss Brooks did not abandon the black-and-tan theme. *In the Mecca* (page 23) has "The ballad of Edie Barrow" who "fell in love with a Gentile boy. / All creamy-and-golden fair"; and, of course, it ends with the usual heart-breaking result of such an affair for the "alien" girl.

We note that most of these pieces on color prejudice are written in the ballad form. We also note that in these ballads, whether on the color theme or in a poem like "The Ballad of Rudolph Reed" (based on the Chicago housing riots), the language is simple and strong, and the passion even stronger. Miss Brooks has told us that the ballad form should have the "beat inevitable," should have "blood," should have "a wildness cut up and tied in little bunches."[4] In some of these ballads we get the impression that Gwendolyn Brooks has somehow stepped into the picture and, forgetting her usual restraint, expressed intense personal feeling.

One of Miss Brooks's most unforgettable and most subtly conceived characters is the title figure in "The Sundays of Satin-Legs Smith."[5] A superb creation, with his wonder suits in "yellow and wine," all drapes, his scented lotion, his artificial flower, and his "hysterical ties," Satin-Legs could easily have become another Sporting Beasley (Sterling Brown's character), heroically and defiantly rising above the drab and sordid Bronzeville environment through sheer sartorial splendor. But Miss Brooks does not yield to that temptation. Satin-Legs, like Beasley, has the peacock syndrome, but unlike Beasley he is not heroic; he does not actually dress his way out of the drabness of Bronzeville. For his creator he is still a self-deceived figure of dry hours and emptiness—a symbol of both the sterility of ghetto living and of twentieth-century life in general.

With the publication of *In the Mecca* (1968), Gwendolyn Brooks begins a new period in her literary career. Like many young and middle-aged writers, she has come under the influence of the Black Aesthetics Movement, a movement which began about 1960, and her commitment to blackness is very evident in her last two publications. We note that the dedication for *In the Mecca* is "to the memory of Langston Hughes; and to James Baldwin, LeRoi Jones, and Mike Alexandroff, educators extraordinaire"; and the title poem itself is inscribed "In Tribute—" to, among others, Don Lee. With Don Lee and LeRoi Jones as "educators," she has had significant teachers for her new commitment.

The title poem of *In the Mecca* relates the search for Ms. Sallie's missing Pepita, and the finding of the child's body under the cot of Jamaican Edward, one of the dwellers in the Mecca. But this pathetic little story is secondary to the poet's major purpose: the looking into the lives and thoughts of the several types who live in this decayed slum apartment house. Through the search for Pepita, Miss Brooks presents a number of fascinating characters, all of them somehow the victims of the Mecca. She also brings to the reader some sense of the vibrancy, the drama, and that peculiar tenseness which seems to stay with black ghettos. This old Mecca, of course, is more than just a run-down apartment house for Negroes; it is a microcosm of the ghettos of all the Northern cities. Its blight, never stated but implied, is the blight that comes from being black and poor.

In a series of subtle yet striking portraits, portraits done with a few short but extremely deft and suggestive lines, Gwendolyn Brooks catches and crystallizes the peculiarity, the misery, the ambition, the desire, the frustrations, and all of the other dominant weaknesses and strengths of her many subjects; for example, "Great-great Gram hobbles, fumbles at the knob, / mumbles. . . ." From her slave past she remembers best the earthen floor of the family cabin and "Something creebled in that dirt" that the children could "pop" and "squish" with their bare heels.

When she describes the teacher, Alfred, however, Miss Brooks could have been thinking of herself:

> Ah, his God!—
> To create! To create! To blend with the tight intenseness
> over the neat detail, come to
> a terrified standstill of the heart, then shiver,
> then rush—successfully—
> at that rebuking thing, that obstinate and
> recalcitrant little beast, the phrase![6]

Among the tenants in the Mecca, the poet places Don Lee and tells us that he wants:

> not a various America.
> Don Lee wants
> a new nation
> under nothing; . . .
> wants
> new art and anthem; will
> want a new music screaming in the sun.

Presumably, Miss Brooks now wants the same thing.

Following the "wants" of Don Lee, she has another tenant, Amos, saying a prayer for America:

"Bathe her in her beautiful blood.
A long blood bath will wash her pure. . . .
Slap the false sweetness from that face.
Great-nailed boots
Must kick her prostrate, heel-grind that soft breast,
outrage her saucy pride . . .
Let her lie there, panting and wild, her pain
red . . .
with nothing to do but think, think
of how she was so grand,
flogging her dark one with her one hand,
watching in meek amusement while he bled.
Then shall she rise, recover.
Never to forget."

Although the thoughts of a character must not be ascribed to its creator, these lines—and those which tell about "Way-out Morgan" who "listens to Blackness stern and blunt and beautiful," collects guns, and "predicts the Day of Debt-pay shall begin," the day of the avenging blood bath, do tell us how far along the revolutionary line the author has traveled. The contrast between these sentiments and those expressed in "The *Chicago Defender* Sends a Man to Little Rock" is startling.

*In the Mecca* contains in addition to the title poem nine other pieces—among them one on "Medgar Evers," one on "Malcolm X," and one on "The Blackstone Rangers."

In her most recent published collection, *Riot* (1969), Gwendolyn Brooks continues her journey into blackness. The slim volume of twenty-two pages was published by the Broadside Press, which represents many young, black, revolutionary poets. The volume is a poem in three parts. According to the back cover of the work: "it arises from the disturbances in Chicago after the assassination of Martin Luther King in 1968."

The titular poem compresses into a page and a half the life and death story of John Cabot, a blue blood. In his short compass Gwendolyn Brooks presents with great skill what the black revolution means to an unprepared upper-class white America. The poem is Gwendolyn Brooks at her best. The second poem in *Riot,* "The Third Sermon on the Warpland (Phoenix)," is written in the poet's obscure style. It seems to give vignettes of the riot and to suggest through its phoenix symbol that good will come with the upheaval:

The Black Philosopher will remember:
"There they came to life and exulted,
the hurt mute.
Then it was over . . ."

A small volume of twenty-three pages, Gwendolyn Brooks's latest verse publication (at this writing), *Family Pictures,* was published by the Broadside Press in 1970. The initial pcem, "The Life of Lincoln West," is a heart-tearing account of the cruelties encountered by an ugly little black boy. He finds some comfort, however, when a man refers to him as "the real thing"; that is, he was "Not like those diluted Negroes you see so much of on / the streets these days." The poem seems to be a parable, and one can interpret it in several ways.

In another piece. "Young Africans," Miss Brooks shows once more her new black position. Concerning the young Africans, she says: "And they await, across the Changes and the spiraling dead, / our black revival, our black vinegar, / our hands, and our hot blood." The poem is a very strong affirmation of the revolutionary perspective. Advocating the "hard-heroic" and a "fine fury," Gwendolyn Brooks continues her trek into the heart of blackness.

Miss Brooks calls *Maud Martha* (1953) a novel, and it is certainly more of a novel in form than Toomer's *Cane.* The work, however, is a series of vignettes, penetrating vignettes, which delineate movements in the lives of dark-skinned Maud Martha and her light-skinned husband Paul. It also describes the lives of many other characters, all of them poor, who live in her "kitchen-ette building." The material is similar to that found in Miss Brooks's earlier poems and in her work *In the Mecca. Maud Martha* gives a low-keyed but subtle picture of the experiences and adjustments of an intelligent, sensitive, poor, black girl in a world where "white is right." Although it has few high spots, *Maud Martha* is one of Gwendolyn Brooks's most sensitive and understanding works. The reader leaves the little volume with a deeper-than-surface insight into the lives of poor black folk in the 1930s and 1940s.

As has been said, *Maud Martha* is a series of vignettes or episodes, but they cling together tenaciously to form a unified picture of the joys and sorrows of this young married couple in a Northern ghetto, with their color differences just one of the crosses they have to bear. The problem of color prejudice within the race comes up often in the works of Gwendolyn Brooks.

Gwendolyn Brooks, like Robert Hayden, is a brilliant craftsman in verse; also like Hayden, she has changed her techniques and verse forms as she has matured. Though never slavishly conventional, in her early works, Miss Brooks employed most of the conventional verse forms, a few of them not often used today. For example, in *Annie Allen,* she has a series of skillful tercets ("Sunday chicken," "old relative," and "downtown vaudeville"); and in "The Anniad," she makes use of a variant of Chaucer's rime royal. In recent years, as stated above, Gwendolyn Brooks has abandoned her former integrationist position and moved steadily towards a black nationalist posture. With this ideological change, there has come a parallel shift in verse techniques. Influenced by the young black revolutionary writers of the 1960s, Miss Brooks has given up, not all, but many of the conventional forms used in her early publications. For one thing, like other modern poets, she employs rhyme very sparingly. Perhaps her most popular form now is the kind of flexible, unrhymed verse paragraph found in the volume *In the Mecca.* These verse paragraphs are naturally of varying lengths, and their moods and verse forms change with the subject matter involved. For example, when she writes about Don Lee, her lines reflect some of the techniques of Don Lee; and when she relates "the ballad of Edie Barrow," she uses rhyme and a ballad-type line.

Miss Brooks often writes short, highly chiseled, one-idea lines, some only one word in length; note for example these verses from "The Chicago Picasso":

> We squirm.
> We do not hug the Mona Lisa.
> We
> may touch or tolerate . . .

Note the alliteration in the last line. It is found also in other poems, including "The Second Sermon on the Warpland": "Salve salvage in the spin. / Endorse the splendor splashes." Perhaps the most effective element in her poetic technique is word-choice. With strong, suggestive, oftentimes unusual words—words that startle the reader—Gwendolyn Brooks weaves a brilliant poetic tapestry. Never sentimental, never a mouther of clichés, she brings to any subject the freshness and excitement which characterize good poetry—and good poets.

# NOTES

1. *Annie Allen* (New York: Harper, 1949), p. 49.
2. *The Bean Eaters* (New York: Harper, 1960), p. 38.
3. *A Street in Bronzeville* (New York: Harper, 1945), p.21.
4. *The Bean Eaters* (New York: Harper, 1960), p. 19.
5. *A Street in Bronzeville* (New York: Harper, 1945), pp. 24–29.
6. *In the Mecca* (New York: Harper and Row, 1968), pp. 6–7.

WILLIAM H. HANSELL

# Essences, Unifyings, and Black Militancy: Major Themes in Gwendolyn Brooks's *Family Pictures* and *Beckonings*

*Family Pictures* and *Beckonings,* two collections of Gwendolyn Brooks's poetry published in the 1970s, if considered thematically and stylistically, are very much like collections of her verse published in the late 1960s.[1] The call for militancy and communal unity, the celebration of blackness, Black heroes, and the role of the poet—all are major concerns. In a somewhat more traditional vein, of course, Brooks also has written love poems, elegies and eulogies, in a wide range of tones.

This study, moving from minor to major themes, will attempt to demonstrate that midway through the decade of the 1970s, Brooks continues to be inspired by the same subjects that were the burden of her poems in earlier periods. More specifically, the bulk of her work in the recent period is all but indistinguishable from such collections as *In the Mecca* and *Riot,* both of which appeared in the late 1960s.[2]

The few poems devoted to love and religion express characteristic attitudes. In a blues idiom, "Steam Song" (*Beckonings*) voices an abandoned woman's response to a "Good Song":

> That Song boil up my blood
> like a good Song can.
> It make this woman want to
> run out and find her man.

"Friend" (B), another love poem, is far removed from "Steam Song" on the spectrum of emotion; it calculatingly evokes a twilight mood:

---

Reprinted from *Black American Literature Forum* 11, no. 2 (Summer 1977). Copyright © 1977, Indiana State University.

It is the evening of our love.
Evening is hale and whole.
Evening shall not go out.
Evening is comforting flame.
Evening is comforting flame.

"A Black Wedding Song" (B) insists, as Brooks has often insisted in the past, that the "World" is a great enemy to lovers:

For war comes in from the World
and puzzles a darling duet—
tangles tongues,
tears hearts, mashes minds;
there will be the need to forgive.

In an early poem about a minister called "the preacher: ruminates behind the sermon," the minister's compassion was portrayed as far more important than any formal religious function he served. Brooks seemed to imply that extending love and sympathy to sufferers outweighed any other service the man might render. She seems to repeat that belief in "Song: The Rev. MuBugwu Dickinson Ruminates Behind the Sermon" (*Family Pictures*). The major difference between the poems, perhaps, is that in "Song" the preacher, insisting that just being good is not enough, urges political action. And as the title in the more recent poem indicates, Christianity is more definitely rejected because, as the poem says, it "is what you learned when . . . little and 'a fool,' / you sat in Sunday School."

When Brooks takes up again art and the role of the artist, the reaffirmation of her ideas is self-evident. For example, an elegy to her brother opens *Beckonings*. Entitled "Raymond Melvin Brooks," the poem celebrates his love of work and life and people, but most of all, the poet stresses her brother's love for and capacity to beautify the immediate and commonplace:

He knew how to put paint to paper—
made the paper speak and sing.
But he was chiefly a painter of days and the daily,
with a talent for life color, life pattern:
a talent for jeweling use and the usual,
a talent for practical style.

Everywhere one looks in either her prose or verse, one finds irrefutable evidence of the importance to her of the immediate and commonplace. Thirteen years ago, for example, Arthur P. Davis commented at length upon her primary concern with the commonplace lives of ordinary people in her immediate environment.[3] Brooks herself, in a 1969 "Interview," declared her intention "to respond to her climate."[4]

Moreover, the aesthetic theory implied in the elegy is almost a transcription of a recent article which appeared in *Black Books Bulletin*.[5] In the article, Brooks has general praise for the energy and creativity of several young poets; yet she also expresses a fear that formal and technical matters have been gaining precedence over things she considers more important.

> I observe [she writes], too many little indications that some of our singing brothers and sisters, in the worrying grip of current frustrations and vagueness, are willing to settle for "the pretty little thing," the handsome harmony, the obscure conundrum. I like prettiness, I like music, I like games and puzzles. But I don't think we Black poets can afford to forget what, in 1967, 1968, 1969, we bravely decided we are *about*. The issues remain too large; the threats continue; the sewers deepen and reach for us with an ever more ravenous hunger.

Brooks then goes on to condemn her own youthful "errors" in the direction of "prettiness": "Reminds me of certain little timidities of my *own* in the late Forties—and I was *wrong!*"

The Black hero has been a preoccupation of Brooks's throughout her career; and the collections under consideration reaffirm her view that true Black poets are of necessity Black heroes. Her tribute to Paul Robeson, in a poem in *Family Pictures,* somewhat like her praise of Malcolm X and Medgar Evers, stresses his masculine defiance of stereotypes, his rejection of amelioristic strategies, and his commitment to Afro-American unity. The poem states that Robeson's true meaning was

> that we are each other's
> harvest:
> we are each other's
> business:
> we are each other's
> magnitude and bond.

Robeson, to add a final word, in addition to radical criticisms of the United States, is also from an earlier generation and may be a reminder to the present generation that Black militancy has a distinguished history. Another poem in *Beckonings,* entitled "To John Oliver Killens in 1975," also states the poet's commitment to art that inspires "black solidarity" and "kindness."

One section of *Family Pictures* is entitled "Young Heroes" and is made up of the following three poems: "To Keorapetse Kgositsile (Willie)," "To Don at Salaam," and "Walter Bradford." The central idea of "Willie," an abstract and difficult poem, is that Willie is a hero and poet largely because he understands that art improves life. Since Afro-Americans are threatened with genocide ("a scientific thinning of our ranks"), the Black poet must teach that the only viable response is to unify in order to resist violently. According to the poem, "Afrika" sends the message that "Blackness is a going to essences and to unifyings." The alternative could mean cultural or racial extermination.

"To Don at Salaam" has the directness and simplicity and concreteness of Brooks's finest poems. Unlike the poems to Kgositsile and Bradford, which stress in explicit terms their contribution to Black nationhood, "To Don at Salaam" is, on the surface at least, more like a love poem. The "Don" in the poem (in all likelihood Don Lee, poet, editor, and critic, among other activities, and who is now Haki R. Madhubuti) epitomizes the honesty, beauty, integrity, and controlled force of the authentic Black poet.

The third and last of the "Young Heroes" is a poem entitled "Walter Bradford," in which Bradford is saluted as a dynamic person who conceivably could jolt even the most inert people into motion by virtue of a seemingly uncontainable energy. The poem itself is playful although the tribute is no doubt seriously intended.

As if asked to supply a set of characteristics diametrically opposed to those of the Black hero, Brooks responds with a poem in *Beckonings* entitled "Horses Graze." "Horses Graze" seems at first to celebrate a view of life which is almost absolutely acquiescent. Walt Whitman's famous celebration of the insouciance of animals and his desire to live among them in order to escape human beings, whose discontentments often make life miserable, comes to mind; for "Horses Graze" seems to approve animal satisfaction, until her satirical intention is recognized, and the full force of her contempt is poured out on creatures who "love" indiscriminately and "eat" and "eat" and "eat." And Brooks very deliberately gives her poem universal meaning:

In Sweden,
China,
Afrika,
in India or Maine
the animals are sane;
they know and know and know
there's ground below
and sky
up high.

The distinction between up and down may be the only one they're capable of making.

On a more whimsical and optimistic note, wonderfully simple and direct advice is given to her "children" in " 'When Handed a Lemon, Make Lemonade.' " The poem from *Beckonings* allows her to observe in her homeliest manner that "trouble" can be turned into a valuable and useful possession and should in no way be denied or rejected; therefore, "When Handed a Lemon, Make Lemonade."

In both *Family Pictures* and *Beckonings,* Brooks continues to explore and expose the mystery of blackness. A poem in *Family Pictures,* "The Life of Lincoln West," for example, is a balladlike recreation of a Black child's escape from shame and self-hatred to the conviction that his blackness is a source of pleasure and pride. But before he learns that, he lives with the daily agony of parents who can just barely tolerate his presence and schoolmates, a white teacher, and his attractive next door neighbors who don't want to be seen with him when their more "acceptable friends" come to play. Lincoln's redemptive experience comes in a theater when an astonished white man, recoiling from Lincoln, accidentally blurts to him that he is indeed the "real thing." Those words, the "real thing," bewilder the boy at first, but gradually he is reassured, in the words of the poem:

When he was hurt, too much
stared at—
too much
left alone—he
thought about that. He told himself
"After all, I'm
the real thing."

It comforted him.

"Elegy in a Rainbow" (*Beckonings*) seems to say that the nature of "the Black Nation," or simply of blackness, is a mystery that rational analysis would kill. Like thoughts of Christmas to a child, blackness must be treated as a special possession "that no one else can see." Clearly, some individuals are denied initiation into the mystery. Possibly it is Afro-Americans alone who can know the truth; or it is also possible that the truth is known only by individuals who can know it by virtue of their intuition.

The following works as well as some others reveal Brooks's unequivocal belief that a struggle of a violent nature is going on and will continue. She has, of course, throughout her career been aware of the full range of racial conflicts and other social evils, and these awarenesses are evident in her poems. However, her belief that the response to such conditions would have to be violent is more recent, appearing in unequivocal terms in the mid-1960s. Partially accounting for the change, as Dudley Randall has written, was "the influence of her association with militant young Chicago South Side writers."[6] In fact, Brooks said in 1969 that her future poems would "include [individuals] who do not think they're thinking about the great fight that's going on,"[7] and that idea is of major importance in a short poem with a long title in *Beckonings*: "Five Men against the Theme." "Five Men" condemns as a class all who are passive or exploitative in response to the "warfare" going on; conversely, it praises men with the strength and determination to act. From *Beckonings,* the poem "The Boy Died in My Alley" portrays an individual who tries to pretend he does not see the horrors which occur all around him. The poem reveals a mind futilely attempting to ignore what the "red floor" of the alley plainly states. Perhaps "The Boy Died in My Alley" is somewhat optimistic in the sense that, like the narrator of the poem, others also will come to accept the truth and act accordingly.

"Young Afrikans" (*Family Pictures*) declares that change will require violence and that the violence will be necessary to compel everyone, the willing and the unwilling, to face the "Blacktime":

> Taking Today (to jerk it out of joint)
> the hardheroic maim the
> leechlike-as-usual who use,
> adhere to, carp, and harm.
>
> And they await,
> across the Changes and the spiraling dead,

> our black revival, our black vinegar,
> our hands, and our hot blood.

Passivity, the poem says, is "harm"; there is no equivocation. True heroes, called "flowers," must be militant and violent"

> If there are flowers flowers
> must come out to the road. Rowdy!—
> knowing where wheels and people are,
> knowing where whips and screams are,
> knowing where deaths are, where the kind kills are.

As in *Beckonings,* the final poem in *Family Pictures,* which is entitled "Speech to the Young," appeals to youth to scorn humiliating compromises. Young people Brooks urges to live their lives even while fully participating in bringing about the necessary changes, just as in an earlier poem the narrator-mother had commanded her son to "Go down the street."

Since "Boys. Black." contains all her major themes in the 1970s, it seems appropriate to examine it in detail. Urging young Afro-Americans to announce the beginning of a new age, the poem begins:

> Boys. Black. Black Boys.
> Be brave to battle for your breath and bread.
> Your heads hold clocks that strike the new time of day.
> Your hearts are
> legislating Summer Weather now.
> > Cancel Winter.

From actions which will probably be violent, the narrator derives some hope in the belief "there's fertile ground beneath the pseudo-ice." In the same poem, "Afrika"—always spelled with a "k"—is held out as an essential inspirational source, even if to the young men Afrika had been little more than a name on a map.

> Boys, in all your Turning and your Churnings,
> remember Afrika.
> Call your singing and your bringing,
> your pulse, your ultimate booming in
> the not-so-narrow temples of your Power—
> call all that, that is your Poem, AFRIKA.

> Although you know
> so little of that long leaplanguid land,
> our tiny union
> is the dwarfmagnificent.
> Is the busy simple thing.

Like Countee Cullen in "Heritage," Brooks believes that even if the connection between Afrika and Afro-Americans seems insignificant—a "tiny union"—yet it is real and important: "the dwarfmagnificent."

Brooks goes on to state that the young men should "Enact our inward law." That phrase "inward law" is explicit evidence she is relying upon a Black mystique, asserting, without explaining, a racial quality. Living, as the poem says, "in the precincts of a nightmare," the young can feel confident that change, however achieved, will at least not be worse than present conditions. And at this point in the poem the young men are urged "to be with your sisters" in the work.

The next section of the poem deals with several threats to their success, and the narrator duly identifies each threat and offers a possible response. They are told to beware of false leaders:

> Because
> the eyeless Leaders flutter, tilt, and fail.
> The followers falter, peculiar, eyeless too.

After warning against false leaders, Brooks informs the young men that religious scruples should not impede the struggle. The passage is somewhat difficult, perhaps more abstract than it had to be (even if the poem is subtitled "a preachment"). She seems to say that Black youth must act in the knowledge that there are no absolutes, no certainties, and she urges the young to use "Force"

> whether
> God is a Thorough and a There,
> or a mad child,
> playing
> with a floorful of toys,
> mashing
> whatwhen he will. Force, whether
> God is spent pulse, capricious, or a yet-to-come.

Formal religious doctrine, I believe these lines declare, must be secondary in the struggle because whether God exists or not, whether God is evil or not, whether God has died or not yet come are all beside the point.

Two further cautionings follow. The first probably contains an allusion to Dr. Martin Luther King, Jr., more particularly suggesting his influence was neutralized and that any reform movement can become nothing more than what the poem calls an "imitation coronation."

> And boys,
> young brothers, young brothers—
> beware the imitation coronations.
> Beware
> the courteous paper of kingly compliments.

The final snares they're warned against are the "easy griefs." They are told it is not enough to shout "ATTICA" in the streets and then go running home to watch "Gunsmoke."

"Boys. Black." concludes with lines which declare unashamedly that love and faith have motivated the poet to speak and that, indeed, love and faith must also be their guiding impulses:

> I tell You
> I love You
> and I trust You.
> Take my Faith.
> Make of my Faith an engine.
> Make of my Faith
> a Black Star. I am Beckoning.

Even though the "Black Star" probably was intended in part to revive memories of Marcus Garvey, Brooks modifies the "Black Star" into a symbol not simply of material wealth or of a way back to Africa but of spiritual faith in the capacity of the young to be the agent of their own salvation.

In sum, *Family Pictures* and *Beckonings,* both of which were published in the 1970s, richly demonstrate that Brooks, whether writing about love, religion, blackness, militancy, or racial unity, continues to instruct her audience in the same manner as in her distinguished works in the late 1960s, most notably *In the Mecca* and *Riot.* Continuing to employ her distinctive, often complex style, she explores and celebrates the essence of blackness and those Blacks who lead or who are only in the process of discovering appropriate "life patterns" in contemporary America.

## NOTES

1. (Detroit: Broadside Press, 1970; Detroit: Broadside Press, 1975). All quotations are from these works unless otherwise indicated.

2. *In the Mecca* (New York: Harper and Row, 1968); *Riot* (Detroit: Broadside Press, 1969).

3. "Gwendolyn Brooks: Poet of the Unheroic," *CLA Journal* 7 (1963): 114–25.

4. George Stavros, "An Interview with Gwendolyn Brooks," *Contemporary Literature* 11, no. 1 (Winter 1970): 1–20.

5. *Black Books Bulletin* 3, no. 2 (Fall 1975): 16–18.

6. "Black Poetry," in *Black Expression,* ed. Addison Gayle, Jr. (New York: Weybright and Talley, 1969), p. 114.

7. Stavros, p. 13.

HOUSTON A. BAKER

# From "The Florescence of Nationalism in the 1960s and 1970s"

During the earlier decade, black writers did suggest that their roles might be different from those of white authors. And they often looked to the Third World. They were patently aware that redefinitions were in order. But they maintained always a reserved and, in some cases, a passionate attachment to the West. Ellison and Wright knew the shortcomings of Europe and America, yet both accentuated what they saw as redeeming qualities of Western history. Baldwin, working in a similar vein, proposed the Western artistic heritage as a means of achieving the mysteries of the self. And many black authors who gathered to discuss their function spoke in solemn tones of the future day when the great Western promise of equality would be fulfilled. Few assumed a truly nationalistic voice. Politics were forbidden at the Sorbonne, and in New York the most radical strategy to emerge was exile—in Africa, or in an African sensibility defined by Negritude. While foreshadowings of the revolt to come were apparent in the 1950s, black writing during the decade remained fundamentally Western in outlook and tone. No black writer in full possession of his senses wanted to be just like his white predecessors and contemporaries, but many insisted, sometimes vigorously, that their past, present, and future had to be comprehended in Western terms.

Their insistence does not, I think, constitute irony, paradox, or treachery. It simply illustrates (in a very Barakan way) that the American mechanisms designed either to placate the dispossessed or to win them to a belief in an "apprenticeship for freedom" are always operative. Their prototypes can be seen in the laws, bills, statutes, and assurances mentioned in conjunction

From Houston A. Baker, Jr., *The Journey Back: Issues in Black Literature and Criticism* (Chicago: University of Chicago Press, 1980), 106–13. Reprinted with permission.

with Douglass. They are always presented in the form of invitations to join a company of white dreamers. Moreover, there was a slight suspension during the 1950s of the extreme violence and repression that blacks had come to regard as daily fare since the end of the nineteenth century; a mild breathing space opened for an instant. The real irony lies in the fact that the black masses took what America intended as a momentary gesture—*Brown v. Board of Education*—as a sanction for their unprecedented surge forward. Suddenly, there were hundreds of thousands of blacks demanding "Freedom Now!" When the media reported in lurid detail the bitterness and intensity of this movement, it must have shocked older black writers to discover that theirs was a passionate people indeed. The existence of a mass black audience, with its mind set on something quite different from the traditional forms of high art, must have been even more surprising.

The confrontations that came in the wake of the accelerating black liberation struggle have been sketched above. Their consequences were severe enough to convince some of the most ardent black disciples that the West could not survive the test at hand. In the early years of the 1960s, therefore, talk of "black Western man" rapidly subsided. It was replaced by prophecies of the last days of the American empire, and the newly emergent black audience was a prime consideration. These addresses were avowedly political and militantly activist in orientation. A new identity, a new nation, seemed possible because black people, in ever-increasing number, were demanding both. In sum, black writers of the 1950s were not certain they had a country. They worked, perhaps too often, in a world of abstractions that included not only their most esteemed values, but also their hypothetical or implied Western audience. In the 1960s and 1970s, on the other hand, black spokesmen were convinced that their real audience, like the nation to come, was black, and their values and canons were designed to accord with this conviction.

The strength of this conviction, moreover, was sufficient to bring about significant shifts in the work of several black writers from earlier generations. Gwendolyn Brooks, winner of the Pulitzer Prize for poetry in 1950, offers an example. In the mid-1960s, Brooks was indisputably the most celebrated living black American poet. She had been lauded by the Midwestern Writer's Conference, the John Simon Guggenheim Memorial Foundation, and countless other agencies of American arts and letters. Her dazzling word-magic had secured the favor of white publishers and reviewers alike. She describes herself in *Report from Part*

*One* as an "old girl"—one from the very select group of black writers who hade made their way in the white literary establishment. She goes on, however, to detail her experiences at the 1967 Fisk University Writers' Conference:

> Coming from white white white South Dakota State College, I arrived in Nashville, Tennessee, to give one more "reading." But blood-boiling surprise was in store for me. First, I was aware of a general energy, an electricity, in look, walk, speech, *gesture* of the young blackness I saw all about me. I had been "loved" at South Dakota State College. Here, I was coldly respected. . . . Imamu Amiri Baraka, then "LeRoi Jones," was expected. He arrived in the middle of my own offering, and when I called attention to his presence there was jubilee in Jubilee Hall.
>
>   All that day and night . . . an almost hysterical Gwendolyn B. walked about in amazement, listening, looking, learning. *What was going on!*[1]

Her bafflement soon became the certainty that "there is indeed a new black today. He is different from any the world has known" (*Report* 85). She also discovered that the artists in the group were directing their energies to the creation of a new nation and their voices to an audience radically different from any she had ever conceived of. Discussing her interaction with black writers in Chicago, she says:

> Well, right around the corner is a tavern, and one Sunday afternoon, some of the poets decided to go in there and read poetry. I went with them. One of them went to the front of the tavern and said, "Say folks, we're going to lay some poetry on you." . . . The poets started reading, and before we knew it, people had turned around on their bar stools, with their drinks behind them, and were listening. Then they applauded. (*Report*, 152)

Jolted from what she calls "a sweet ignorance," Brooks cast her lot with the new generation. Conducting poetry workshops in Chicago's South Side black community, meeting with developing writers in her home, and moving among black people intent on their own nation, she came to a new resolve: "My aim, in my next future, is to write poems that will somehow successfully "call" (see Imamu Baraka's "SOS") all black people: black people in taverns, black people in alleys, black people in gutters, schools, offices, factories, prisons, the consulate; I wish to reach black people in pulpits, black people in mines, on farms, on thrones" (*Report*, 183).

Since 1967, Brooks has indeed reached out to a black audience. Her early poem "Negro Hero," written "to suggest Dorie Miller," a black ship's steward who rushed on deck to man the guns during an enemy attack in World War II, begins:

> I had to kick their law into their teeth in order to save them.
> However I have heard that sometimes you have to deal
> Devilishly with drowning men in order to swim them to shore.[2]

And her long poem of the same period, "The Anniad," contains the following wry reflection on its heroine:

> Think of thaumaturgic lass
> Looking in her looking-glass
> At the unembroidered brown;
> Printing bastard roses there;
> Then emotionally aware
> Of the black and boisterous hair
> Taming all that anger down.[3]

The difference between the foregoing and Brooks's more recent work is illustrated by a figure like Way-out Morgan of *In the Mecca:*

> Way-out Morgan is collecting guns
> in a tiny fourth-floor room.
> He is not hungry, ever, though sinfully lean.
> He flourishes, ever, on porridge or pat of bean
> pudding or wiener soup—fills fearsomely
> on visions of Death-to-the-Hordes-of-the-White-Men!
> Death!
> (This is the Maxim painted in big black
> above a bed bought at a Champlain rummage sale.)[4]

Just as Way-out Morgan—for all his rummage-sale furniture and too-intense revolutionary display—is a quantum leap from the Negro hero, so Mary Ann of "The Blackstone Rangers" is light-years away from the sensitive and troubled Annie Allen: "Mary is / a rose in a whisky glass" (*Mecca*, 47).

The ironies that Brooks directed at supercilious whites and the detached, subtle amusement with which she approached some black subjects in earlier work[5] are absent in poems like "Malcolm X," "Medgar Evers," and "The Second Sermon on the Warpland." Her more recent poetry stands in fine contrast to products of "the western field." The phrase comes from the first poem of a two-part dedication in *In the Mecca*. Entitled "The Chicago Picasso," it states:

> Art hurts. Art urges voyages—
> and it is easier to stay at home,
> the nice beer ready.
>> In commonrooms
> We belch, or sniff, or scratch.
> Are raw.
>
> (*Mecca*, 40)

Written to commemorate the unveiling of a Picasso sculpture, the work continues by detailing the demands exercised by those tangible artistic objects before which the individual viewer squirms. While the poet concludes with the romantic notion that art—like a flower in the western field—is its own excuse for being, she goes on to demand more. Her second poem, "The Wall," offers a representation of an entirely different type of art.

A spirit of communality and participation marks the crowd that comes to celebrate the "Wall of Respect," which was painted on a building at 43rd and Langley in Chicago to honor black heroes—including Brooks. Instead of the one-to-one (or individualistic) relationship between object and viewer seen in "The Chicago Picasso," the aesthetic experience in "The Wall" is shared by "hundreds of faces, red-brown, brown, black, ivory" (*Mecca*, 43). The poet's uncertainty about her role in the group disappears when the members "yield me hot trust, their yea and their Announcement / that they are ready to rile the high-flung ground" (*Mecca*, 43). Like a condemned person pardoned an instant before execution, the speaker gladly accepts these reassurances. She and her audience blend as the poem concludes:

> An emphasis is paroled.
> The old decapitations are revised,
> the dispossessions beakless.
>
> And we sing.
>
> (*Mecca*, 43)

The "emphasis" which is "paroled" is not only the past life of the speaker. The new energy of the masses is also "paroled" or set in words. The poet, in other words, affirms the ideals of her audience. Past oppression is transcended and transformed as the entire group finds its voice in art.[6]

In *Riot,* a three-part poem written in response to civil disorders in Chicago, Brooks further demonstrates her intention to "call" black people. The poem begins with the demise of John Cabot, a manicured white dilettante. It ends with a resonant black love song. The substance of the middle section is captured by the following lines:

> GUARD HERE, GUNS LOADED.
> The young men run.
> The children in ritual chatter
> scatter upon
> their Own and old geography.[7]

But like other writers who moved with black America during the 1960s, Brooks shows clear signs of disillusionment in her work of the 1970s. *Beckonings* begins with "The Boy Died in My Alley," which portrays the speaker as one who has failed in her obligations to her fellows. The work also implies a pervasive and meaningless violence ("the Wild") that seems immemorial in the black community. *Beckonings* closes with the poem "Boys. Black." which urges young blacks to redeem the time. But in this work—unlike in "The Wall"—it is the poet who is the strong force yielding grace:

> I tell You
> I love You
> and I trust You.
> Take my Faith.
> Make of my Faith an engine.
> Make of my Faith
> a Black Star. I am Beckoning.[8]

The sentiments are stirring, but they are far from the assured forecasts of *In the Mecca* and *Riot.* "To John Oliver Killens in 1975" addresses the coordinator of the writers' conference from which the poet dates her conversion. It reflects, in disconsolate terms, the sobered mood of black America in the mid-1970s:

John Killens,
look at our mercy, the massiveness that it is not.
Look at our "unity" look at our
"black solidarity."
Dim, dull, and dainty.
Ragged. And we
grow colder; we
grow colder.
See our
tatter-time.

You were a mender.
You were a sealer of tremblings and long trepidations.
And always, with you, the word kindness was not
a jingling thing but an
eye-tenderizer, a
heart-honeyer.

Therefore we turn, John, to you.
Interrupting self-raiding. We pause in our falling.
To ask another question of your daylight.

(*Beckonings*, 7)

While one can not say that an "improvement" in Brooks's art resulted from her allegiances of the 1960s, one can justifiably infer from her most recent volume that she placed as much faith in the imminence of a new black nation as did her younger contemporaries. *Beckonings* reveals a moving attempt at reassessment, the poet's tribute to those who have maintained the faith ("Five Men against the Theme 'My Name Is Red Hot. Yo Name Ain Doodley Squat' "), and an urgent plea to those who will move our black tomorrows.

NOTES

1. *Report from Part One* (Detroit: Broadside Press, 1972), pp. 84–85. [References for quotations are given in parentheses in the text.]
2. *Selected Poems* (New York: Harper, 1963), p. 19.
3. *Ibid.*, p. 39.
4. *In the Mecca* (New York: Harper and Row, 1968), p. 28. The Mecca was a huge apartment building in Chicago that, at one stage in its history, was reported to contain some two thousand occupants. Ms. Brooks's poem explores what she represents as some of the lives of these occupants.

5. See my essay "The Achievement of Gwendolyn Brooks," *Singers of Daybreak* (Washington, D.C.: Howard University Press, 1974), pp. 43–51.

6. I wish to thank Professor Arnold Rampersad for sharing with me his insights on "The Wall."

7. *Riot* (Detroit: Broadside Press, 1969), p. 15.

8. *Beckonings* (Detroit: Broadside Press, 1975), p. 16.

HARRY B. SHAW

# Maud Martha

Miss Brooks is known almost entirely for her poetry. Her lone novel, *Maud Martha,* published in 1953 during the early period of her work, was not very successful. Miss Brooks says that she was too meticulous, "utilizing the possibility of every word" just as she did with her poetry and that she does not think the novel is in her "category."[1] In 1953 Miss Brooks was still forming her ideas and had not had the "great awakening" that was to come in 1967. Therefore, her novel does not include some of the themes that were popular in her poetry after 1967, such as rebirth and survival through violence.

Virtually the same poetic style, however, and use of the vignette occur in the novel as in the poetry. The same scenes and experiences inspire the same kind of characters in her poetry and prose. Each chapter presents a vignette from the life of Maud Martha. While some of the poetic themes are missing from the novel, it is somewhat more socially inspired than the early poetry but less politically inspired than her poetry after 1967.

The novel is a thinly disguised autobiographical account that depicts a black woman in a ghetto situation similar to that where Miss Brooks grew up and lived. While Miss Brooks has no sister, Helen is the embodiment of all the light-skinned or white girls with whom Maud Martha seemed to sense perpetual rivalry. The invention of Helen can be seen as a need to bring the conflict or the trouble of a quiet, unassuming, dark-skinned black woman closer with more permanence and constancy. So the fair-skinned, beautiful Helen was invented, not as a friend with whom comparisons could occasionally be made, but as a sister-foil whose daily presence was a constant reminder of the problem. Society, then, becomes parents treating their daughters differently—heightening the effect. Maud's near obsessions with color, features, and hair are paralleled in Miss Brooks's autobiog-

Reprinted with permission of Twayne Publishers, an imprint of Macmillan Publishing Company, from *Gwendolyn Brooks* by Harry B. Shaw. Copyright © by G. K. Hall & Co., 1980.

raphy, *Report from Part One,* and in her poetry.[2] There is no real plot in the novel but the order of the vignettes suggests a chronological progression from childhood, to courtship and marriage, and from marriage to motherhood. Indeed the themes that run through *Maud Martha,* in the absence of a plot, are what give the novel any cohesion. What little direction there is comes from the general movement of her thematic picture. The novel considers how Maud Martha looked at the world and how she thought the world looked at her. *Maud Martha* is a story of a woman with doubts about herself and where and how she fits into the world. Maud's concern is not so much that she is inferior but that she is perceived as being ugly.

While there are themes of death, negative displacement, survival, exaltation of the commonplace, the black-and-tan motif, and escape, they are all filtered through the point of view of an insecure, self-disparaging black woman who feels that she is homely and, therefore, uncherished because she is black and has nappy hair and "Negro features." She measures herself and her work against the standards of the world and feels that she comes out short inevitably—that white or light beauty often triumphs, though somehow unfairly—and that the depravation of the beholder is to blame. The book is also about the triumph of the lowly. She shows what they go through and exposes the shallowness of the popular, beautiful, white people with "good" hair. One way of looking at the book, then, is as a war with beauty and people's concepts of beauty. Indeed sometimes this war takes the forms of exaltation of the commonplace, escape through diversion or death, sour grapes or negative displacement, choking environment.

Although the vignettes of *Maud Martha* afford many examples of themes and subthemes, there are four main themes in the book: death, negative displacement, survival of the unheroic, and the war with beauty.

## I. *Death*

The theme of death in *Maud Martha* is treated similarly to the way it is handled in Miss Brooks's poetry. In both the poetry and in the novel death is presented as an event that is part of family life. The deaths of relatives or close friends are favorite subjects and are often presented from the point of view of a child. The numerous depictions of and references to death in *Maud Martha,* as in the poetry, suggest the importance of spiritual and physical death.

Chapter 4, "Death of Grandmother," illustrates Maud's awe and esteem of death as a little girl watching her grandmother die. As in Miss Brooks's poetry (especially "Old Relative") Maud is both fearful of and fascinated with the idea of death. The harshness of the sounds and other details of the dying signifies the importance and the repulsion it has for Maud. Yet she describes her grandmother in terms of envy. Her grandmother "enjoyed" a kind of glory and importance because she was dying. The others all seem foolish compared to the grandmother; she is a queen, is exalted:

> This woman, this ordinary woman who had suddenly become a queen, for whom presently the most interesting door of them all would open, who lying locked in boards with ther "hawhs," yet towered, triumphed over them, while they stood there asking the stupid questions people asked the sick, out of awe, out of half horror, half envy. (p. 13)[3]

Miss Brooks often sharply contrasts the living with the dead in order to dramatize or heighten the effect of death. In Chapter 4 she especially calls the reader's attention to this contrast by saying:

> She who had taken the children of Abraham Brown to the circus, and who had bought them pink popcorn, and Peanut Crinkle candy, who had laughed—that Earnestine was dead. (p. 14)

The same technique is used in chapter 7. Tim is presented as robust and then in juxtaposition as dead. The sharp purposeful contrast helps to heighten the sense of loss through death. In "Tim" Maud again appears to be torn between fear of and fascination with death.

Occasionally the theme of death is conveyed through an incidental reference of imagery which lets the reader know that the idea of death is prominent or perhaps latent with Maud. In chapter 6, "Howie Joe Jones," Maud describes him as looking like an "upright corpse." His singing does not salve the eyes and sores of those who come to watch and hear him. The audience, though momentarily enlivened, returns to its grimness as it leaves the theater:

The audience had applauded. Had stamped its strange, hilarious foot. Had put its fingers in its mouth—whistled. Had sped a shininess up to its eyes. But now part of it was going home, as she was, and its face was dull again. It had not been helped. Not truly. Not well. For a hot half hour it had put that light gauze across its little miseries and monotonies, but now here they were again, ungauzed, self-assertive, cancerous as ever. The audience had gotten a fairy gold. And it was not going to spend the rest of the night, being grateful to Howie Joe Jones. No, it would not make plans to raise a hard monument to him. (p. 18)

If he is an upright corpse, "how can he imbue them with life?"[4]

Howie Joe Jones was distraction, a temporary escape from "death" but thoughts of death itself are presented as another means of escaping. The quickness with which Maud accepts the thought that she might die in "Maud Martha's Tumor" shows her ambivalent fear-fascination with death. While she seems to seize death as a way out of the grayness of her life, she is at the same time terribly frightened by death. Her contemplation of death reveals that "she was ready. Since the time had come, she was ready. . . . Her business was to descend into the deep cool, the salving dark, to be alike indifferent to the good and the not good" (p. 104). Her viewing death as a refuge bespeaks more of her view of life than of death. Like the "men of careful turns, haters of forks in the road," she is weary of having to make choices and wants to be "indifferent to the good and the not good."

Yet her joy at learning that she is not going to die demonstrates her real desire to live and love.

"You mean—I'm not going to die."
She bounced down the long flight of tin-edged stairs, was shortly claimed by the population, which seemed proud to have her back. (p. 104)

Maud's flirtation with death seems to be a silent, anomic protest against the stultifying conditions of her life.

The connection between Maud's living conditions and death are first made in chapter 14, "Everybody Will Be Surprised." The chapter involves Maud Martha and Paul, her fiancé, planning the kinds of conditions under which they will live. Paul's dreams of having the "swanky flat" are more than offset by his firm pragmatism about living within his means. While he literally believes, for instance, that the "*Defender* will come and photograph it," he plans to consider buying "four rooms of furniture for eighty-nine dollars" and to rent a stove-heated or a basement flat because it would be cheap. Maud's reaction is first to protest and then to imagine that she sacrifices for her man. She seems to contemplate even sacrificing her life or inviting a kind of death. "She though of herself, dying for her man. It was a beautiful thought" (p. 46).

Maud's sense of having invited a kind of death is borne out in chapter 15, "The Kitchenette." When Maud and Paul move into the Kitchenette, Maud's enthusiasm is reflected in the use of the colors green, red, and white. After a few weeks, however, the apartment becomes a place of grayness with roaches, odors, sounds, and colors combining to "kill" her hopes and enthusiasm. The prominence of the color gray suggests death, as in Brooks's "kitchenette building" and other poems:

> The color was gray, and the smell and sound had taken on a suggestion of the properties of color, and impressed one as gray, too. The sobbings, the frustrations, the small hates, the large and ugly hates, the little pushing-through love, the boredom, that came to her from behind those walls (some of them beaverboard) via speech and scream and sigh—all these were gray. And the smells of various types of sweat, and of bathing and bodily functions (the bathroom was always in use, someone was always in the bathroom) and of fresh or stale lovemaking, which rushed in thick fumes to your nostrils as you walked down the hall, or down the stairs—these were *gray*.
> There was a whole lot of grayness here. (p. 49)

The grayness in the lives of Maud and Paul is attributable to the ennui that accompanies their powerlessness. Paul, after all, had such grandiose dreams that he is utterly distressed to find nothing of significance was happening to him or was about to happen. Paul's failure to be invited to be a member of the Foxy Cats Club in chapter 27, "Paul in the 011 Club," is suggestive of his general failure. Maud shares his sense of failure as she observes Paul and summarized his thoughts:

> The baby was getting darker all the time! She knew that he was tired of his wife, tired of his living quarters, tired of working at Sam's, tired of his two suits. (p. 105)

That the thought of even their baby is depressing rather than buoying to the couple indicates the depths of their spiritual death.

## II. *Negative Displacement*

The effect of the couple's despair is intensified whenever comparisons are made between their present circumstances and past circumstances or expectations. The reader is made aware of a negative displacement through Maud Martha's sense of loss as she reflects on her condition. Paul's crudeness as described in chapter 16, "The Young Couple at Home," increasingly disappoints her. His sleeping through a musicale, "clowning" playfully in public, not masking his need to use the bathroom, and falling asleep again leave Maud less than pleased. The titles of the books they choose to read reflect their respective tastes. Significantly he chooses *Sex in the Married Life,* which, as he nodded, "was about to slip to the floor [but] . . . she did not stretch out a hand to save it" (p. 52). The conditions of their lives had combined unhappily with their respective dreams to form a disillusionment and a self-rejection. Maud chooses *Of Human Bondage,* which suggests her feelings about her condition.

Beyond Paul's crudeness, however, the physical surroundings of the flat itself affect Maud's sense of loss. When she compares the flat with what she was accustomed to with her parents, she experiences a negative displacement. When Paul informs her that he was thinking of a stove-heated flat, she responds, "Oh, I wouldn't like that. I've always lived in steam" (p. 45). It is obvious that she considered the move a step down.

At the time of their marriage, however, she is willing to endure a temporary lowering of her condition as a "sacrifice" for her man and as testimony of her love. Later she becomes disillusioned even with love: "People have to choose something decently constant to depend on, thought Maud Martha. People must have something to lean on. But love of a single person was not enough" (p. 74).

Maud's insecurity and disillusionment are in sharp contrast to the security she felt when she was living with her parents. In chapter 22, "Tradition and Maud Martha," she chronicles her disappointments in her marriage, lamenting the lack of wholesome traditions. She contrasts the ritual, security, and happiness of her life with her parents with the grayness, insecurity, and inconstancy of her life with Paul.

## III. *Survival of the Unheroic*

Maud Martha comes to realize that even through disillusionment and spiritual death life will prevail. She notices that children in the spring are indomitable even amidst bleakness. In chapter 2, "Spring Landscape: Details," she observes the children "mixed in the wind" as part of the bleakness but also as rays of hope. The tentative promise of the sun is like the unsure promise of the children. "Whether they would fulfill themselves was anybody's guess" (p. 7). The children are not subdued by the drab, cramped environment. Rather like Maud's commonest flower, they "come up, if necessary, among, between, or out of—beastly inconvenient! The smashed corpses lying in strict composure, in that hush infallible and sincere" (p. 127).

Maud's tendency, nevertheless, like the tendency of the mother in "The Children of the Poor," is to shield, to protect her children from the harshness of the environment. For instance, in Brooks's poem "What shall I give my children? who are poor," the mother laments her powerlessness:

> My hand is stuffed with mode, design, device.
> But I lack access to my proper stone.
> And plenitude of plan shall not suffice
> Nor grief nor love shall be enough alone
> To ratify my little halves who bear
> Across an autumn freezing everywhere.
>
> (*World,* 100)

The same frustration and "baffled hate" are expressed by Maud after her daughter, Paulette, has been virtually ignored by Santa Claus in a department store:

> . . . Maud Martha wanted to cry.
> Keep her that land of blue!
> Keep her those fairies, with witches always killed at the end, and Santa every winter's lord, kind, sheer being who never perspires, who never does or says a foolish or ineffective thing, who never looks grotesque, who never has occasion to pull the chain and flush the toilet. (p. 125)

Hidden in this plea is the need to shield the eyes of her children from the realities of life. The characters of Brooks's poetry often engage in diversions that distract them from certain unpleasant realities. Howie Joe Jones has been shown to be just this type of distraction for Maud Martha and the other patrons at the Regal. Maud Martha's infatuation with New York is a different kind of "bandage" for her eyes. She is able to "escape" to New York in her imagination.

Brooks depicts the "survival" of poor people through the everyday devices of escape and distraction. She shows Maud identifying with and taking comfort in a hardy but common flower, the dandelion. The idea that life can spring from death flourished in Brooks's poetry after 1968, but had been expressed in similar ways in *Maud Martha*.

## IV. *War with Beauty*

As she identified with the dandelion in chapter 1, "Description of Maud Martha," Maud expresses her basic need to be cherished. This chapter also lays the foundation for the struggle that occupies much of the novel. The struggle to feel cherished while knowing she was plain "was the dearest wish of Maud Martha Brown."

Immediately the comparison is made with Helen who is described as having "heart-catching" beauty. Helen symbolized the light-complexioned black woman and even white women who enjoyed favors because of their color. Maud resents this disparity of treatment and stature as vehemently as Brooks's personae in "the ballad of chocolate Mabbie" and "Ballad of Pearl May Lee." The issue of color and its effects occurs throughout Brooks's poetry.

Beginning in childhood with Emmanuel's harsh rejection of Maud in favor of offering Helen a ride in his wagon, the instances of the advantages enjoyed by Helen and other lighter and "more beautiful" women continue throughout the novel. Even Maud's brother, Harry, and her father favor Helen. Although Helen does nothing to deserve their loyalty as Maud does, they cherish her while paying little attention to Maud.

Each incident involving color and beauty becomes a painful memory to Maud. Her tone betrays her resentment of Helen as she reflects on the favoritism shown to Helen:

> Helen was still the one they wanted in the wagon, still "the pretty one," "the dainty one." The lovely one. (p. 28)

Maud tries not to blame her family by saying she understands, but her "noble understanding" does not make the burden any lighter. Harry runs errands and opens doors for Helen but not for Maud. Their father prefers Helen's hair, worries about Helen's homework and her health, and thinks the boys dating Helen are unworthy.

In chapter 13, "Low Yellow," the ravages of the "war" begin to show as Maud denegrates herself. Obsessed with color, features, and hair, she thinks Paul, her fiancé, would prefer a light-complexioned girl with curly hair. She imagines that Paul is self-conscious about being with her in public and that Paul wants people to know "that any day out of the week he can do better than this black gal." The passage that follows shows just how completely both Maud and Paul had ascribed to a "white" standard of beauty.

> "I am not a pretty woman," said Maud Martha. "If you married a pretty woman, you could be the father of pretty children. Envied by people. The father of beautiful children."
>
> "But I don't know," said Paul. "Because my features aren't fine. They aren't regular. They're heavy. They're real Negro features. I'm light, or at least I can claim to be a sort of low-toned yellow, and my hair has a teeny crimp. But even so I'm not handsome."
>
> No, there would be little "beauty" getting born out of such a union. (p. 42)

In the minds of Maud and Paul, black or "Negro" features—dark skin, and nappy hair—are clearly considered ugly while beauty is associated with fine, regular features, wavy hair, and light skin. With these odds against her, Maud settles for being "sweet" instead of pretty.

Although Maud resigns herself to not being pretty, her resentment and her war with beauty continue. She repeatedly shows not only her resentment but also her envy and idolization of the white world, especially white women. Their opulence is contrasted repeatedly with the poverty and wretchedness of the blacks. This theme appears in many of Brooks's poems, such as "The Lovers of the Poor," "Beverly Hills, Chicago," and "Strong Men, Riding Horses." In chapter 18, "We're the Only Colored People Here," both Maud and Paul show their deference to whites as they self-consciously attend a movie downtown at the World Playhouse. The comparisons they make reveal their feelings of inferiority:

> The strolling women were cleverly gowned. Some of them had flowers or flashers in their hair. They looked—cooked.

Well cared for. And as though they had never seen a roach or a rat in their lives. Or gone without heat for a week. And the men had even edges. They were men, Maud Martha thought, who wouldn't stoop to fret over less than a thousand dollars. (pp. 56–57)

Maud Martha extends the comparison beyond what she sees to what she imagines and she also extends her resentment from purely physical attributes to possessions and living conditions:

But you felt good sitting there, yes, good, and as if, when you left it, you would be going home to a sweet-smelling apartment with flowers on little gleaming tables; and wonderful silver on night-blue velvet, in chests; and crackly sheets; and lace spreads on such beds as you saw at Marshall Field's. Instead of back to your kit'n't apt., with the garbage of your floor's families in a big can just outside your door, and the gray sound of little gray feet scratching away from it as you drag up those flights of narrow complaining stairs. (p. 58)

Maud Martha does not like life and feels that the main reason for her deprived circumstances is her appearance. Hence her obsession with skin color, features, and hair texture. She is quite self-disparaging in chapter 19, "If You're Light and Have Long Hair." When Maud and Paul are invited to attend the Annual Foxy Cats Dawn Ball, Maud immediately thinks that Paul does not want to go with her because of her appearance. Her insecurity is heightened when Paul dances closely with Maella, who was "red-haired and curved, and white as a white." She feels that Paul merely tolerates her and that he has to "jump over" the wall of her color in order to appreciate her inner qualities:

But it's my color that makes him mad. I try to shut my eyes to that, but it's no good. What I am inside, what is really me, he likes okay. But he keeps looking at my color, which is like a wall. He has to jump over it in order to meet and touch what I've got for him. He has to jump away up high in order to see it. He gets awful tired of all that jumping. (p. 65)

At times frustration, whether from real of imagined causes, leads Maud to feeling like fighting, making the war open and physical. At the ball, for instance, she considers going over to Maella and scratching her upsweep down or spitting on her back or screaming. More often, however, she is content to consider herself in a psychological war with beauty or with those who are considered beautiful. Because to Maude white women fall into this category, she uses every opportunity to claim little victories at their expense. Chapter 29, "Millinery," depicts such a victory as Maud shops for a hat. Sensing the condescension of the woman manager, Maud decides to disabuse her subtly of any notions she may have that Maud could be taken lightly because she was black. She allows the manager to use all her devices and techniques in an effort to sell the hat at the listed price of $7.95. When the manager concludes that Maud would not pay more than five dollars, she offers to consult the owner. Maud coolly refutes the manager's claim that the effort to reduce the price could be made because Maud was an old customer by saying, "I've never been in the store before." Undaunted, the manager feigns a consultation with the owner and returns with the happy news that the reduction would be possible. ". . . Seeing as how you're such an old customer . . . he'll let you have it for five." Maud's relish of triumph can be seen in the closing passages of the chapter:

> "I've decided against the hat."
> "What? Why, you told—But you said—"
> Maud Martha went out, tenderly closed the door.
> "Black—oh, black—" said the hat woman to her hats—which, on the slender stands, shone pink and blue and white and lavender, showed off their tassels, their sleek satin ribbons, their veils, their flower coquettes. (pp. 111–12)

Perhaps the ultimate encounter with a white woman occurs in chapter 30, "At the Burns-Coopers'," when Maud hires out as a maid. The situation is very similar to that in the poem "Bronzeville Woman in a Red Hat." Driven by extreme poverty while Paul is temporarily unemployed, Maud determines to endure the condescension of Mrs. Burns-Cooper. When, however, Mrs. Burns-Cooper and her mother-in-law reprove Maud with a stern look because the potato parings are too thick, Maud decides never to return to the job:

> They just looked. . . . As though she were a child, a ridiculous one, and one that ought to be given a little shaking, except that shaking was—not quite the thing, would not quite do. One held up one's finger (if one did anything), cocked one's head, was arch. (pp. 115–16)

Maud even disdains trying to explain her reasons for quitting, although she knows Mrs. Burns-Cooper will be puzzled. She, however, has a simple explanation for herself:

> Why, one was a human being. One wore clean night-gowns. One loved one's baby. One drank cocoa by the fire— or the gas range—come the evening, in the wintertime. (p. 116)

Maud Martha would indeed have difficulty explaining these reasons to Mrs. Burns-Cooper. Yet these reasons underlie every theme in the book. *Maud Martha,* in essence, depicts a sensitive young woman grappling with the difficult problem of reconciling her human need to be cherished with society's aesthetic preferences and insensitivity which appear virtually to exclude her from the ranks of the cherishable. Her recognition of her problem and her attempts to solve it manifest themselves in the four main themes of death, negative displacement, survival of the unheroic, and the war with beauty.

These themes, along with the use of vignettes, a common setting, and similar characters, appear in both *Maud Martha* and Brooks's poetry. In the poetry the themes are emeshed in carefully drawn pictures and words while the novel is characterized by "naked" themes for the most part. The vignettes of the novel, while drawn from a common storehouse of experiences, appear less "finished" than those of the poems. These differences arise from Brooks's restriction of the novel to presenting all the vignettes from Maud Martha's point of view, whereas she varies the personae of the poems to fit the different situations. Ultimately, however, the themes, presented from a single point of view, not only provide the unity within *Maud Martha* but help to tie the novel to the larger body of Brooks's literary works.

## NOTES

1. George Stavros, "An Interview with Gwendolyn Brooks," *Contemporary Literature* 2 (Winter 1970): 16.

2. Ida Lewis, "Conversation: Gwen Brooks and Ida Lewis," *Essence,* April 1971, p. 28.

3. *Maud Martha* (New York, 1953). All page references to this book appear parenthetically in the text.

4. See Stavros, p. 15.

PATRICIA H. LATTIN AND VERNON E. LATTIN

# Dual Vision in Gwendolyn Brooks's
# *Maud Martha*

Since its publication in 1953, Gwendolyn Brooks's *Maud Martha* has been a novel in search of a critic. Major studies of the black American novel have either completely ignored it or have included only brief, general remarks.[1] Noel Schraufnagel is typical when he devotes a page to *Maud Martha*, briefly mentioning a few episodes and concluding that "Maud Martha is the type of enduring black woman that has become a stereotype."[2] Only Barbara Christian recognizes significant value in Brooks's novel. Although she does not provide an extensive analysis, Christian speaks favorably of the novel as a work that "heightens our awareness of the wonderfulness of the commonplace." Christian also recognizes the importance of family life and cultural roots for Maud. In contrast to Schraufnagel, she correctly perceives that Maud Martha "is not reduced to a stereotype either in the grand heroic style or the mean downtrodden mode. . . . In *Maud Martha*, Brooks deflated the mystique of heroism and grand defeat by illuminating the commonplace and thus created a new type of black woman character."[3] The only full-length critical article on *Maud Martha*, Annette Oliver Shands's "Gwendolyn Brooks as Novelist," is not perceptive.[4] Shands treats the novel only as opportunity to quote parallels from Brooks's poetry. The comparisons are obvious and fail to provide the reader with any insights into *Maud Martha* as a work of fiction.

We are therefore left with a critical void. One reason is that critics have in general not written as much on black women writers as on their male counterparts.[5] Also, Gwendolyn Brooks's going on to win a Pulitzer Prize as a poet and not as a novelist has encouraged critical studies of her poetry, not her novel. Had she written and won the prize for a later novel, certainly her first novel

*Critique* 25 (Summer 1984): 180–88. Reprinted with permission of the Helen Dwight Reid Educational Foundation. Published by Heldref Publications, 1319 Eighteenth Street, N.W., Washington, D.C. 20036-1802. Copyright © 1984.

would have garnered more critical attention. In the present study, we hope to make clear that *Maud Martha* is a significant work of fiction deserving serious attention.

Discussion of *Maud Martha* must begin with a recognition of what the novel is not. In 1940, Richard Wright told the story of Bigger Thomas growing up in black Chicago not far from where Maud Martha was to grow up.[6] In 1953, the year *Maud Martha* was published, Ralph Ellison added the story of his protagonist harassed from the south to New York City.[7] Judged by the standards of these two complex, powerful urban novels, *Maud Martha* could easily be dismissed. Maud does not experience the same intense search for identity that Bigger and Ellison's protagonist experience. Nor does the novel have comparable violent struggles between the black and white worlds, broad philosophical discussions of black nationalism, or tragic conflicts between characters. Maud Martha's stage is not the newspapers or courtrooms or Bigger's stage or the packed auditorium and street battles where Ellison's unnamed protagonist plays his role. Maud's stage is the home in which she grew up, the schools she attended, the kitchenette where she lives after marriage, and most often her own mind and heart as she struggles to be creative and to be an individual in a gray, oppressive world.

A reader cannot, therefore, approach *Maud Martha* expecting the epic or tragic dimensions of *Native Son* or *Invisible Man*. *Maud Martha* must be judged by its own standards. It is a unique work. With a very loose organization consisting of a series of short vignettes, and with lyrical language never far from poetry, this short novel has a deceptively light and simple exterior which belies the complexity of the interior. Although on the surface a comedy of the commonplace, *Maud Martha* is also a novel that looks directly at racial discrimination and its effects on Blacks, and anger often simmers underneath its calm surface. The protagonist, however, possesses a dual vision that allows her to see simultaneously beauty in ugliness, life in death, and a positive way of living by which one can maintain one's self-respect and creativity in the face of overwhelmingly negative forces.

Brooks's *Maud Martha* is first of all a comedy of the commonplace. Underlying the author's story is the constant recognition that the world is not populated with tragic or epic heroes. People exist in everyday settings, seldom reaching even the height of melodrama. Maud herself comments that "on the whole . . . life was more comedy than tragedy. Nearly everything that happened had its comic element. . . . Sooner or later one could find something to laugh at. . . . The truth was, if you got a good Tragedy out of a lifetime, one good, ripping tragedy, . . . you were doing well."[8]

Maud has intuitively appreciated the common everyday world since she was a child. For example, she has always had a special feeling for dandelions, the flower she sees most often in her back yard. She would have liked to have "a lotus, or China asters or the Japanese iris, or Meadow lilies" (127), but she nevertheless loves the common, ordinary dandelion, which she thinks of as "Yellow jewels for everyday, studding the patched green dress of her back yard" (128). In contrasting herself with her sister Helen, who has "heart-catching beauty," Maud identifies with the dandelion: in its everydayness "she thought she saw a picture of herself, and it was comforting to find that what was common could also be a flower" (128). Maud's subtle consciousness of beauty in the everyday leads her as a child to like "painted music," which she thinks of as "deep blue, or delicate silver" (127), and to have a special sensitivity for the colors of the evening sky and the light it radiates. As an adult, Maud takes pleasure in simple events like putting a good white cloth on her second-hand table, bringing out some white cups and saucers, and serving her mother gingerbread and cocoa. She increasingly learns "to love moments. To love moments for themselves" (204).

Maud's struggle to grow up, black and female, in the white-dominated Chicago of the 1930s and 1940s is a day-to-day struggle made up of small events. These small events, however, generally reflected on silently and internally, create an awareness of racial segregation and its effects that is as great as that of Bigger as he is surrounded by whiteness or of Ellison's protagonist as he realizes his recurring nightmare with its engraved letter that reads "Keep This Nigger-Boy Running."[9] As a child, Maud is aware of the color line when she goes with her mother for an evening walk "East of Cottage Grove" and sees so many white faces. Nothing happens on the walk, and the reader's interest in the event lies with Maud's later reaction to the walk. Asleep, she dreams of an escaped gorilla, and awake, lying in her bed, she instinctively associates the white world with her fear of the night, which she sees as "always hunched and ready to close in on you" (135). Over east of Cottage Grove, she thinks, "that matter of mystery and hunchedness was thicker, a hundredfold" (135–36). Years later, when Maud and her husband attend a movie at the World Playhouse, with its all-white staff and audience, very little happens. No confrontation occurs. In fact, ex-

cept for Paul's buying a ticket, there is no communication be-
tween the couple and the whites. However, the reader feels with
Maud as she is nervous, uncertain, and afraid, yet also defiant
and assertive. She hates Paul a little when he remarks that they
are "the only colored people here" (201), and she is angry that
Paul is afraid to ask the "lovely and blonde and cold-eyed"
woman about tickets. In the darkness of the movie house, she is
happy with the idea of being there, of feeling that she is an equal
with all the others. However, when the lights go on, the spell is
broken. Although she wants to communicate with the whites
around her, sharing perceptions of the film, she and Paul speak to
no one, and no one speaks to them. The most they can really
hope for as they leave is that they will not see any "cruel eyes"
and that no one will "look intruded upon" (204).

The reader feels with Maud as she experiences fear, anxiety,
and doubt not unlike that felt by Wright's Bigger Thomas when
he goes out to eat with Jan and Mary. The difference between
Bigger and Maud is not their emotions but rather understanding
of the emotions and their ability to control them. Blinded by his
anger and fear, Bigger wants to blot out the world he cannot
change or even understand. On the other hand, Maud's aware-
ness of the racism and injustice which threaten her ability to exist
in a creative fashion challenges her to control her anger and frus-
tration so that she can continue to develop and grow as a "good,"
loving human being. For example, Maud knows that her hus-
band Paul has accepted the "white is better" philosophy and that
he can never fully love her because she is darker than he. She
knows that for Paul, as for many black men of the period, "Pretty
would be a little cream-colored thing with curly hair" (179), and
when, at the Foxy Cats Club dance, Paul leaves her to dance with
"someone red-haired and curved, and white as a white" (211),
Maud knows Paul is rejecting her on the basis of her blackness.
"What I am inside, what is really me, he likes okay. But he keeps
looking at my color, which is like a wall. He has to jump over it
in order to meet and touch what I've got for him. He has to jump
away up high in order to see it. He gets awful tired of all that
jumping" (213–14). She does not, however, reject Paul because
of his weakness; she lives with him in full understanding of why
he is as he is. Haunted by the "white mountain" similar to the
wall Maud sees Paul trying to jump, Bigger Thomas wants to
"strike something with his fist," like Ahab attacking the white
whale, and his overpowering frustration and rage are spent only
after he has killed and been apprehended. Maud has thoughts of

scratching, spitting at, and screaming at Paul's light-skinned dance partner but does not give in. Maud seems to realize that she will never have the opportunity to defy the gods and mountains responsible for her oppression, so she, like Paul, will simply keep jumping at the wall.

In this connection, it is important for a reader to recognize that Maud is not naive. The early Brooks has often been accused of failing to see racial oppression, and a superficial reader could use Maud Martha to support such a view of Brooks. In fact, Maud is clearly aware of ugliness and oppression, but she chooses to defy with grace, to live as best she can. She also recognizes and regrets that she and others often fall short even of the goal of defiance. For example, Maud once observes a disturbing incident while having her hair done in the beauty shop. When a white saleswoman says to the black shop owner, Sonia Johnson, "I work like a nigger to make a few pennies" (265), Sonia says nothing to the saleswoman and, in fact, keeps on smiling at her. Maud's reaction is to think that she must have heard wrong: surely the saleswoman did not say what she thought she heard. When Sonia Johnson later tries to explain to Maud that "They don't mean anything against me. . . . Our people is got to stop getting all stepped up about every little thing, especially when it don't amount to nothing" (267), Maud Martha says nothing in reply. "She kept on staring into Sonia Johnson's irises" (268). Maud may appear on the surface to be as blind as Sonia. In fact, however, she is recognizing in herself and in Sonia an ever-present wish to avoid one's "duty" to fight against insensitivity and racism. The constant pressure to react, to defend, to correct, to attack a world that segregates and degrades Blacks is overwhelming, and sometimes one cannot help avoiding the conflict by pretending not to hear (Maud) or by rationalizing (Sonia). This is the day-to-day reality, the world of black/white existence that is as real as the race-riot at the end of *Invisible Man* or as Bigger's killing of Mary and Bessie in *Native Son*. One lives and dies minute by minute, holding on, and for most people, Maud comes to realize, "nothing at all happens . . . most people merely live from day to day until they die" (275).

The complexity of Maud Martha's reaction to racism is perhaps best illustrated in the Christmas incident in which the white Santa Claus ignores her daughter Paulette, causing the child to ask, "Why didn't Santa Claus like me?" (300). Maud resists the urge to take her scissors from her purse and "jab jab jab" Santa

Claus' eyes. However, she realizes that she cannot resolve the incident in her mind, as her sister Helen would have been able to do, "Because it really would not have made much difference to Helen" (301). Nor can she forget it or dismiss it from her mind, "put off studious perusal indefinitely" (301), as she knows her husband Paul would have done after his initial twitching and cursing, "the first tough cough-up of rage" (301). "She could neither resolve nor dismiss" (302). She regrets that she has difficulty expressing the "scraps of baffled hate in her" (302), but at this moment she can only think of protecting her child's innocence. She hopes that tonight will not be the time the child will start asking questions. She hopes to allow Paulette to live a little longer in the world of "fairies, with witches always killed at the end, and Santa every winter's lord, kind, sheer being who never perspires, who never does or says a foolish or ineffective thing, who never looks grotesque, who never has occasion to pull the chain and flush the toilet" (302). The struggle within Maud is powerful and significant. She is learning to live without giving up her imagination, her quest for beauty and love. At one point Maud thinks that "everything can be done with a little grace. I'm sure of it" (192). As with most real people, Maud's rites of passage are not heralded by trumpets and fanfare, but they are nevertheless real and meaningful.

When Maud does carry out an act of resistance against racism, she exhibits insight premature for her times: even before the 1954 Supreme Court decision and before the Civil Rights Movement, she understands that one can resist evil and discrimination by refusing to be part of the system. Her husband laid off from work, Maud goes to work as a cook for a white woman. After being reminded to use the back door next time, and after being treated all day "As though she were a child, a ridiculous one, and one that ought to be given a little shaking" (288), Maud knows that she cannot go back the next day, even though the wages are good. Although she cannot singlehandedly change the system, she can turn away and say "No, in thunder!" She can make a conscious decision not to be further dehumanized by these particular people at this particular place. She compares her act to that of one who "walked out from that almost perfect wall, spitting at the firing squad. What difference did it make whether the firing squad understood or did not understand the manner of one's retaliation or why one had to retaliate" (289)?

Maud's attitude toward this act of passive resistance underscores what should be clear by this point: alongside her recognition of racism and human weakness, Maud has developed an awareness of both the significance and insignificance of an individual's existence. She has managed to combine a subtle cynicism with a genuine acceptance of the human condition. Refusing to go back to her job is like spitting at a firing squad not only because it has positive significance for one's inner being but also because in many respects it is totally meaningless. Our acts are absolutely significant for ourselves, and yet they are also common and meaningless in the long march of history. With this dual vision, Maud is able to make her individual acts significant, maintaining her humanity, grace, and dignity in the face of the absurdity and violence of the world, to which she is never for one moment blind. She knows that, like the snowball bush in her parents' backyard, on which the snowballs got smaller and smaller until both the blossoms and the bush disappear, without her even noticing that it was gone, our life is beautiful but nevertheless followed by death, which will probably not be noticed by most people. Santa is "every winter's lord" and also a racist who does "flush the toilet." Her husband Paul is a fool who falls asleep at concerts and goes to the library only to look up the word "bastard" in the card catalog, but he is also sometimes a loving human being, a man who suffers from the day-to-day oppression of his employer, and a part of history that after his death "doubtless fewer than five people would think of . . . oftener than once a year" (276). Both the richness and the absurdity of life seem to sustain Maud's existence. She has learned to see both sides without either being drowned in maudlin tears or consumed by anger.

It is not an overstatement to say that in *Maud Martha* Brooks suggests a positive way of life that can help one maintain one's self respect and creativity in the face of the racism and death which surround one. One can create in spite of the deadening realities of life. The novel is full of images of traps, walls, being cornered, and lying in a coffinlike bed. In the middle chapter of the novel (chapter 17), Maud's marriage and life in her kitchenette have become a trap. As the reader focuses on Maud in her dingy apartment, the camera shifts, and we see Maud capturing a mouse that has been eluding her for days. Having captured the mouse, however, she begins to empathize with the creature, thinking that it may have a family and that it is regretting all the pleasure it will miss. She lets the mouse go. One can profitably contrast this scene with the opening scene of *Native Son,* where Bigger Thomas violently kills a fighting, frightened, cornered rat and then sadistically torments his sister with its dead body. In his limited, poverty-stricken, oppressed life, Bigger is as trapped as the rat. In contrast, Maud, at this midpoint in the novel, experiences an epiphany and "sees" that she has power "to preserve or destroy." She "sees" that she need not blindly succumb to circumstances but that she can in her own fashion create value and meaning. Through her "simple restraint" she has created. "She had created a piece of life" (197). By letting the creature go, she has been not only an artist/creator but also a moral "good." Uniting art and morality, she sees herself as having "a godlike loving-kindness" (197). Clearly for Brooks everyday existence can be invested with meaning and beauty.

Essential to the positive way of life Brooks suggests are the elements of love and the sense of place. Brooks seems to imply that these elements are not only necessary for the development of our "precious private identities" but also for the survival of Blacks as a people. Whereas Bigger Thomas grows up with little sense of "family," Maud grows up surrounded by love reinforced by an almost mythical understanding of her place in time and space. Her parents are always stable anchors for her. Going to the bathroom at night, the child Maud is reassured by seeing her parents lying close together in the bed, their earlier quarrel forgotten. "Why, how lovely!" Maud thinks (135). She was close to her grandmother alive, and the memory of her dead grandmother sustains her. Maud continues the line of love by showing deep care and concern for her own daughter, Paulette. Maud also developed a strong attachment for every detail of the house where she grew up, and the possibility of losing it during the depression was a frightening experience. Part of her unhappiness with the kitchenette apartment she lives in after marriage is that she is living with other people's furniture and the landlord will not allow her to use her own. One must, she knows, become familiar with places and things, possessing the sense of place that so many urban dwellers have lost.

Like Joseph Campbell, Brooks also realizes the importance of custom and ritual to humans' spiritual survival. Campbell despairs that modern America has no ritual or myths and therefore sees us as doomed.[10] Wright's Bigger Thomas appears to have grown up in a lifestyle devoid of ritual, seeing time as meaningless and life as merely a series of events. Maud's life, however, has been full of rituals, one version of what she calls "posts" in chapter 21. Her life has been recorded by celebrating Christmas with tree-decorating, black walnut candy, cups of hot cocoa, and shortbread; by Easter, when eggs are dyed, the children recite in the Sunday School Easter program, and everyone changes from winter to spring underwear; by "October customs" of yellow pumpkins, polished apples, and ghost costumes; by birthdays of carefully wrapped presents and cakes, candles, and ice cream. Maud regrets that Paul is a man "who never considered giving his own mother a birthday bouquet, and dropped in his wife's lap a birthday box of drugstore candy (when he thought of it) wrapped in the drugstore green" (232). She hates having to celebrate Christmas night serving beer and pretzels to Paul's friends, inhaling their smoke, and watching "the soaked tissue that had enfolded the corner Chicken Inn's burned barbecue drift listlessly to the rug" (233). She remembers a past in which each season, each event had its own colors and tastes, and she wants this for her husband and child: "to found—tradition . . . to shape, for their use, for hers, for his, for little Paulette's, a set of falterless customs. She wanted stone" (228). Ultimately, the rituals of her everyday life and her sense of time and place sustain Maud.

In *Maud Martha,* Brooks has created a female character unique for the time period. Within the comedy of the commonplace, she allows us to see the effects of racism, the occasional absurdity of human behavior, and the quest of one individual for beauty, love, and meaning. *Maud Martha* remains a fresh novel even today because it balances the individual's struggles and hopes with an understanding of human mutability and limited existence. Although the novel ends on a positive note, as Maud awaits the birth of her second child and as the weather bids her "bon voyage," this is tempered by the dual vision created within the novel, and the reader realizes that the seasons will change. We recognize that Maud has won human dignity for herself in the daily struggle against inertia, grayness, and hate. Suggesting that such is possible is a significant contribution for any novel to make.

## NOTES

1. The novel is ignored, for example, by Roger Rosenblatt, *Black Fiction* (Cambridge: Harvard University Press, 1974); C. W. E. Bigsby, *The Black American Writer* (Deland, Fla.: Everett/Edwards, 1969); Bigsby, *The Second Black Renaissance* (Westport, Conn.: Greenwood Press, 1980); Herbert Hill, ed., *Anger and Beyond* (New York: Harper and Row, 1966); Addison Gayle, Jr., *The Way of the New World: The Black Novel in America* (New York: Doubleday, 1975).

2. Noel Schraufnagel, *From Apology to Protest: The Black Novel* (Deland, Fla.: Everett/Edwards, 1973), p. 93.

3. Barbara Christian, *Black Women Novelists* (Westport, Conn.: Greenwood Press, 1980), pp. 69–71.

4. Annette Oliver Shands, "Gwendolyn Brooks as Novelist," *Black World* 22, no. 7 (June 1973): 22–30.

5. See Deborah E. McDowell, "New Directions for Black Feminist Criticism," *Black American Literature Forum* 14, no. 4 (Winter 1980): 153–59. She states the case clearly: "When Black women writers are neither ignored altogether nor given honorable mention, they are critically misunderstood and summarily dismissed."

6. Richard Wright, *Native Son* (New York: Harper and Row, 1940).

7. Ralph Ellison, *Invisible Man* (New York: Random House, 1953).

8. Gwendolyn Brooks, *Maud Martha,* in *The World of Gwendolyn Brooks* (New York: Harper and Row, 1971), p. 291. All future quotations from *Maud Martha* will be from this edition and will be cited in the body of the text.

9. Ellison, p. 26.

10. Joseph Campbell has expressed this view on public television, in the concluding chapter of *The Hero with a Thousand Faces* (New York: Meridian Books, 1949), as well as in numerous other places.

R. BAXTER MILLER

# "Define . . . the Whirlwind": Gwendolyn Brooks's Epic Sign for a Generation

For Mari Evans

For twenty-three years, Gwendolyn Brooks tried to write her epic *In the Mecca* (1968). Her portraits of the Black community began with *Street in Bronzeville* (1945) and continued with *Annie Allen* (1949), *Maud Martha* (1953), and *Bean Eaters* (1960). But these books did not fulfill her ambition to write in the heroic genre. An epic should rank with the classics; it should portray the narrator's journey, the obstacles encountered, and the final vision of victory.

Brooks tried to write a Black epic in the title poem of *Annie Allen* but failed. Because the style was too lofty for the theme, an unintentional mock epic resulted. She had heeded the critics too carefully; their requests had led her to substitute Germanic mythology for the Black folk life that she knew. If Latin and Greek diction replaced the Black vernacular, the folk voice would not be evident.

Before Brooks attempted an epic again, she wrote *Maud Martha*. In this autobiographical novel, she practiced the technique of focusing upon the life of one woman and the characters and problems come upon. Brooks tested, too, her skill for creating an undramatized narrator, the fictional self conceived in the work, who can enter characters' minds or withdraw into objectivity.[1] Her next book, *The Bean Eaters* (1960), continued some good poems, especially those concerning the 1950s, yet few of these verses demonstrated majestic finish and thematic depth. The poems did not rival the fine sequences of sonnets that end her first two volumes. Once again she wanted to attempt a long poem. Could free verse and ballad succeed where rhyme royal and sonnet had not? The next book would tell. A year after its

From *Black American Poets between Worlds, 1940–1960,* ed. R. Baxter Miller (Knoxville: University of Tennessee Press, 1986), 160–73. Reprinted with permission of the University of Tennessee Press.

publication (1969), George Starvros, an interviewer for *Contemporary Literature,* would question: "Let me ask you about the character in your poetry and in your novel *Maud Martha. In the Mecca,* your most recent volume, portrays life in a large city building. *A Street in Bronzeville* gave similar vignettes of people in the city. The same, I think, can be said of all your work." Brooks replied, "It's a fascination of mine to write about ghetto people there."[2] One can evaluate her success in this effort, first in light of the Anglo-American tradition of poetry, next in the paradox of the American Dream, and finally in some skillful use of techniques such as Christian myth, parody, and narrative distancing. *In the Mecca* is a most complex and intriguing book; it seeks to balance the sordid realities of urban life with an imaginative process of reconciliation and redemption.

Before an explication of the title poem, one needs to know some background. In her interview with Starvros, Brooks comments:

> when I was nineteen, and had just gotten out of junior college, I went to the Illinois State Employment Service to get a job. They sent me to the Mecca building to a spiritual adviser, and he had a fantastic practice; lucrative. He had us bottling medicine as well as answering letters. Not real medicine, but love charms and stuff like that he called it, and delivered it through the building.[3]

Brooks's explanation here closely correlates with the description of Mecca that appears on the back of her title page:

> . . . a great gray hulk of brick, four stories high, topped by an ungainly smokestack, ancient and enormous, filling half of the block north of Thirty-fourth Street between State and Dearborn . . . The Mecca building is U-shaped. The dirt courtyard is littered with newspapers and tin cans, milk cartons and broken glass. . . . Iron fire escapes run up the building's face and ladders reach from them to the roof. There are four main entrances, two on Dearborn and two on State Street. At each is a gray stone and threshhold and over each is carved "THE MECCA." (The Mecca was constructed in 1891, a splendid palace, or showplace of Chicago).[4]

The date of 1891 is significant because it designates the post-Darwinian world. In American history, industrialization had ended the dream of an agrarian world. The Chicago Mecca, in this light, becomes ironic when one considers the other Mecca, the holiest city of Islam and birthplace of Mohammed. Having wanted to write two thousand lines, Brooks settles for slightly more than eight hundred.[5] She says: "This poem will not be a statistical report. I'm interested in a certain detachment, but only as a means of reaching substance with some incisiveness. I wish to present a large variety of personalities against a mosaic of daily affairs, recognizing that the *grimmest* of these is likely to have a streak or two streaks of sun."[6] The intention is to expand a dramatization of individual scene into universal type so as "to touch every note in the life of this block-long block-wide building would be to capsulize the gist of black humanity in general."[7]

The simple plot and structure of "In the Mecca" (the poem) present an urban setting. For convenience one can divide the narrative into three sections. Part I sets forth the return home from work of Mrs. Sallie Smith, mother of nine. The focus here is on the neighbors that she encounters and on the characterizations of her children. In the second part, the shortest, the woman notices that Pepita, one of her girls, is missing. This prompts the first search through the tenement and allows for further characterization and biblical parody. Part II also concerns the paradox of American myth. The longest section is Part III, which constitutes almost half of the verse. Here the police retrace the Smiths's search. Because of its themes and styles, Part III is probably the richest. The following contribute to its power: militant declarations, interracial lovemaking, rhetorical questions, and Christian myth. The poem ends with the discovery of Pepita's corpse under the bed of Jamaican Edward.

"In the Mecca" represents opposite strains of the Anglo-American tradition. One finds a naturalistic version of Walt Whitman, by way of the industrial age, and the redemptive, if frustrated, potential that characterizes the world of T. S. Eliot. But these influences work so that the peculiarities of the Black American experience transform them into a new and creative vision. By adapting to the social forces of the 1960s, the poet uses a new milieu. Her canvas is a most demanding time in American history. For this and other times, Gwendolyn Brooks holds to light the soundness of body and mind against the decline of courage and assurance, a lapse which emerged with modernity and the shadow of the Holocaust. She continues to believe that imaginative and verbal power challenge and balance finally the danger which posits the insignificance of human life and the indifference to human extinction. For her generation, the defining emblem is ultimately the whirlwind, the collapse of self-confidence, the failure to transform social ill once more into epic victory and to reclaim from the time before the Holocaust, and the later accusation of "reverse discrimination" in the United States, the heroic and bluesesque will of Black hope. Whereas for Margaret Walker, cleansing has been the metaphor for the perspective in which woman takes on historical and cosmic evil, the depth here every bit as great as Melville's "mystery of iniquity," for Brooks the sign is medication. The artistic process itself plays out the action of healing, while the poem serves as both epic quest and sacramental liberation.

Melodie Mary, one of Mrs. Sallie's daughters, shows this turmoil. She likes "roaches, / and pities the gray rat." To her, headlines are "secondary," even though she knows that "blood runs like a ragged wound through the ancient flesh of the land." The imagery implies the naturalism of Richard Wright and others, for to such writers people are manipulated by forces beyond their control. Yet Brooks's point is not that life is crushed inevitably, it is, rather, that even the most lowly insect is sacred. Such a proposition returns a reader to Emerson's belief that each individual reflects all Being. It leads similarly to Whitman's indebted idea that a leaf of grass indicates Eternal Reality. In her description of Melodie Mary, the narrator disorients the reader.[8] Although the imagery indicates naturalism, the statement suggests transcendentalism. To Mary, the deaths of roaches signify what pervades all Life. The naturalism after 1850 tempers the romantic vision, when the undramatized narrator withdraws from Mary's mind:

> Trapped in his privacy of pain
> the worried rat expires,
> and smashed in the grind of a rapid heel
> last night's roaches lie.

This suggestion of the post-Darwinian universe reinforces the date of 1891 on the copyright page. Similarly it recalls the imagery that helps depict Prophet Williams, an "engine / of candid steel hugging combustibles." Mrs. Sallie describes three of her children—Emmett, Cap, and Casey:

> skin wiped over bones
> for lack of chub and chocolate

and ice cream cones,
for lack of English muffins
and boysenberry jam.

The ensuing question is a twentieth-century one and could suit well the wasteland: "What shall their redeemer be"? That Brooks's version has a concrete setting in Chicago adds to the intensity of her effect.

The poverty of the three children mentioned above is as real in the second part as in the first. The levels of the narrator's dramatization in verse in the second part move from the particular to the general: personal, racial, urban, and human. By giving a setting of the city, the narrator implies a need for the pastoral, since the human mind conceives by contrasts. It is striking, indeed, to find in her compressed style, resembling that of Pound and Eliot, the truth of Thomas Gray. Still it was this eighteenth-century poet of graveyards who wrote once on the same theme of death concerning the human potential and the genius that can redeem reality.

> And they [the children] are constrained . . .
>    upon fright and remorse and their stomachs . . .
>    are rags of grit.
>    . . . . . . . . . . . . . . . . . . . . . . . . . . . . .
>    many flowers start, choke, reach up,
>    want help, get it, do not get it,
>    rally bloom, or die on the wasting vine.

From the narrator's observation, the plot reverts to a drama of poetry, where Mrs. Sallie still performs the lead. The image and tone suggest both the Old Testament and the folk ballad "No More Auction Block." In the first part, one finds an emphasis on lost children; in the second, there is an implication of Black death, which is archetypal. The present only foreshadows Pepita's end: "One of my children is gone" (15).

That Don Lee, a poet of the 1960s, appears in "In the Mecca" recreates him as a man of its imaginative world as well as a man of history. The Lee in the poem lives at the midpoint between mimesis and reality. He wants "not a various America / Don Lee wants / a new nation / under nothing" (21). One must remember that this Lee is a tenant in the building described, as are all of the other characters. Should the reader elect to jump from the mimetic world to the historical one, he may get into trouble. Like the real Lee (Madhubuti), he may find that only one portrait in the poem is truly distinguished:[9]

> Way-out Morgan is collecting guns
> in a tiny fourth-floor room.
> He is not hungry, ever, though sinfully lean.
> He flourishes, ever, on porridge or pat of bean
> pudding or wiener soup—fills fearsomely
> on visions of Death-to-the-Hordes-of-the-White-Men!

Madhubuti, of course, has his own followers and his ideology. Here, however, the latter spoils his opportunity to appreciate fully the range of Gwendolyn Brooks. She does depict Morgan with the imagery and power necessary to make him real. But she portrays John Tom, too (no incidental name), St. Julia Jones, and others who have different beliefs. All live in this decaying city; only through imagination can the reader constantly sustain their opposing visions. But in *Mecca* sustenance is all.

The final two hundred lines show once more the influence of Eliot. The refrain, in particular, indicates a sordid world that has profaned what once was sacred: "How many care, Pepita?" The prostitutes and harlots are unconcerned, as the phallic imagery shows: "the obscene gruntings / the dull outwittings / the flabby semi-rhythmic shuffling." Equally obscene are those people, young or old, who make vulgar love. Preoccupied with their own lives, past and present, the characters lack any answers, and the narrator will have to give her own. These inhabitants of the city can no more acknowledge the sacredness of procreation than Alfred, the confused poet, can see that divinity is already within him:

> Hush.
> An agitation in the bush.
> Occluded trees.
> Mad life heralding the blue heat of God
> snickers in a corner of the west windowsill.

Other characters inhabit this Mecca, Brooks's wasteland, though they number too many to receive more than passing attention. Among them are Dakara, the reader of *Vogue;* Aunt Tippie and Zombie Bell, who are undramatized; Mr. Kelly, the beggar with long gray hair; Gas Cady, a grave robber; the janitor, a "Political Person"; Queenie King, an "old poem silvering in the noise"; and Wallace Williams, proclaimer of his virility. To all, the narrator's answer to the rhetorical question applies equally: "these little care, Pepita, what befalls a / nullified saint or forfeiture (or child)."

Set against this background, the description of Alfred becomes particularly significant, for it suggests that the world has passed from hope to hopelessness. For his authorities, Alfred cites Baudelaire, Browning, and Neruda, but his best trick is to parody Whitman. To affirm the redemptive potential of the human spirit, the nineteenth-century poet wrote: "Good-bye and hail! my fancy." To deprive humankind of such belief, Alfred expresses the opposite: "*Farewell, and Hail! Until farewell again.*" Tension separates the literary vision of the past from that of the present.

Other observations show that this is less the world of Thomas Gray and Walt Whitman than that of T. S. Eliot. Consider Aunt Dill, who wears *Tabu* perfume. Little Papa, probably her husband, has been dead for nine years, and all of her children were stillbirths. As a woman who loves God, she reminds the reader of St. Julia. More importantly, she illustrates the paradox that Pepita faced: to grow into a woman who should be shunned or to die in the innocence of youth. Dill

> Is not
> true-child-of-God—for are we ever to
> be children?—are we never to mature,
> be lovely lovely? be soft Woman
> rounded and darling . . . almost caressable . . .
> and certainly wearing *Tabu* in the name of the Lord.

Usually ambivalent in attitude, Alfred hates Mecca, when he confesses,

> something, something in Mecca
> continues to call! Substanceless . . .
> . . . . . . . . . . . . . . . . . . . .
> an essential sanity, black and electric,
> builds to a reportage and redemption.
> . . . . . . . . . . . . . . . . . . . .
>      A material collapse
> that is Construction.

From Alfred, however, one will hardly get the opinion of the undramatized narrator or the implied author. Since the beginning, Brooks has portrayed him as a weak man and an inadequate intellectual. Pepita, on the contrary, is a true poet, just as Alfred is a false one. Despite her youth, she responded to life with sincerity and sensitivity: " 'I touch'—she said once—'petals of a rose. / A silky feeling through me goes!' " (31). For a brief moment the reader receives an alternative vision set against the urban chaos of squalor and hopelessness.

The urban setting reveals the paradox of the American dream. At the beginning, the narrator shifts the focus from her reader to a persona. By combining the imperative and the expository, the verse commences: "Sit where the light corrupts your face. / Miës Van der Rohe retires from grace. / And the fair fables fall" (5). Thomas Earl, one of Mrs. Sallie's children, loves an American folk figure. In tone, however, the narrator questions the validity of John Chapman, now transformed into American legend. She does not mention Mecca, Saudi Arabia, but its reputation for uncultivability suits well the imagery and myth:

> It is hard to be Johnny Appleseed.
> The ground shudders.
> The ground springs up;
> hits you with gnarls and rust,
> derangement and fever, or blare and clerical treasons.

Characterizations in the narrative parody American myth. Melodie Mary, Thomas Earl, and Briggs have "gangs rats appleseed." Examine each word within the quotation mark, first as an entity and then as a whole. Each of the first two images implies the urban experience, but the last suggests the frontier. The collectivity of the line leaves the reader with two questions. Is the idea that "gangs" or "rats," as social reality, corrupt myth and dream, "Appleseed," beyond recognition? Or can myth, "Appleseed," redeem the ghetto from "gangs" and "rats"? By their very disjunction such inquiries mislead, for the purpose here is to create not a separation of perspectives but a unity composed of alternative points of view.

One must measure American ideals against the social reality of Mecca. In one scene Emmett, a daughter of Mrs. Sallie, seizes the telephone from John Tom. Considered on various levels of meaning, this incident becomes complex. In a fine wordplay on time and the American Dream, the narrator recreates the folk legend of the submissive Black: "Despite the terror and the derivation, / despite the not avuncular frontier, / John Tom, twice forty in 420, claims / Life sits or blazes in this Mecca." When the narrator intervenes, Tom has provoked already the "calm and dalliance" of law. On a second level, the narrator becomes unintentionally ambiguous. An exclamation that concerns the size of Pepita results in the American Dream ironically rendered. The twist is that one can be small in thoughts as well as in dimensions: "How shall the Law allow for littleness! / How shall the Law enchief the chapters of / wee brown-black chime, wee brown-black chastity." With the arrival of the impersonal policemen begins a second trip through the Mecca, one which ends in the discovery of the dead child. The officers and the character Amos have different ideologies, since the latter is a bitter militant. He says of a personified America: "Bathe her in her beautiful blood."

"In the Mecca," the title poem, portrays the urban scene through a straight or ironic use of Christian myth and through parody. Throughout the plot, the verse changes the point of view between the narrator and her characters. The situation of Briggs, another of Mrs. Sallie's children, reworks a central motif in *Maud Martha*: at some point human concern passes from social reality—a difficult concept with which to deal—to religion and forgetfulness. The narrator first enters into the character's mind and then withdraws. In the initial description of the young man there comes ironic detachment, but after the reader learns about his problems with the gangs in his neighborhood, the vision comes from within: "Immunity is forfeit, love / is luggage, hope is heresy." The narrator, nevertheless, can step back from the character and speak directly; she can explain human psychology brilliantly: "there is a central height in pity / past which man's hand and sympathy cannot go."

Reviewing the first 254 lines of the poem shows that they have described, first, Mrs. Sallie's return home; second, her children; and third, Alfred, the neurotic artist. But line 255 begins the inciting incident, which both the poem and its reader must resolve. Where is Pepita, Sallie's ninth and mising child? The abrupt shift from the narrator's heightened style shocks when Sallie's children reply emphatically in the Black vernacular: "*Ain seen er I ain seen er I ain seen er* / Ain seen er I ain seen er I ain seen er."[10]

Like most characters in Mecca, Loam Norton worries more about his own concerns than about Mrs. Sallie's daughter. He remembers Belsen and Dachau, the prison camps of World War II, and possibly his own children. But in a parody of the Twenty-third Psalm the narrator interrupts and holds the stage:

. . . The Lord was their shepherd.
Yet did they want.
Joyfully would they have lain in jungles or pastures,
walked beside waters. Their gaunt
souls were not restored, their souls were banished.
. . . . . . . . . . . . . . . . . . . . . . . . . . . . .
Goodness and mercy should follow them
   all the days of their death.

For her character St. Julia Jones, the narrator parodies with equal
fidelity the same passage. There the effect was less a religious
cynicism than a folk joy. Sallie Smith saw Julia, who asked:

"Isn't our Lord the greatest to the brim?
The light of my life. And I lie late
past the still pastures. And meadows. He's the comfort
and wine and piccalili for my soul.
He hunts me up the coffee for my cup.
Oh how I love that Lord."

When Alfred dreams of being a red bush "In the West Virginia
autumn," the image implies the appearance of the Lord to Moses
(Exodus 2:3). The narrator knows that man, by being alive, is
already divine; Alfred doubts: "the bush does not know it flames"
(22). The force of the ending comes from a repetition of this tone.
Jamaican Edward "thrice denies any involvement with Pepita,"
just as the Peter of the New Testament (Matt. 26:4) refuses to
acknowledge Christ. The girl lies beneath Edward's cot in the
dust. Despite differences in sex and age, she resembles Jesus.

    If the title poem, Part I of *In the Mecca,* shows the callousness
of the people in the ghetto, Part II, "After Mecca," offers a
corrective or redeeming vision.[11] Here Brooks takes historical
figures from the 1960s and elevates them to a level of myth
where they transcend life.[12] First she describes Medgar Evers,
the Civil Rights leader assassinated in 1963. Never settling for a
mere recording of history, she transforms fact into a tercet of
prophecy: "Roaring no rapt arise-ye to the dead, he / leaned
across tomorrow. People said that / he was holding clean globes
in his hands." In this section, Brooks goes beyond description to
symbolism. She reshapes history to make it reflect social vision,
created form, and human imagination. Next she portrays Mal-
colm X, the Black leader slain in 1965. The emphasis, however,
should fall not upon history alone but upon Malcolm's role as a

political magician. Since the beginning of the volume, such a type of human being has evolved. An artist, like a magician, seeks to create a new order of reality, although the former wants to change the physical world and the latter to institute an imaginative one. By the power of words, the writer seeks to mesmerize her reader with the spell of form. Alfred was a poet, if not a great one; by her life and death, Pepita was more exemplary. The narrator of the verse in "In the Mecca" was, too, for only in her role as seer and harmonizer could she find irony and avoid despair. To envision Malcolm means to reconstruct the many types that precede, as word-maker, ironist, visionary, and prophet:

> . . . in a soft and fundamental hour
> a sorcery devout and vertical
> beguiled the world.
>
> He opened us—
> Who was a key,
>
> who was a man.

At the end of *In the Mecca* redemptive vision depends upon two poems: "The Sermon on the Warpland" and "The Second Sermon on the Warpland" (hereafter "Second Sermon"). The first demonstrates Brooks's ability to portray reality initially from one point of view and then from another, which clarifies the original. The poet reverts to her habit of coining words, as necessary. What does "Warpland" mean? If the word "Sermon" parodies Christ's speech on the Mount, "Warpland" implies not geographical place but military design—a "war planned"—and the problem of distortion, the "warp land." Yet the several strengths, the speakers in the verse, express the opposite yearnings of the human spirit: "Say that our Something in doublepod contains / seeds for the coming hell and health together" (49). The voice of a Black militant, shortly afterward, recalls Amos or Way-out Morgan in the title poem. But in this world of pervasive irony and contradiction, speech must end in an oxymoron.

> Prepare to meet
> (sisters, brothers) the harsh and terrible weather;
> the pains;
> the bruising; the collapse of bestials, idols.
> . . . . . . . . . . . . . . . . . . . . . . . . . . . . .

the seasoning of the perilously sweet!
the health! the heralding of the *clear obscure!* [emphasis mine]

To this voice, Brooks adds a corrective or balancing resonance. Perhaps her greatest gift is a talent for creating opposite viewpoints within the same poetic world. With equal adeptness she can imagine the militant and renew the meaning of Christ's words to His disciple, Peter (Matt. 16:18). In both instances she stresses universality within the framework of the Black American experience. To one who has read *In the Mecca* as an objective correlative, the narrator here becomes Pepita, resurrected and grown into womanhood. The figure is older and maternal:

> "Build now your church, my brothers, sisters. Build.
> · · · · · · · · · · · · · · · · · · · · · · · · · · · · · · · ·
> Build with lithe love. With love like lion-eyes.
> With love like morningrise.
> With love like black, our black—
> luminously indiscreet;
> complete; continuous."

Immediately following this poem, "Second Sermon" results in a final triumph for the human imagination: "This is the urgency: Live! / and have your blooming in the noise of the whirlwind" (51). The verse has four parts. The first gives the theme quoted last; the second emphasizes the need to give form, to "stylize the flawed utility" (52). In the third division one discovers the chaos against which the imagination conceives. At the end (IV), comes a description of Big Bessie, who stands in the wild weed.

What a metaphor that whirlwind is. From it, one can look at various angles and see diverse personalities, including the arrogantly indifferent, inhumanely callous, and hopelessly contemplative. The narrator's voice reaches back to the end of *Annie Allen*. There, for the first time in Brooks's verse, a speaker possessed some intuitive truth which neither the characters in the poem nor the readers outside fully understood. The observer here [II] is not a well-rounded character; she is, rather, the Imaginative Mind that resolves disparities:

> Not the easy man, who rides above them all,
> not the jumbo brigand,
> not the pet bird of poets, that sweetest sonnet,

shall straddle the whirlwind.
Nevertheless, live.

The third and fourth parts show that imaginative vision can save the listeners in the world of Mecca. By perceiving this world, in its contradictions and ironies, the observer has ordered chaos. Is this the final paradox?

> All about are the cold places,
> all about are the pushmen and jeopardy, theft—
> all about are the stormers and scramblers but
>
> . . . . . . . . . . . . . . . . . . . . . . . . . . . .
>
> Live and go out.
> Define and
> Medicate the whirlwind.

The noblest virtue of Big Bessie, the woman who concludes the volume, is imagination. Without disillusionment, she can look at life and survive. Brooks owes part of the imagery to Langston Hughes's Simple: "Big Bessie's feet hurt like nobody's business / but she stands—bigly—under the unruly scrutiny, stands in the / wild weed" (54, emphasis added). By vision and endurance, the Big Bessies redeem the city in which the Pepitas are slain.

For twenty-three years, Gwendolyn Brooks had sought this balance of vision. In *A Street in Bronzeville,* she had been a poet of the unheroic,[13] but the folk religion lingered. It manifested itself at the end of *Annie Allen* and subsided in *Maud Martha* and *Bean Eaters* only to reappear more intensely in *Mecca.* By then Brooks had practiced ironic detachment and varying distance of narration. Drawing upon Christian myth and different strains of Anglo-American poetry helped her to enrich an epic in which the narrator is heroine. From a certain vision of Chicago as wasteland, Brooks moved to a double perspective of destruction and creation; from Pound and Eliot, her journey led back to Whitman. But the reason is not that Whitman is especially important. It is only that he is romantic in some way that Black folk are: rebelling against constraint, hoping for natural redemption from the depths of an industrial age. If the city corrupts the romantic vision, does it matter? Revealing the paradox of the American Dream suffices, for to show one's reader paradise is not the only way to save his soul.

In the aesthetic formulations, Gwendolyn Brooks remains the

talented poet. She imposes the personal voice upon the sources and archetypes of the literary generation. Through the quest for epic form, she combines the impulse toward architectonic space with prophetic invocation, fusing at once the written and the spoken word. Often when she draws upon Judeo-Christian, historical, and folk sources, through the ornate style or through the vernacular, she opposes the id to the superego, balancing the contradictory tensions which inform human existence. With metaphoric power and intellectual depth, she reconfigures the events of modern history into complex symbol. Whatever her invaluable contributions to the current era, especially from 1945 to 1986, her poetry still signifies two generations past. Yet her language subsumes and transcends historicity.

## NOTES

1. See Wayne C. Booth, *The Rhetoric of Fiction* (Chicago: University of Chicago Press, 1961), pp. 149–63, 211–34.

2. Quoted in George E. Kent, "The Poetry of Gwendolyn Brooks," *Black World,* Part I (September 1971): 30–43. Kent writes: "The depth of her responsiveness and her range of poetic resources make her one of the most distinguished poets to appear in America during the twentieth century."

3. George Starvros, "Interview with Gwendolyn Brooks," *Contemporary Literature* (March 28, 1969); reprinted in Gwendolyn Brooks *Report from Part One* (Detroit: Broadside Press, 1972), p. 162.

4. Gwendolyn Brooks, *The World of Gwendolyn Brooks* (New York: Harper and Row, 1971).

5. Gwendolyn Brooks, "Work Proposed for 'In the Mecca,' " *Report from Part One,* p. 189.

6. Ibid.

7. Ibid., 190.

8. Part of my thinking about Brooks as a poet who disorients the reader has its origin in Hortense Spillers, "Gwendolyn the Terrible," seminar paper for the MLA Convention, December 1975.

9. Don L. Lee, "Gwendolyn Brooks: Beyond the Wordmaker— The Making of an African Poet," in Brooks, *Report from Part One,* p. 22.

10. See George E. Kent, "The Poetry of Gwendolyn Brooks," Part II, *Black World* (October 1971), pp. 36–48, 66–70.

11. To my knowledge, the only article focusing on the volume as a whole is William H. Hansell, "Gwendolyn Brooks' 'In the Mecca': A Rebirth into Blackness," *Negro American Literature Forum* 8 (Summer 1974): 199–207.

12. To discriminate among myth, romance, and realism, see Northrop Frye, *Anatomy of Criticism* (Princeton: Princeton University Press, 1957).

13. Arthur P. Davis, "Gwendolyn Brooks: Poet of the Unheroic," *CLA Journal* 7 (December 1962), pp. 114–25. See George E. Kent, "Aesthetic Values in the Poetry of Gwendolyn Brooks," in *Black American Literature and Humanism*, ed. R. Baxter Miller (Lexington: University Press of Kentucky, 1981); R. Baxter Miller, " 'Does Man Love Art?': The Humanistic Aesthetic of Gwendolyn Brooks," in *Black American Literature and Humanism*, ed. Miller, pp. 95–112.

# D. H. MELHEM

## *In the Mecca*

*In the Mecca*[1] was conceived about 1954 as a teen-age novel. It drew upon Brooks's early, firsthand experience in the Mecca Building as secretary to a patent-medicine purveyor. On December 21, 1958, the poet submitted [to Elizabeth Lawrence, her editor at Harper's] parts of two books: verse from "Bronzeville Men and Women" (later *The Bean Eaters*), and a novel, "In the Mecca." Lawrence didn't care for "Mecca" as a novel. She felt Brooks's discipline in poetry to be a handicap in the larger, freer area of prose. The poet accepted the criticism, noting that she wanted to try writing a verse novel with historical background. The editor responded enthusiastically. In December 1961 she met with Brooks in Chicago and was given a completed version of "In the Mecca" as a novel. Still not favorably impressed, Lawrence suggested that the poet continue in the medium of poetry. On August 22, Brooks reported progress with a poem of "2,000 lines at least, thick with story and music and sound and fury and I hope idea and sense—based on life 'in the Mecca.' "

Writing for the young did not represent a passing interest. *Maud Martha, Bronzeville Boys and Girls,* and, later, *Aloneness, The Tiger Who Wore White Gloves,* and *Very Young Poets* reflect Brooks's welcomed role as mother and teacher. All these books, in fact, excepting *Maud Martha* (for Henry, Henry Jr., and Nora), are dedicated to her children. In 1954, when she began working on the young adult novel, Henry Jr. was fourteen and Nora was three. Brooks's alertness to the ideas and welfare of young people, expressed also through her poetry workshops and the bestowal of numerous literary prizes and other benefits, never diminished. The anthology *To Gwen with Love* (1971), mainly of poems by young black poets, witnesses the bond, "her most cherished award."[2]

While Brooks worked on the poetic conversion of "In the

From *Gwendolyn Brooks: Poetry and the Heroic Voice* (Lexington: University Press of Kentucky, 1987), 153–89. Copyright © 1987 by D. H. Melhem. Reprinted with permission of the University Press of Kentucky.

Mecca," *Selected Poems* was issued. Lecture and reading commitments throughout the United States became heavy. Upon the retirement of Elizabeth Lawrence in 1964, Genevieve ("Gene") Young, who did not pretend to familiarity with poetry, became Brooks's editor. Brooks and Young enjoyed a warm and mutually respectful relationship throughout the production of *In the Mecca*. The poet had been planning to leave Harper's for some time because of her interest in the new black publishing companies, and did leave after Young's departure in 1970 to join J. B. Lippincott.

In 1964 the Illinois Bell Telephone Company commissioned Brooks to write a poem about Chicago. "I See Chicago," a strongly alliterative variation of a Petrarchan/Shakespearean sonnet, appeared in *Time* magazine under the puzzling caption "Vers Libre." The poet also completed a chapter of her autobiography. She continued to travel and write until 1966, when she suffered a mild heart attack, followed by influenza. After the illness, she labored assiduously on *In the Mecca* until, in January 1967, she anticipated completion by midyear.

In the spring, the Second Fisk University Writers' Conference seeded a new psychopoetic awareness for Brooks. The new Black consciousness and its surging creativity; meeting Walter Bradford, the Blackstone Rangers, and the students she organized into a workshop—these register in the style and matter of *In the Mecca. Jump Bad*, Brooks's workshop anthology, is livened by Black speech, consciousness, and pride in African heritage. The poet also responded to her students' talent and thought with the second dedication of *In the Mecca,* "In Tribute," where their names appear.

On September 1, Brooks mailed the manuscript to Young and wrote her two days later, including a three-page revision. Editorial reaction was somewhat negative at Harper's; Lawrence's opinion was again solicited. She made known her reservations to Brooks, with hopes for a larger and more diversified volume, one that was less stylized in language (Oct. 4). In a letter to Young bearing the same date, Brooks agreed that ten poems should be added; an improvement, the new editor subsequently assured. In the November correspondence, Dudley Randall is mentioned as planning to print "The Wall" as a broadside, already having done so with "We Real Cool."

Brooks sent several new poems, including "Two Dedications," to Gene Young on November 8 and enclosed newspaper clippings of the events. The poet considered the works "art reports." The editor suggested, with the concurrence of Ann Harris, then poetry editor, that some newspaper account precede each poem. Brooks agreed in a telegram received at Harper's March 5, 1968; she carefully selected and edited the epigraphs which appear. As printed by Dudley Randall's Broadside Press (1967), "The Wall," without epigraph, shares the immediacy of a journalistic account.

*In the Mecca* was so well received in the summer of 1968 that by September a second printing was ordered and in November, a third. In February 1969, Brooks was nominated for a National Book Award; she has never received one. James N. Johnson warmly reviewed *In the Mecca,* stating, "No white poet of her quality is so undervalued, so unpardonably unread."[3]

By August 1969, Brooks had located her publishing allegiance in the black press. She informed her editor that Dudley Randall would publish her next book, *Riot,* and that she planned to do no further teaching. It interfered with her own writing and kept her in Chicago; she liked to travel. In June she sent the editor a photo of herself with her hair natural, the style she had adopted in February.

There was little personal correspondence with Harper's after the departure of Young in October. On December 14, 1970, the *New York Times* carried an article headlined "Yale Conference Studies Role of Black Woman," by Thomas A. Johnson, who stated that Brooks's future work would be published by Broadside Press. The last book published by Harper's, *The World of Gwendolyn Brooks,* involved a minimum of correspondence, that between Roslyn Targ, her first and last literary agent (they are no longer associated), and her last editor at Harper's, Ann Harris. At first the plan was to exclude *In the Mecca.* But Brooks firmly and correctly insisted that the omission would disregard her development and ignore her contemporary vitality.

Brooks notes that she and Harper's "parted company" with mutual respect and understanding. At all times, she avows, her former publisher has treated her with consideration, cooperation, and kindness.

## "In the Mecca"

*In the Mecca* bears the spiritual imprint of the turbulent 1960s. Added to the Civil Rights Movement, the mass politicizing of the decade mounted an enlarging opposition to the Vietnam War. Early in the period, widespread street demonstrations against nuclear testing helped expedite the 1963 Nuclear Test Ban Treaty. The year of Martin Luther King's "I Have a Dream" speech at the Lincoln Memorial (Aug. 28, 1963) saw the assassinations of President John F. Kennedy (Nov. 22) and Medgar Evers, the NAACP leader (June 13). Brooks wrote poems about both victims; the one for Evers appears in *In the Mecca*. Hazards to civil rights workers, both white and black, were tragically enacted in the murders of Michael Schwerner, Andrew Goodman, and James E. Chaney by members of the Ku Klux Klan in Philadelphia, Mississippi, June 22, 1964.

The assassination of Malcolm X on February 21, 1965, in Harlem held great meaning for the future of integration. The Black Muslim minister had turned away from separatism after his pilgrimage to Mecca in the spring of 1964. Dr. C. Eric Lincoln told the press that "for the Negroes in America, the death of Malcolm X is the most portentous event since the deportation of Marcus Garvey in the 1920s."[4] Brooks's poem "Malcolm X" significantly appears in "After Mecca."

Riots in Watts, the black ghetto in Los Angeles, August 11–16, 1965, resulted in the death of thirty-five people and considerable property damage, calling attention to the miserable economic conditions of the residents. Anti–Vietnam War protests increased in size and intensity throughout 1966 and 1967. Draft card burnings and antidraft demonstrations grew widespread. The black ghetto of Newark experienced a devastating riot in 1967. During this turbulence, Brooks attended the Fisk University Conference that impressed her so deeply. The following year, the murder of Martin Luther King and the ensuing urban riots, specifically those in Chicago, inspired *Riot,* her first volume with Broadside Press.

Two indications of the breadth, indeed, the poetic breath to which *In the Mecca* would expand greeted the reader of the 1968 volume. Reprinted in the omnibus, they constitute the jacket quotation from Brooks and the two sets of dedications. On May 31, 1968, Young sent the author a copy of the jacket material which had already gone to the printer, and assured her that changes could still be made. Brooks wrote back immediately, relieved that she could alter her statement, and happily inscribed the final version on the letter itself in both ink and type: "I was to be a Watchful Eye; a Tuned Ear; a Super-Reporter." She was concerned that the semicolons and capitals be maintained. The statement confirms Brooks's own view of her work as quasi-divine reportage—close to the actual text of existence—a spiritual closeness indicated by the "Eye" of the soul as well as of the body, the "Ear" attuned to the urgencies of her people. The "Super-Reporter" relates to the "Teller" and to the prophetic voice.

## Composition, Language, Themes, Images, Characters

Of the two portentous dedications, the first honors the memory of Langston Hughes, along with James Baldwin, LeRoi Jones (Amiri Baraka), and Mirron ("Mike") Alexandroff who, as president of Columbia College, Chicago, gave Brooks her first teaching job, a poetry workshop. The four-part epigraph, appearing between the two dedications, quotes author John Bartlow Martin; a Blackstone Ranger, Richard "Peanut" Washington; a Chicago political activist, Russ Meek; and "A Meccan," cited in Martin's article on the Mecca Building, "The Strangest Place in Chicago."[5]

"In the Mecca," the title poem, is by far Brooks' longest single work. Its 807 lines are divided into fifty-six stanzas of uneven length, ranging from one to fifty-three lines. The multiform verse is mostly free. Incantatory modes, parallel constructions evoke the chanted sermon. Random, slant, and internal rhyme and varied metrical patterns enhance a formal freedom with counterparts in African polyrhythm. Some compounding, more alliteration, and rich imagery limn the highly figurative contours of the heroic style. The most apparent departure from the past, outside the variety of embedded forms, meets the eye at line initial. Brooks abandons conventional capitalization; words that begin sentences take capitals as they would in prose. Other capitals lend occasional emphasis, but mainly indicate the abundance of names—people, places, real and imaginary objects, ideas, items of dailiness, identities that crowd the life of the Mecca as its inhabitants crowd its apartments.

From time to time, the poet's voice modulates from objective narration to subjective, to *style indirect libre,* to protagonist-Teller. Yet the shifts cohere. Through Brooks's purposeful vision, the real and fictive worlds interact to present a social panorama. The dramatic poem "In the Mecca" exposes the detritus of a competitive system and comments indirectly upon American capitalism, the price of its success and failure. Brooks's black world mirrors the psychic isolation of its white environment. Like the pool players in "We Real Cool," embattled Mecca residents arm themselves with indifference.

The setting is the "great gray hulk of brick four stories high," as described by John Bartlow Martin in his article cited above. Built in 1891, it was "a splendid palace, a showplace of Chicago" with carpeted stairs and goldfish bowls in the lobby. By 1912, it housed the black elite. But the Depression of the 1930s hastened its decline into a slum building with fire escapes cluttering the façade. The Mecca was the location for one of Brooks's earliest jobs, secretary to a patent-medicine man, mildly recalled by "Prophet Williams," who sells magic remedies in the poem. In 1941, the Illinois Institute of Technology bought the building and, despite opposition, tore it down nine years later to extend facilities on the site.[6] The Mecca Building was cleared as a slum.

The narrative framework is simple. Mrs. Sallie Smith goes home to the Mecca. A poor woman, mother of nine children, she work as a domestic. Filled with fantasies of reversing roles ("And that would be my baby . . . I my lady"), she "loves and loathes" her employer's pink "toy-child," who is indulged with the material things denied her own family. A good mother, she can afford only ham hocks, "six ruddy yams," and "cornbread made with water" to feed her brood. She is an expansive woman, suggested by the children's names, Yvonne, Melodie Mary, Cap, Casey, Thomas Earl, Tennessee, Emmett, Briggs, Pepita—a cosmopolitan mélange indicating both city life and a possible variety of fathers, none of them mentioned. Mrs. Sallie's introductory reverie ends with the narrator's comment, expendable, "What else is there to say but everything?" (unilinear st. 16). When she thinks of Pepita, the two sentences in bold-looking capitals are set off as a stanza: "SUDDENLY, COUNTING NOSES, MRS. SALLIE SEES NO PEPITA. WHERE PEPITA BE?" Typography stresses both grammar and emotion. A common Black English construction makes its first appearance in Brooks's work: "invariant *be*."

Nothing first that the study of Black English was initiated by William A. Stewart's work from 1962 on, William Labov gives attention to the copula in his major study *Language in the Inner City*.[7] Labov sees BEV ("black English vernacular") as "a distant subsystem within the larger grammar of English" (63–64). What he calls "invariant *be*" or *be$_2$*, the use of *be* to indicate " 'habitual' behavior: durative or iterative depending on the nature of the action" (51), is differentiated from *be$_1$*, "the ordinary finite *be* which alternates with *am, is, are,* etc." Disagreeing with Stewart and Dillard on a Creole origin for *be$_2$*, Labov observes: "The closest analogy is with the Anglo-Irish *be,* stemming from the Celtic "consuetudinal or habitual copula." Both Labov and

Dillard argue convincingly for BEV as a coherent system which, as dialect in the former and language in the latter, displays the logical features of a bona fide grammatical structure, exemplified by Mrs. Sallie's speech.

Her frantic pilgrimage through the Mecca forms the action. In the course of Mrs. Sallie's search for her daughter, Brooks sketches a representative number of tenants and addresses a broad range of contemporary and philosophical subjects. The technique—flexible, cinematographic—cuts to vignettes, close-ups, and landscapes while moving the narrative.

The religious impulse of "In the Mecca" is cued by the homiletic epigraph set apart on the verso page preceding the poem: "Now the way of the Mecca was on this wise." This line was originally the last line of the poem and remained there as late as September 1967 in a revised fragment sent to Harper's. The transposition, of course, lends a biblical tone. A parable is forthcoming; the Mecca Building will become a social paradigm.

The opening lines,

> Sit where the light corrupts your face.
> Miës Van der Rohe retires from grace.
> And the fair fables fall.

invite a reverie of the past, nearly two decades before. Then the Miës Van der Rohe-designed Illinois Institute of Technology still faced the Mecca Building, which was already a roiling ghost of its splendor. The lines also connote the failure of religion, art, and politics in confronting American life.

Brooks packs her images with meaning: the revelatory light (natural and heavenly light, reason) that will become physical in the "Don Lee" section, is powerless to sanctify, being itself tainted. Modern art, expressed by Miës Van der Rohe, who has produced exemplary new architecture in Chicago, cannot save the Mecca. Indeed, modern art turns away. It would replace the building with a structure detached from the environment, like the surrealist's "careless flailed-out bleakness" in the "Catch" poem.

"Fair" mainly connotes beautiful or pleasing to the eye, light, just, so that the lovely fables of the American Dream are also fables of fairness. The collocation of "light," "face," and "fair" suggests some association with whiteness as skin color. Brooks says she did not intend "fair fables" as a reference to whiteness, however. An ironic semantic note is that "fair," usually associated with blondness and light skin among whites, carries, along with "light," a parallel regard for skin color among blacks, where the range of hue actually varies from white to brown and black. "Fair" is noteworthy in the "Amos" passage (st. 43), the prophetic denunciation of American society that must remove her "fair fine mask."

Immediately following, "The ballad of Edie Barrow" tells of a "fair" wealthy lover who will marry a "Gentile" girl "come fall, come falling of fall" while he retains his black mistress. Repetition of "fall" connects with the theme of a declining white culture. "Fall" also summons the fall from innocence in the Garden of Eden, Edie's paradisaic innocence (like that of Annie Allen). Her treacherous lover destroys her ingenuous hopes, revealing them as "a fair fable."

The fall of the fables—tales of the American success system—accompanies the resonant image of the Mecca Building. In recreating the demolished edifice, Brooks offers a new legend, infused with anger, compassion, despair, and hope, as she imbricates past, present, and future. The name "Mecca," that of the holy city to which Muslims turn in prayer, has acquired the connotation of a special focus or goal. Combining literal and figurative referents, the building achieves its bitter apotheosis as Brooks's central image. Its crumbling magnificence, housing the decay of religious, economic, and moral energy, becomes a powerful symbol of deteriorated spiritual and economic health. Yet dialectial forces within the decay work toward regeneration.

Religion in the Mecca is a hodgepodge of cant, self-seeking, and the sale of indulgences; it represents and parodies what passes for religion in much of American society, as elsewhere. Alfred scores the betrayal of "trinities"; Jamaican Edward "thrice denies" his guilt (cf. "thrice-gulping" in "Leftist Orator"), recalling folk-tale numerology and Peter's denial of Jesus. Concern with religion permeates the narrative. "St. Julia Jones" prays with enthusiasm; Mrs. Sallie, "all innocent of saints and signatures," wryly observes her, "content to endorse / Lord as an incense and a vintage," no more vital than a nostalgic fragrance (though "vintage" subtly echoes "the grapes of wrath" in Julia Ward Howe's "Battle Hymn of the Republic"). Sallie herself retains the dignity and loving strength of a fundamental religiosity. From the outset, as she climbs the "sick and influential stair" of her environment, Brooks regards her with compassionate amusement as a "prudent partridge," a game bird who becomes "a fugitive attar and a district hymn." Both "attar" and "hymn," the floral and the religious musical attributes (the former fleeting, mortal, the latter local and sacred), endow Sallie with a native, humanistic grace.

The critical stance toward formal religion scatters. It appears in the parodic usage of the Twenty-third Psalm in the "Loam Norton" stanza (26), its furious outcry against the suffering that Belsen and Dachau prisoners were permitted to endure. Like the allusion to the civil war in China (st. 10), where Melodie Mary, who likes roaches "and pities the gray rat," is only mildly touched by headlines about the foreign children, the concentration camp reference is vital to the scope of the poem. For the work reaches far beyond the Mecca into violence and absence of caritas in the world. This breadth lends aesthetic validity to the villain as a nonnative black man, "Jamaican Edward," since the conceptual framework moves beyond American society to the world of heroes, villains, and victims.[8] Moreover, the Anglo-Saxon name Edward means "guardian of property," here both destroyer and emblem of destructive materialism. Pepita, on the other hand, in Spanish means "a grain of pure gold" or the seed of a fruit.

Unhappy Thomas Earl clings to his life-asserting fantasy-identity with Johnny Appleseed in the midst of "hells and gruels," where the ground gives forth not increase in the spring but "gnarls and rust, / derangement and fever, or blare and clerical treasons" (st. 13). This is a time far removed from the renewal promised by religion and nature. Of Sallie's children, the poets asks, "What shall their redeemer be?" and answers, "Greens and hock of ham." Physical needs must precede spiritual ones. The children are hungry.

In the next passage, Alfred, teacher and intellectual, views "The faithless world! / betraying yet again / trinities!" (st. 15), a world without charity, offering no meaningful Christianity that will feed its hungry children. Prophet Williams, widower, lustful fraud, advertises his nostrums, potions, charms, and lucky numbers "in every Colored journal in the world." People seek his magic to cope with problems, material needs, and desires. Yet Brooks views the Mecca residents compassionately. They move through "martyred halls"; their fate borders that of the concentration camp inmates of Belsen and Dachau in a deeply moving reflection by Loam Norton. His name denoting earth, he is one of the few caring individuals in the Mecca.

The martyr theme colors the blood imagery of the Loam Norton passage. The ghastly sacrament of concentration camp victims, like the blood of Chinese Civil War victims in the

Melodie Mary stanza, later transforms into the blood of tormentors, when Amos and "Way-out Morgan" seek vengeance (sts. 43 and 50). The martyr theme recurs in burning images: "Insane Sophie," who sees fires running up and down a world aslant in a macabre dance; Sallie, who comforts herself with the thought that "Pepita's smart" while "Knowing the ham hocks are burning at the bottom of the pan" (st. 29). We have encountered the burning food image in "A Bronzeville Mother" and "The Chicago *Defender*." Here again, the victim is a child, her martyrdom portended in the homely image of the burned dinner. ("Hocks" may further suggest Pepita's physical defect, discussed later.) Burned bacon and wheat toast in the previous poems similarly point to the near-casual violence in daily life. The innocent victim theme recurs in the now-familiar chicken image (Briggs is a gang member who must "choke the chickens" to prove his manhood), and the cockroach and insect images (cf. Melodie Mary, Great-Gram, and the discovery of Pepita).

Religion, martyrdom, innocence broadly subsume under caritas, observed as a major theme in Brooks. "How many care, Pepita?" becomes a rhetorical question. The difficult, circumscribed lives, "the hollowed, the scant, the / played-out deformities? the margins?" (st. 46) have little to offer of their spent selves. *Vogue* is a grotesque here. Darkara looks at its improbable world of haute couture. She studies a picture of playboy Laddie Sanford, who says, "I call it My Ocean. Of course, it's the Atlantic" (st. 47). The self-indulgent rich are as detached emotionally as they are physically from the Meccas around them.

Like the depression and apathy discerned by Freud as anger deflected toward the self, indifference within the Mecca charts a survival tactic of oppressed people. Psychologically, loss of affect may signal its repression. Feelings make one vulnerable. The Mecca, so crammed with misery, injustice, poverty, and squalor, can lacerate the undefended heart into a screaming rage.

This rage, the extreme of and alternate to apathy/coolness, surges variously at three critical points: the descriptions of Amos, Way-out Morgan, and Don Lee. Amos, namesake of the prophet of a vengeful God, demands a blood bath, a "good rage" to wash America pure (st. 43). The "good rage" recalls "the whirlwind of good rage" in "Riders to the Blood-red Wrath." It relates to the Don Lee stanza (41)—which calls for "a new music screaming in the sun"—and to the Way-out Morgan stanza (50) summoning a terrible vengeance as he collects guns in his fourth-floor room. Rage also looks to the whirlwind image in "The

Second Sermon on the Warpland." Like Amos, who is weary of gradualism (" 'Takes time,' grated the gradualist. / 'Starting from when?' asked Amos"), these activists propose desperate remedies. The three represent phases of rage: prophecy, destruction, and construction. "In the Mecca" moves from expression to interpretation; from questions to possibilities for action.

The Don Lee stanza, about two-thirds into the poem, together with stanza 54 near the end, forms the pivot of hope countering Pepita's fate as the pivot of despair. It illustrates, moreover, the alternating or antithetical structure of the poem. And it gives insight into the important light imagery previously discussed in "Big Bessie" and the "Catch" poems. Big Bessie does not want her son to be misled by illusive "candles in the eyes." Don Lee, however, becomes a symbol of positive action, desiring "a physical light that waxes," one that grows from the efforts and commitment of black people themselves. As the poem's blood imagery turns from victim to oppressor, so does the light imagery move from its revelatory function in the first line, "Sit where the light corrupts your face," to the "least light" given off by the environment as Sallie contemplates her shabby kitchen, toward fulfillment as human energy. Removing her hat, Sallie confesses, overwhelmed, " 'But all my lights are little!' " (st. 7), ironic coupling of small hopes and small children.

In contrast with Big Bessie and Sallie, Don Lee "is not candlelit" like the former or frustrated by the "least light" of the latter. He calls vigorously for a new nation "under nothing" (partly alluding to the Gettysburg Address and the revised Pledge of Allegiance), as he "stands out in the auspices of fire / and rock and jungle-flail" (st. 41). Evoking the prophetic image of Shadrach, Meshach, and Abednego (Dan. 3:12–30), a human "physical light that waxes" triumphs over the fiery furnace of political attack, even as light turns to fire in the process of action. The new black, embodied by Lee, will want a "new art and anthem . . . a new music screaming in the sun," partly a reference to his *Don't Cry, Scream* (1969). Light moves from fire to sun in a progression toward the "new black sun"[9] where Brooks will find her "surprised queenhood" several years later. The light becomes physical as it rises to consciousness. Guided truly from within, people illuminate each other. This dynamic transformation of imagery is one of the technical splendors of the poem.

The Don Lee section is bracketed by stanzas on "Hyena," the self-engrossed debutante (39), death (40), and Alfred, the teacher/intellectual/failed artist (42). Directly preceding 39 and 40 is the tribute to Léopold Sédar Senghor, the poet who became the first president of the Independent Republic of Senegal in 1960. The escapist yearnings of Alfred contrast with Lee and the ambition of prophetic Amos in the next section. Transitions are deftly graded.

The call for a "new art and anthem" recognizes that art in contemporary society cannot save the Mecca, nor can its detached contemplation. Art is a palliative, not a cure or an organic endeavor. Returning from work, Sallie surveys her kitchen, the antagonist she would conquer by decoration. The poet comments, "A pomade atop a sewage. An offense. / First comes correctness, *then* embellishment!" (st. 7). This states a moral concern with art in society, with the concept of beauty as a wholeness, "an essential sanity" called for near the end of the poem. The Mecca will not be improved by Darkara's imported *Vogue,* by Alfred's amiable dabbling in the arts, his reduction of literature to an obsession with language and his knowledge of Senghor. Reiteration that Alfred has not seen Pepita, though he can describe the Mecca and praise the poet-president, emphasizes his well-meaning yet ineffectual nature, his inability to relate actively to his own environment.

The Senghor passage (st. 38) begins with Alfred "(who might have been a poet-king)" and dissolves into a description of the man who was both poet and political leader. (The fragment first appeared in *Negro Digest,* September 1964). Pictured in Europe as "rootless and lonely," Senghor is still revered for representing an ideal: the artist as man-of-action, whose art expresses communal needs. Proximity of the important passage to Don Lee, the two bridged by relatively short, emotionally pacing stanzas (Hyena and death) joins historical and dramatic impact near the core of the narrative. Yet Senghor's wistful, exiled call for "negritude," filled with past achievement, cedes to the younger poet's rousing exhortation.

Contemporary world politics, which permit a Mecca at home and concentration camps abroad, cannot save the Mecca. Justice is fugitive. "The Law" visits reluctantly. The final insight, nevertheless, before the dreadful denouement, is given to Alfred in one of the poem's absolute passages. In stanza 54, Alfred, "lean," leans over the balcony and looks out over the wretchedness of the scene. Listening, he is aware that

> something, something in Mecca
> continues to call! Substanceless; yet like mountains,
> like rivers and oceans too; and like trees

with wind whistling through them. And steadily
an essential sanity, black and electric,
builds to a reportage and redemption.
    A hot estrangement.
    A material collapse
that is Construction.

The epiphanic moment recalls William Wordsworth on Mount
Snowden (*The Prelude,* Book XIV), the sense of continuity with
nature through which human life perceives the universal bond.
"Substanceless" implies nonmaterial or spiritual, as in Words-
worth. For the latter, imagination combines with the Platonic
hierarchy leading to intellectual love; in Brooks there is a similar
emphasis on imagination as empathy, but the engagement is more
immediately applicable to daily life. In a destructive environment,
she suggests, black sanity will be curative, not by passive alien-
ation but through a passionate "estrangement" from prevailing
values. "Material collapse" will be the collapse of a materialistic
society. Construction must involve essential change. In leaning
toward Mecca, Alfred inclines toward a new ethos for an entire
social order.

Compare the Alfred of this passage with his introduction at
stanza 4, where we encounter his narrow (though benign) ped-
antry, minor lubricities, and occasional overindulgence in drink-
ing. Alcohol induces a pseudo-mystical insight where "the
Everything / is vaguely a part of One thing and the One thing /
delightfully anonymous / and undiscoverable." The balcony epi-
sode, by contrast, occurs in a state of sobriety, in the sanctuary of
consciousness. Alfred's development critically supports the
theme of possible redemption, reminding that his Anglo-Saxon
name, originally "elf-in-council," means "good counselor." He
reinforces at stanza 48 the poet's appraisal of the Black situation
in the Don Lee passage. His impotent intellectualism, limned in
stanzas 4 and 38, undergoes modification with the insights of 48,
where he turns away from Baudelaire, "Bob Browning," and
Neruda, foreign white poets dealing with foreign matters, to the
need for native "Giants over Steeples." The giants are empow-
ered, super- (as opposed to supra-) human beings who will rise
above the very edifices of religion. Alfred acknowledges both
"confusion and conclusion." Conclusion is not only the end of
things but the *conclusion* to be drawn. Conclusions entail judg-
ment and understanding. From this point Alfred can move to the
moment on the balcony and the pinnacle of insight.

Despite the mild suggestion that Alfred turns toward Mecca as religion, plausible considering the shambles of organized (or disorganized) religion the poem portrays, Mecca remains basically the aspirations and potential of black people housed in the Mecca Building. The ambiguity, however, enriches the poem's texture, both in ironic and spiritual substance. Like the Mahayana Buddhist, however, who eschews Nirvana for the return to help his fellow creatures, Brooks drops from contemplative height to the body of Pepita and the ground of daily life.

## Structure, Narrator, Forms

Although a work of such complexity cannot be reduced to simple patterns, it is helpful to view (and review) the structure in several ways. Partly, as noted above, it is a series of antithetical and graded movements. These alternate between a despairing past and present which interact with hope. They do so by means of the narrative, the narrator, and juxtaposition, by the tesselating of personae and poetic forms. Main characters appear early but the cast continually augments. We draw analogies with art and music: a mosaic of themes with variations, movement toward multi- and polyrhythm, the gradual revelation of tapestry by the shuttle.

Above all, "In the Mecca" is a dramatic quest of a parent for her child. The panorama eddying around her, Mrs. Sallie advances with the tragic aura of a Hecuba or Niobe. She begins with the problem of feeding her children and ends with the murder of one. From start to finish, she must address existential matters, basic and extreme. Thus the work moves dipodally between "How shall I live?" and "What shall I live by?" the two questions being related in the poem as they are in life. The economic, moral, and psychological function like agitated particles trapped in solution. Mrs. Sallie and her mission are the bestirring agents. The distraught mother, more catalyst than developing character, progresses mainly through degrees of alarm. Her reflection in stanza 18 (after noting the absence of Pepita), "I fear the end of Peace," merges with the poet-narrator in harsh irony. Sallie Smith, embattled and harried, has known no peace from the beginning.

The narrator is a strategic tour de force. Though Sallie is the dramatic agent, the poet addresses the reader and the characters. "Sit where the light corrupts your face" notifies us that the poet will participate in the action. At times observing, at times entering in *style indirect libre,* the narrator reacts to character and to plot. She functions as a Greek tragic chorus, embodying moral and social commentary, and acquires a personality. Her delineation advances the heroic dimensions she invokes in others. Moral and intellectual vigor refine the Don Lee section, where her praise enunciates her own ideals and native optimism.

Thus evolve another pair of foci: the drama unfolding around Mrs. Sallie and the poet's sensibility. This double perspective enables the latter to approach, embrace, and observe the former. The dynamics of the poem's hope-despair motifs, set constantly in tension, remain essentially connected. As medium of temporal connections, moreover, the narrator/interpreter joins past, present, and future.

Range and variety of characters in the Mecca bespeak a microcosm. The diversity, in turn, imprints the form. Free verse, metrical verse, random rhyme, slant rhyme, alliteration, the couplet, and the ballad accompany moods varying through sermonic, dramatic, and ironic, and objective and subjective narrative modes encompassing a spectrum of attitudes. Brooks's magisterial prosody summons historical figures from contemporary life, houses present action in a demolished edifice, and images the past in the "Great-great Gram" passage (st. 25, which recalls the system of slavery). Formally she utilizes and renovates the past, drawing it to the present. But her emphasis is contemporary, progressive.

Inclusion of the ballad at three points—in modified form describing Prophet Williams's wife, Ida (st. 3), the material aspirations of Emmett, Cap, and Casey (st. 22), and "The ballad of Edie Barrow" (st. 44), a tale of white betrayal of black love—should be noted. Disguised by block presentation, the poems provide the "clarifying" which Brooks will continue to pursue. In addition to linguistic paring, the ballad strips down narrative to heroic essentials, a prerequisite for mythologizing. Formal blending affects the poem as a whole and, like the poetic voice, serves to unify within diversity. If Brooks had employed the ballad in, say, the Senghor or Don Lee sections, the distinctive form coupled with the elevated subject matter might have detached either one from its context. What the poet has done, then, is meld the diverse elements into an organic entity. Her tact corresponds to the poem's underlying quest for social cohesion.

The ballad is further compatible with the narrative and journalistic modes and with parable ("Now the way of the Mecca was on this wise"). In Brooks's supple narration, personae speak directly or indirectly, as observed and interpreted. Old St. Julia Jones, Great-great Gram, Aunt Dill, Great-uncle Beer, and others tell their own tales through the omniscient observer, reporter, interpreter, prophet. As Brooks herself notes of the growing Black consciousness described in the Alfred balcony passage, there is a building toward "reportage and redemption." The bodily eye, ultimately, accommodates the deeper perceptions of the soul. "Ye shall know the truth, and the truth shall make you free" (John 8:32).

## Dynamics of Narrative Sequence

In narrative sequence, the first stanza introduces the themes of failed art, religion, and politics, or Western ethos; the first sixteen stanzas (and, intermittently, the next fourteen, mainly through action) describe Sallie and her children, alternating with certain key neighbors. Superpious and, significantly, "old" St. Julia Jones and the cynical hypocrite Prophet Williams act as foils to the sincere religiosity and prophecy in the poem. They also permit announcement of Sallie's skepticism and humanistic concern with her children's needs. Stanza 4 introduces two extremes: Hyena, the modish, hedonistic "debutante," and Alfred, the self-engrossed intellectual. They represent two aspects of disengagement from the scene, although Alfred will change. Selfishness in the poem associates with despair; caritas, communality, with hope and psychic health.

The children span egoism, sociability, antisociality. Youth makes them less responsible and defined, but we can see how they, too, will be ground into quotidian ferocities. Melodie Mary likes roaches but is emotionally removed from the children of China's civil war; Briggs belongs to a gang and learns violence (choking chickens); Thomas Earl fantasizes, his generous sympathies deflected by the environment; Tennessee is passive like his cat; Emmett, Cap, and Casey ("skin wiped over bones") are "redeemed" by food (ironically recalling Jesus' "Man shall not live by bread alone," Matt. 4:4 reference to Deuter. 8:3); Yvonne, in her teens, reflects upon her shared lover with a tough satisfaction that she will have her portion. Stanza 15 importantly precedes discovery of Pepita's disappearance. The passage presents Alfred's "faithless world" reflection and reverts to skepticism of the introductory stanzas. Thus weighted, the stanza ironically describes the indulged child of Sallie's rich employer. Wealth, like the egocentricity of Hyena and early Alfred, the religious fanaticism of St. Julia

Jones, and the religious fraud of Prophet Williams, flaunts another extreme and contrast. Moving from Sallie to the others and back, Brooks's technique widens consciousness.

Stanza 17 acts as a stop of full tension. When Sallie asks, "WHERE PEPITA BE?" her terrified question casts the story into chiaroscuro. Stanza 18 refers to the child as

> our Woman with her terrible eye,
> with iron and feathers in her feet,
> with all her songs so lemon-sweet,
> with lightning and a candle too . . .

Stanza 30 will clarify that she is "halted." Within the elemental and human terms of her description, "candle" and "halt" relate her to Big Bessie's son in the "Catch" poems, the "bright lameness from my beautiful disease" of romantic illusion. The penultimate stanza will reveal Pepita's love of beauty, perhaps implicated in her death, and the "petals of a rose" which she once touched and for which her mother will try.

Highlighted by the ballad of adolescent wants (st. 22), the children's dreams intensify impressions of social evils grown immediately menacing. As the children acknowledge the unknown peril to their sister, they become "constrained." The word, appearing three times in stanzas 20 and 23, suggests force, the unnatural restraint involved in the murder itself. In stanza 23 the family is suddenly activated; the frieze of their emerging terror gives way to the charge "down the martyred halls." The adjective not only recognizes the martyr theme initially portended by the name "St. Julia Jones." It projects an associated guilt on to the external environment of the Mecca Building.

While the search for Pepita begins at stanza 23, Mrs. Sallie's pilgrimage actually beings in stanza 2, where she seeks rest at home, peace from her chores and anxieties. Economic struggle determines her life; survival and conflict rudely foreground the tragedy. Choked chickens (st. 11), Belsen and Dachau (st. 26), and burning ham hocks in the pan (st. 29) foreshadow the sacrifice. Directly follows the second description of Pepita: "the puny—the halted, glad-sad child" (st. 30). Particularly shocking at this point comes the reality of Pepita: an undernourished, lame little girl. The question of brute survival of the "fittest," subtly yet unmistakably raised, extends the urgency into an awesome, pernicious dimension. Suddenly the world seems threatening and cruel to the family. Succeeding stanzas on the police and Aunt Dill turn acerbic.

Summoned, the police dally and present "a lariat of questions," recalling the "lariat lynch-wish" and the "scythe / of men" in "The *Chicago Defender*." Mrs. Sallie "wants her baby" in a screaming variation on the rhyme "And that would be my baby" in stanza 15. Aunt Dill (st. 36) dispenses solace as dour as her name, recounting a child's murder from the week before. Her account heightens tension and adds to the violent context. "The Law" (st. 37) searches in vain. At stanza 38 Alfred, whose moderate character eases transitions both in himself and the action, has not seen Pepita. But he can speak of Senghor, "the line of Leopold." This crucial moment offers, at nearly the nadir of despair, a kind of hope, not personal, not even complete (Senghor is pictured in exile), but a generalized aspiration for all black people.

The abrupt shift to Hyena's self-indulgence (st. 39) underscores her dislike of "a puny and a putrid little child." Her lack of sympathy and her hostility parallel the next stanza's ultimate negative, uttered by the narrator, beginning, "Death is easy." Death and denial of caritas foreshadow the denouement. More immediately, they permit stunning contrast with the following Don Lee stanza's upward swing to a vigorous hopefulness. Stanza 42 contemplates Alfred musing over semantics. Action recoils from the constructive stance of 41 toward the prophesied violence of Amos (43). This shift partly anticipates the closing violence. At the same time, it offers a transforming potential, the blood bath that will regenerate the country.

There is a further, unmediated transition to "The ballad of Edie Barrow" (st. 44), the young black woman betrayed by a rich white man, "a Gentile boy." This lyrical interlude poises before the wider hope/despair oscillations in the last third of the poem. It illustrates white perfidy and the exploitation of blacks—and of women generally (the lover also manipulates his future bride)—by white society. At the same time, it broadens the work to include lyrical expression of a major theme.

"Gentile boy" lends typology to the action. The subtle parallel between blacks and Jews (cf. "The Ghost at the Quincy Club"), the latter already seen as concentration camp victims, etches the Mecca as an oppressive ghetto. Martin Luther King similarly utilized the parallel in one of his sermons, "The Death of Evil upon the Seashore," in alluding to the Supreme Court decision of Brown vs. Board of Education of Topeka, 1954. "A world-shaking decree by the nine justices of the Supreme Court," he stated, "opened the Red Sea and the forces of justice are moving to the other side."[10]

The cynicism of false Prophet Williams in stanza 45 acts as a foil to the sincerity of apocalyptic Amos in 43. Stanza 46 is introduced by a variety of minor characters who lead to the powerful description of insane Sophie. She sees "the fires run up" in a world askew. Violence and purgation forge her consciousness which, in turn, expresses her mad environment. Besides epitomizing the burning and apocalyptic imagery, the Sophie passage again instances the failed religion theme. Her "Mad life heralding the blue heat of God / snickers in a corner of the west windowsill." She resembles "Wezlyn, the wandering woman" in the stanza, who prowls the halls of Mecca at night "in search of Lawrence and Love," reiterating the failed art and caritas themes. (D. H. Lawrence's individualist solutions would little avail the socioeconomic morass of the Mecca.) The "blue heat of God"—the pure flame of religion and hope—burns closer to Sophie's madness and Amos's apocalyptic cleansing than it does to organized religion. Sophie knows she has failed herself, the love she has "promised Mother," and the world. She has the pristine insight that endows saints, fools, and frequently the insane. The most withdrawn character, she epitomizes both rejection and its consequences. In the west windowsill, she snickers her commentary on the religious and moral valetude of the West.

Stanza 47 veers from psychic atrocity to a listing of minor figures who do not care, people like Darkara who studies *Vogue*. Characters are deftly imaged; or else their vivid names ("Aunt Tippie," "Zombie Bell") join others more amply cited ("Mr. Kelly with long gray hair who begs / subtly from door to door"). Stanza 48 presents Alfred's growing consciousness, his turning away from foreign poets toward the need for "Giants over Steeples" and "A violent reverse." This new reaching braces the possibility of changes invoked by Amos and Don Lee. Stanza 49 reverts to the policemen as they question two sisters, whose caring limits itself to Gustav Mahler (composer of "Kindertotenlieder" or "Songs on the Death of Children") and tea. The next stanza portrays Way-out Morgan. Vengeance-seeker, victim of white violence, Morgan remembers his mob-raped Sister and murdered comrades. He collects guns, preparing for "Ruin." This glimpse of havoc foreshadows Pepita's death and, like the Amos passage, further politicizes the action.

Stanza 51 retrenches to Marian's repressed violence. An unappreciated housewife, she sublimates her anger by fascination with crime. The next stanza glances at meek, forgetful Pops Pinkham. Aunt Dill (st. 53), revisited, collects items including "bits of brass and marble," listed and held as lovingly as Way-out Morgan hoards guns. Self-considered a "woman-in-love-with-God," she gives no real assistance to Sallie, whose anxiety (and the reader's) she intensifies. This postscript on inadequate religion precedes Alfred's introductory statement in stanza 54, "I hate it. Yet . . ." and his epiphanic moment on the balcony. His insight counters the shabbiness of conventional faith with the possibility of constructive belief. From this height, narrative plunges toward Pepita's body "lying in dust with roaches," finally discovered under the cot where her murderer sits as he is questioned by police. The swift antithetical movement locates the strongest dramatic impact.

Yet Brooks's magnificent tapestry has already lifted the child into mythos. "Hateful things sometimes befall the hateful / but the hateful are not rendered lovable thereby" understands without condoning the murderer. Caught with subtly webbed sounds, the closing stanza leaves epitaph and apotheosis:

> She whose little stomach fought the world had
> wriggled, like a robin!
> Odd were the little wrigglings
> and the chopped chirpings oddly rising.

Pepita's physical reality, a hunger bravely confronting life— and death—has been ended. But the robin also means spring and renewal, paradox of the heartbreaking lines. The feminine endings support the continuing movement. Although her frailty was mortally exploited, Pepita's inviolate spirit, become bird, will not be subdued. (The word "odd" will recur in "The Life of Lincoln West"; the two contexts bear comparison.) The small stanza reverts the panoramic scope to personal scale, while it expresses an altered reality, permanently rendered.

"In the Mecca" is a great work deserving the closest study. It takes strength from controlled, formal diversity, from the detailed presence of Mecca in the world and the pressures of life, and from the poet's urgency that fuses craft and intelligence to its dimensions. Particulars of black experience draw its themes into a universal vortex. As a black mother, Mrs. Sallie projects an identity of hope and sorrows. Above the rubble of the physical site, the poem creates a Mecca that is something past, something present, infusing both with meaning and hope, with fair black fables that may revive its shattered realities.

## NOTES

1. Gwendolyn Brooks, *In the Mecca* (New York: Harper and Row, 1968); reprinted in *The World of Gwendolyn Brooks* (New York: Harper and Row, 1971) from which these citations are taken.

2. Addison Gayle, Jr., "The World of Gwendolyn Brooks," *New York Times Book Review,* January 2, 1972, p. 4.

3. James N. Johnson, "Blacklisting Poets," *Ramparts* 7, no. 9 (1968): 54.

4. C. Eric Lincoln, as quoted in *The Autobiography of Malcolm X* (1964; reprint New York: Grove Press, 1966), p. 444.

5. John Bartlow Martin, "The Strangest Place in Chicago," *Harper's Magazine* 201 (December 1950): 86–97; reprinted in *This Is Chicago: An Anthology,* ed. Albert Halper (New York: Henry Holt, 1952), pp. 42–60.

6. Ibid., ed. note, p. 42. A laboratory was planned for the site, which now extends the Illinois Institute of Technology.

7. See William Labov, "Contraction, Deletion, and Inherent Variability of the English Copula," *Language* 45 (December 1969); reprinted in *Language in the Inner City: Studies in the Black English Vernacular* (Philadelphia: University of Pennsylvania Press, 1972), Chap. 3. A more general guide is J. L. Dillard, *Black English* (New York: Random House/Vintage, 1973). Its controversial thesis traces Black English to African sources via pidgin English and Creole.

8. The issue is raised in M. L. Rosenthal's review, "In the Mecca," *New York Times Book Review,* March 2, 1969, 14–16. He writes: "It is as though, despite the familiar squalor and violence and terror . . . it would be unbearable to point up a native son's guilt as well." Rosenthal is perturbed by Brooks's "stylistic distortions," such as alliteration, internal rhyme, and "whimsical and arch observations that distract from its horror almost as if to conceal the wound at its center."

9. Gwendolyn Brooks, *Report from Part One* (Detroit: Broadside Press, 1972), p. 86.

10. The sermon appears in Martin Luther King, Jr., *Strength to Love* (New York: Harper and Row, 1963), pp. 58–66.

JOYCE ANN JOYCE

# Gwendolyn Brooks: Jean Toomer's November Cotton Flower

As epigraph to Part I of her very important book *When and Where I Enter: The Impact of Black Women on Race and Sex in America,* Paula Giddings cites Toni Morrison's evaluation of her character Sula. Morrison says, ". . . she /Sula/ had nothing to fall back on; not maleness, not whiteness, not ladyhood, not anything. And out of the profound desolation of her reality she may well have invented herself." Despite the nurturing and encouragement Gwendolyn Brooks received from her mother, who was responsible for the young Gwen's meeting and receiving the help of James Weldon Johnson and Langston Hughes, despite the fact that her work appeared in two anthologies by the time she was twenty, despite the fact that Langston Hughes dedicated several newspaper columns and a book of short stories to her, despite the fact that Gwendolyn Brooks has received at least nine literary awards including a Pulitzer and two Guggenheims, despite the fact that she has served as poetry consultant for the Library of Congress, Gwendolyn Brooks, a Black American woman poet, had no choice but to invent herself. She has emerged as one of America's most distinguished poetic voices in spite of the history of racism and sexism that characterizes all levels of American society. Whereas it was little short of a miracle that Phillis Wheatley could read at all, perhaps it is equally miraculous that Black women pioneers like Sojourner Truth, Harriet Tubman, Ida B. Wells, Frances Harper, Mary Church Terrell, Charlotte Hawkins Brown, and Eva Bowles were successful at inventing themselves. For in their struggles to combat the impact of racism and sexism on the lives of Black women, they had no history of Black women predecessors to serve as role models to guide them. Analogously, Gwendolyn Brooks's eleven books of poetry, her novel, her autobiography, and the critical acclaim that

From Haki R. Madhubuti, ed., *Say That the River Turns: The Impact of Gwendolyn Brooks* (Chicago: Third World Press, 1987), 80–83. Reprinted with permission.

now enthusiastically affirms her work rose out of the dearth of an American landscape hostile to the social, economic, and emotional well-being as well as the creative productivity of the Black American woman.

Against America's historical background, which attempts to stifle the spirit and creativity of the Black woman, Gwendolyn Brooks has evolved with the same beauty and impact as the flower in Jean Toomer's "November Cotton Flower":

> Boll-weevil's coming, and the winter's cold,
> Made cotton stalks look rusty, seasons old,
> And cotton, scarce as any southern snow,
> Was vanishing; the branch, so pinched and slow,
> Failed in its function as the autumn rake;
> Drouth fighting soil had caused the soil to take
> All water from the streams; dead birds were found
> In wells a hundred feet below the ground—
> Such was the season when the flower bloomed.
> Old folks were startled, and it soon assumed
> Significance. Superstition saw
> Something it had never seen before:
> Brown eyes that loved without a trace of fear,
> Beauty so sudden for that time of year.

Gwendolyn Brooks began to bloom in a season when the literary scene was even more dominated by white males than it is today. Like the cotton flower, she struggled against the drought of male censorship from one of her own kind. When Richard Wright, serving as reviewer for Harper and Brothers, negatively critiqued the poem "the mother" from *A Street in Bronzeville* because of its emphasis on abortion, he evidenced the kind of male misunderstanding of issues that affect the lives of women. Yet rather than yield to the aridity of Wright's limitations, Gwendolyn Brooks, like the strong flower which fights the deadening effects of the cold natural world, explained to editor Edward Aswell that the emphasis in her poem is not so much abortion as it is the poverty and environmental conditions that produced ambivalence in the mother's attitude toward being a parent. Interestingly enough, Wright, who moved to Paris so that his daughters could escape the stifling effects of racism in American society, failed to grasp the essence of "the mother."

Wife, mother, nurturer of her parents, poet, leader of poetry workshops, and bearer of monetary gifts to young poets,

Gwendolyn Brooks assumed her own significance. Her brown/ black eyes captured "without a trace of fear" the complexity of being a Black woman in America when the mainstream American poetry arena was dominated by demigods like T. S. Eliot, John Crowe Ransom, Robert Penn Warren, Allen Tate, Randall Jarrell, e.e. cummings, Karl Shapiro, and Stanley Kunitz. Having bloomed under the light of Robert Hillyer's *First Principles of Verse,* Brooks brought to modern American poetry her own peculiar sensibility, which manifests at once the embodiments of both Wallace Stevens's blue guitar and the African griot's drum. Even though they have the visual and stylistic attributes of a Euro-American poetic tradition, her earlier ballads, free verse poems, and the sonnets reveal the same feelings of racial integrity and record the same malaises of racism as those poems published after 1967 when Brooks's blackness confronted her "with a shrill spelling of itself." Yet this blackness, Brooks's absorption of the psychic patterns of her ancestral heritage, has made its identifiable mark on all her poetry.

Despite its use of medieval and Renaissance language to evoke the chivalric mood, "The Anniad," found in Brooks's second volume, *Annie Allen,* shares with the poem "To Black Women" from *To the Diaspora,* Brooks's tenth volume, a strong ending which suggests the Black woman's resolute will to survive. One strongly, stylistically Euro-American and the other distinctly Afro-American, both poems channel the experiences of the poet's cultural heritage through the blue guitar of her creative imagination, producing complementary visions of Black women in American society. These poems, looked at together, serve as a single example of how Gwendolyn Brooks's poetry provide rich insights into the diversity and fluidity of the Black experience. Even though her works reveal a sharpened consciousness in the late 1960s, Gwendolyn Brooks has always been a Black priestess of words who conjured up herself by absorbing the best of the Euro-American poetic tradition and assimilating this tradition into her indigenous Black cultural experience.

She began this formidable task at a time when it was not only far from fashionable, but also iconoclastic for a black women to dare to infiltrate the modern American poetry arena. Thus "folks were startled." Nonetheless, the November Cotton Flower, like Jean Toomer before her, demonstrated majestically how racial themes become an element of the Black writer's craft. The end result of the merger of imitative techniques characteristic of a Euro-American tradition with the Black priestess's peculiarly

Afro-American stylistic innovations thrusts Gwendolyn Brooks, a Black American woman poet, to the forefront of the American literary scene. Put simply, this Black woman writer, who had no role models to follow and who began writing at a time when it was customary for the Black writer to borrow the master's tools, reshaped those tools and made them yield to the magic of her ancestral heritage. Even though thirty-seven years have passed since Brooks received the Pulitzer Prize and even though she has served as an inspiration and teacher to many Black women poets who follow her, the historical significance of her contribution and what she symbolizes remain "Beauty so sudden for [this] time of year."

GERTRUDE REIF HUGHES

# Making It *Really* New:
# Hilda Doolittle, Gwendolyn Brooks,
# and the Feminist Potential
# of Modern Poetry

Newness was the central concept of modernism. In their legend-
ary attempts to "make it new," modern Anglo-American poets,
like modern novelists and visual artists in general, wanted to
challenge every aesthetic complacency and cultural institution
they could identify. They broke spatial wholeness into Cubist
fragments, they disrupted temporal sequence, and they tried to
integrate the status of subject with that of object.[1] For all its
innovations, literary modernism was deeply conservative in one
important respect: it failed to question male entitlement and
white supremacy. Rather than challenge Eurocentric and an-
drocentric values, the high modernism of Pound, Eliot, Joyce,
and Williams left these values securely in place.

The masculinist bias of modernism becomes evident when
gender is used as a category of analysis. Until recently, accounts
of modernism ignored questions of gender, though the Woman
Question and women's suffrage were known contemporary is-
sues and though feminists like Gertrude Stein and Virginia Woolf
helped to create modernism in Anglo-American literature. Now
that women have become visible, it is clearer that modernism is
not neutral but gendered. On the one hand, according to Sandra
Gilbert and Susan Gubar, the "determinedly anticommercial
cast" of the highbrow innovations for which modernism is
known functioned as a kind of white men's club designed to
exclude the women writers whose increasing commercial promi-
nence in the twentieth century threatened male writers.[2] On the
other hand, some women saw a feminist potential in modernism

From *American Quarterly* 42, no. 3 (September 1990): 375–401. Copyright ©
1990, American Studies Association. With permission of The Johns Hopkins
University Press and Gertrude Reif Hughes.

from the start. As Carolyn Burke has shown, a technical experiment like Gertrude Stein's splicing "contains a poetics of gender hidden within its apparently formalist concerns"; and, as Maureen Honey and Gloria Hull argue, the supposedly derivative, Eurocentric poetry of women poets of the Harlem Renaissance, which has been dismissed as sentimental, codes resistance to both racism and sexism.[3]

When modernism is regarded from the point of view of gender relations, both its masculinist bias and its feminist potential become evident. Hilda Doolittle and Gwendolyn Brooks used this potential to challenge patriarchal privilege. Their poems are not isolated instances but exemplifications of how modernism can be fashioned to protest oppressive practices and to revise the mentalities that sponsor them.

The midcentury poems of Doolittle and Brooks offer excellent examples of modernism's feminist potential. Written between 1945 and 1968, before the second wave of feminism and during its beginnings, these poems take as their theme the oppressions of otherness that Simone de Beauvoir's *The Second Sex* described in 1952. Otherness, said de Beauvoir, "is the lot assigned to woman in the patriarchate, but it is in no way a vocation, any more than slavery is the vocation of the slave."[4]

Both Brooks and Doolittle used the high modernist devices and anti-heroic perspectives of Pound, Eliot, Joyce, and Williams to explore women's assigned alterity and to challenge the priority of the first sex. Imagistic, synchronistic, and hard to read, Gwendolyn Brooks's "The Anniad," the heart of her Pulitzer Prize–winning poem sequence, *Annie Allen* (1949), exposed the misogyny of romance conventions by making a woman's struggle to disentangle herself from them the measure, and the menace, of her maturity.[5] In similarly difficult modernist poetry, Doolittle made Helen of Troy, Western culture's most famous sex object, the protagonist, instead of the pawn, in her "epic of consciousness,"[6] *Helen in Egypt,* written from 1952 to 1956 and published just before Doolittle died in 1961.[7] In their hands, the conservative and often misogynistic modernism of Pound and Eliot turned out to have surprisingly liberating uses.

Doolittle and Brooks adapted four poetic elements of masculinist modernism. I call them modernist elements rather than techniques, devices, conventions, or the like, because the word "element" can refer to both the more attitudinal and technical ones, while at the same time suggesting the intrinsic modernness of all four: (1) merging subjects with objects—particularly as in imagist poetry; (2) the deflating attitudes of an anti-heroic sensibility; (3) synchronicity, the creation of strange compounds by radically juxtaposing or compressing what is temporally or spatially far apart; and (4) the characteristic attribute of modernist texts—the infamous obscurity that resists, or seems to resist, interpretation.

At first, these poetic elements seem like naturals for evoking the themes of alienation, fragmentation, and decadence that are associated with high modernism. By collapsing subjects and objects, for example, the poet can evoke a world order in which predicates disappear and the intensity of one individual's impression overwhelms the sense of shared experience. Anti-heroism also perceives community feeling as a lost blessing. Nostalgically, anti-heroism mourns the days when the values of a given society were supposedly so unanimous that a single, recognized representative could champion them. Similarly, synchronicity can promote nostalgia by matching classical subjects with their latter-day counterparts to demonstrate a supposed social and cultural decline. Finally, textual obscurity seems to represent the world as intrinsically baffling and to undermine the hope that understanding can be achieved. Though classical modernist negations often make a gloomy and conservative world picture seem inevitable, modernism also has more progressive uses.

The poetry of Brooks and Doolittle exemplifies these progressive uses of modernism. Rarely considered together,[8] the two poets are extremely dissimilar. Not only do Brooks and Doolittle belong to two different generations, races, and classes—with all the contrasts in experience and interest that such differences suggest—but the resonances of their poetry—one urban and local, the other classical and remote—do not harmonize or correspond. Because these two poets' lives and styles contrast so sharply, it is all the more interesting and suggestive that both should concur in using the elements of modernist negation for creating modernist affirmations of political and spiritual possibility. Different as they are, both Brooks and Doolittle turn the ordinarily conservative and negative features of modernist poetry to radical and hopeful ends.

Privileged, white, emotionally volatile, and physically fragile-looking in a traditionally feminine way, Hilda Doolittle (1886–1961) was a prominent intellectual and expatriate known for her early contributions to imagism and for her relationships to male mentors from Ezra Pound to D. H. Lawrence and from her husband, Richard Aldington, to her personal analyst, Sigmund

Freud. She formed intense romantic relationships with both women and men and was a spiritual quester who explored a variety of esoteric religious traditions.[9]

If Doolittle were the epitome of a pre– and post–World War I American expatriate intellectual, Gwendolyn Brooks—born in Topeka in 1917 but a Chicagoan since early childhood—is an early representative of another twentieth-century type: the apparently conventional, obedient woman who, in the newly politicized America of the late 1960s and early 1970s, discovers a new identity when her consciousness is raised. In *Report from Part One,* the autobiographical memoir she published at age fifty-five, Brooks confided, "It frightens me to realize that, if I had died before the age of fifty, I would have died a 'Negro' fraction," nonwhite instead of black or African, a white-designated Other.[10] Until her experience of black solidarity at the Second Fisk University Writers' Conference in 1967, she said, she "knew there were injustices, and . . . wrote about them, but I didn't know . . . it was all organized" (*RPO* 175). Though the American 1960s radicalized her, her earlier poems, she insists, reveal that she was already "politically aware as she herself insists."[11]

Actually, throughout her career, Brooks, unlike the expatriate Doolittle, has been a "citizen-poet,"[12] mixing the radical with the conventional. A spokesperson for black activism[13] and African separatism, she also has held national positions as poet laureate of Illinois (succeeding Carl Sandburg in 1968) and as consultant in poetry at the Library of Congress from 1985 to 1986.

Brooks uses urban scenes and lower middle class characters in her richly but unobtrusively allusive poetry, and she infuses her narratives with the enraging humiliations of being stereotyped in color-crazed and woman-exploiting, white America. By contrast, almost all of Doolittle's poems take place in stylized locales saturated with legends. Here the awakening consciousnesses of her meditative characters excavate and revise the legendary cultural material, sometimes to exorcise, sometimes to reclaim its power.[14] Despite their sharply differing styles, both Brooks and Doolittle are interested in relations of power: who controls, who benefits, who gets hurt.

Doolittle's poetry explores such questions through eroticized images of nature, as in her routinely anthologized early poems "Heat" and "Oread," but especially through making natural and supernatural worlds interpenetrate as in her long, midcentury poems *Trilogy* and *Helen in Egypt.*[15] For Doolittle, questions of power play themselves out in social and romantic relations between men and women; in relations between mothers and daughters; and in access to spiritual power that may bring inspiration, comfort, understanding, or courage to someone of either gender. In the world of Gwendolyn Brooks social injustices of racism and poverty dictate choices of scene and character. Color and the color line preoccupy her characters' lives, whether heterosexual relations, relations of mothers to children, or racial relations themselves are at stake.

Both poets include men as subjects as well as objects, yet reserve the roles of wise, vital, or resilient knower for women. Doolittle's Helen and Brooks's narrators in *Trilogy,* the indomitable Cousin Vit, Big Bessie, and Mrs. Sallie Smith, all are women whose experiences under patriarchal privilege have made them strong and defiant, women who, refusing to accept its oppressive arrangements, are determined to prevail.[16] Finally, both poets were modernists who made modernism serve various antipatriarchal uses.

## Imagism

A number of surrealist movements shared the modernist method—and ideal—of blurring boundaries between subjects and objects. The symbolist descendants of Baudelaire and Poe—Dadaists, Vorticists, and Imagists—all prized the surrealistic effects that resulted from dissolving grammatical or conceptual distinctions between subjects and objects. They felt that such effects could counteract the impulses of naturalism, which threatened to turn art into documentation, and thus could help save art from Philistine referentiality.[17] Imagism epitomized this characteristically modernist enterprise.

Imagistic poems like Pound's "In a Station at the Metro" and Doolittle's "Oread" fused poetic speaker with poetic topic until, as contemporary critic Oscar W. Firkins complained testily, "the man is abridged into mere vision, [and] the object contracts into pure visibility."[18] Imagist poems were focused so intensely that they seemed contextless. Disembodied and sourceless, such poetry, Firkins warned, is isolated from social and political particularity:[19] "It is destitute alike of a place in a charted globe and a function in a civilized order. It has no history, no prospects, no causes, no sequels, no association, no cognates, no allies" (459).

Described this way, imagism seems hopelessly ahistorical. Yet the technique of unsettling distinctions between subject and object was suited to reconceiving relations between men as subjects and women as objects, which is exactly how Doolittle used it.

In her revisionary Trojan War epic, *Helen in Egypt,* Doolittle removed Helen from her traditional imprisonment within Trojan walls and placed her in Egypt. There Helen muses on the story of love and war and her own infamous role as the trophy who, by being awarded to Paris for his favors to Aphrodite, was then herself awarded the blame for the destruction of Troy. Doolittle put Helen in Egypt to give her protagonist a space from which she can assess the codes that condemn her as both victim and perpetrator of Western culture's classic crime.[20] In sequences of incantatory poems punctuated by prose segments that function like the commentary of a chorus in Greek tragedy, Doolittle's Helen labors meditatively to understand how the forces of love and war get confused and how, if at all, they might be untangled. By removing Helen, Doolittle purposely rendered her, as Oscar Firkins would have charged, "destitute alike of a place in a charted globe and a foundation in a civilized order" because only at so drastic a remove can she assess the "place" she has in the "civilized order" and engage in the heroic labor that Gwendolyn Brooks's protege-mentor, Haki R. Madhubuti (Don L. Lee) has called, "question[ing] the measuring rod" (*RPO* 20).

Egypt, then, represents a place where Helen, and later Achilles, can live "a life / unfulfilled in Greece," and from which they can perhaps "take our treasure, . . . back to the islands, . . . // where desolation ruled" (*HE* 90). In the Egyptian temple of Amen, or Thoth, Helen tries to read "the Amen-script," the hieroglyph that adorns the temple walls. Compressed into an evocative, cryptic compound (like an imagist poem), the hieroglyph baffles her until the moment when vultures, like those pictured in the hieroglyph, fly overhead. The boundary between Helen as reading subject and hieroglyph as object is erased, and suddenly the writing starts to make sense. Ceasing to feel alienated from the hieroglyph, she is now able to read it, and she also realizes that "she herself is the writing":

> . . . when the bird swooped past,
> that first evening,
> I seemed to know the writing,

as if God made the picture
and matched it
with a living hieroglyph.

(HE 22–23)

As a "living hieroglyph," Helen, who is learning to decipher
herself—a conceit that Doolittle uses throughout the poem—is
both reader and text, both subject and object. In order to free her
from imprisonment in alterity, Doolittle makes Helen the reader
and embodiment of an imagist poem—herself.

Brooks's imagistic vignettes restore the subjectivities of people
who have been treated as objects, black women and men, espe-
cially impoverished ones, living in the cities and suburbs of
twentieth-century, white America. Instead of being dislocated
into the kind of metaphysical realm in which, as Oscar W. Firkins
complained, intensity has burned away locality, her poems take
place in the fully historical streets and hallways, bars and beauty
parlors of the slum section of Chicago called Bronzeville.[21] Her
telling snapshots show men as dudes, dandies, and heroes and
women as mothers, daughters, sisters, wives, lovers, whores, and
heads of families. In an extraordinary variety of brief dramas, they
court, go to war, trust or envy one another, and do lots of that
enforced waiting that Brooks pointedly calls "loitering."

Her poetry may not seem imagistic, because it is more mi-
metic, less stylized, than that of classical imagists like Pound,
Doolittle, and Williams, but Brooks's poems, like the more
classical imagistic ones, use precise evocations to convey, not
merely what things look like, but " 'the reciprocity of inner and
outer realities.' "[22] A generation after the founding of imagism,
Brooks, too, strives "for a penetrating kind of seeing which
makes sight insight."[23] Moreover, her poems show that the
imagistic techniques and aims of making subject experience and
object status interpenetrate need not conflict with historicity.
Indeed, as Doolittle found in a different way, where subjectivity
historically has been denied to a group of human beings so that
they are thought of only as objects in someone else's "outer
reality," the process of finding their own subjectivities becomes
a political as well as psychological struggle, and understanding
"reciprocity" among various "inner and outer realities" be-
comes an adventure in cognition that the fusings and reloca-
tions of imagism can register effectively.

To align "inner and outer realities," Brooks frequently em-
beds distinctly unromantic situations in romancelike or balladlike

poems.[24] Take, for example, her emphatic allusions to romance and ballads in her anti-ballad, "A Bronzeville Mother Loiters in Mississippi. Meanwhile, a Mississippi Mother Burns Bacon" (*Bean Eaters*, 1960; *WGB* 317–23). This poem narrates the aftermath of the real-life lynching of Emmet Till in the daily lives of some of its perpetrators and survivors.[25] Yet it works imagistically in several ways.

When a white woman, the Mississippi mother of the title, realizes that her own daily life conforms to the conventions of the ballads she read in school, she starts to read the incriminating ballad of her life as Helen read the hieroglyph. She learns that she has been living according to the conventions of her role as "maid Mild" who gets rescued from a "dark villain" (Emmet Till) by the "Fine Prince" (her husband, the sheriff). As a result, she is responsible for the murder not of a villain but of a fourteen-year-old child. To her increasing horror, she realizes that the role she has been assigned and has accepted has given her an identity she does not want. She herself is the ballad, and the more she sees what dangers its beauties hide, the more she understands her complicity in young Till's murder. Panicked, she feels she cannot survive the tale in which she has been cast.[26] Although the poem lets her read her complicity, it keeps her caught within the killing romance, unable to seek, much less find, a different role to play.

Brooks frequently suggests as in this poem's final scene the sinister, scarcely concealed violence of male entitlement in moments of heterosexual intimacy. Mumbling about making love, the husband "pulled her face around to meet / His," and the Mississippi mother feels physical revulsion as "His mouth, wet and red, / So very, very red, / Closed over hers" (*WGB* 322–23). The Mississippi mother is not allowed to escape from her role as fair damsel, but, locked in her husband's sickening embrace, she does fill with "a hatred for him" that becomes a "glorious flower" (323). Then, in an audacious use of imagistic fusion, Brooks makes the perfume of that blossoming hate overflow this poem and fill the next one—the haunting coda entitled "The Last Quatrain of the Ballad of Emmet Till," which highlights the Bronzeville Mother (*WGB* 324). (Until then, Till's mother, the "loitering" Bronzeville mother of the title, has been silent and, except for a brief mention toward the end, absent in a brilliant representation of the invisibility whites can confer on blacks.)

Imagistically, Brooks separated and linked the two poems so that a white woman's hatred for a man's entitlement to her body and for his white supremacism could become part of a black woman's lament for the son who was killed by their white privilege. Here are the final lines of the anti-ballad and then, from the next page, the entire coda, complete with title, to show how the "glorious hatred" links them.

> She did not scream.
> She stood there.
> But a hatred for him burst into glorious flower,
> And its perfume enclasped them—big,
> Bigger than all magnolias.
>
> The last bleak news of the ballad.
> The rest of the rugged music.
> The last quatrain.

### THE LAST QUATRAIN OF THE BALLAD OF EMMET TILL

> after the murder,
> after the burial
> Emmet's mother is a pretty-faced thing;
> the tint of pulled taffy.
> She sits in a red room
> drinking black coffee.
> She kisses her killed boy.
> And she is sorry.
> Chaos in windy grays
> through a red prairie.
>
> (*WGB* 323–24)

The "glorious hatred" provides a wordless language for the stunned, bereaved mother. When the half rhymes of "taffy" and "coffee" dwindle into the still less congruent rhymes of "sorry" and "prairie" they evoke the chaotic bleakness that stretches ahead, as well as the blood that reddens the past, and perhaps future. As in a classical Imagist poem, all elements merge, and the final predicate falls away. Here, Brooks used imagism to render a historical event placeless and timeless, not because it wasn't historical, but because it was.

## Anti-Heroism

Like imagism, the anti-heroic strain in modern poetry disturbs traditions that habitually devalue women. By challenging accepted ideas of bravery, honor, and heroic action and by focusing on protagonists whom society either rejects or ignores, anti-heroic poetry can portray seriously what is traditionally dismissed.

Not that anti-heroism ordinarily functions this way. In contrast to a conventional hero who represents the interests of his people and, honored by them, leads them into a future that his exploits have secured for all, an anti-hero usually feels misunderstood, belated, impotent. A Hugh Selwyn Mauberley, J. Alfred Prufrock, or Yeatsean "sixty-year-old smiling public man" exists in an alienating, futile world, filled with nostalgic allusions and foiled encounters. Such plots and postures are *anti*-heroic because they define themselves against traditional protagonists in traditional plots.

Anti-heroic plots and postures dramatize the perceived loss of once-shared values, but anti-heroism also can be used to challenge values that are too shared. It can expose narratives that perpetuate dangerous interests. Both Doolittle and Brooks use the anti-hero for this purpose. They focus on stories that endanger women by locking them in "romantic thralldom," to borrow Rachel Blau DuPlessis's phrase.[27] This kind of plot presents women only in relation to men—particularly as lovers—and the passion and vitality of love in terms of the violence and prowess of war. Both Doolittle's *Helen in Egypt* (1961) and Brooks's "The Anniad" (1949) invoke a Western heroic tradition of love and war by alluding to two of its most honored epics, the *Iliad* and the *Aeneid*. Both poems center on women, both narrate the protagonist's quest for a love that does not threaten autonomy, and both—though in very different ways—use female trials and failures to extricate love from war. They reject the respectability of war and celebrate potential, new forms of love.

Brooks's "The Anniad" is a mock-heroic tale of a young woman being courted, captured, and abandoned.[28] Like her predecessor "Chocolate Mabbie" in Brooks's first book of poems,[29] Annie Allen has chocolate-dark skin and dreams naively of "What was never and is not," especially of "the paladin / Which no woman ever had" (*WGB* 83). Brooks's opening snapshot makes it clear that Annie's silly expectations endanger her:

> Think of ripe and rompabout,
> All her harvest buttoned in,
> All her ornaments untried;
> Waiting for the paladin

Prosperous and ocean-eyed
Who shall rub her secrets out
And behold the hinted bride.

(WGB 83)

Young Annie's ripeness is a doomed vulnerability; if her dreams succeed, they will obliterate rather than fulfill her.

Such dreams are dangerous to their dreamers, and so is the culture that sponsors them. Annie's paladin, the nameless though color- and gender-specific "man of tan" who soon arrives on the scene (84), is an agent of this danger, but he is also liable to it himself. After winning and bedding her, he goes off to war where "the reveille / Is staccato majesty" but where he quickly comes "to know / the hunched hells" of actual battle (86).

In "The Anniad," war is an arena for male heroism as marriage is for female heroism, and each betrays its champion. For her part, Annie Allen willingly begins domesticity with her paladin not "in the heaven she put him in" but in the "lowly room" he can afford, "[w]hich she makes a chapel of," and "[w]here she genuflects to love" (85). For his part, the man of tan who had felt his manhood much more validated by war than by marriage, feels emasculated when he returns to civilian life:

> With his helmet's final doff
> Soldier lifts his power off.
> Soldier bare and chilly then
> Wants his power back again

(87)

sings the narrator, blending satire with compassion. Tan man gets sympathy for his battle fatigue, but he gets no mercy for exploiting Annie when he first lays his nightmares in her lap and then abandons her for a series of other women who he vainly hopes will cheer and succor him more effectively. Brooks mocks his "random passion" for these women, none of whose many colors—all lighter than his wife's chocolate—please him for long (88).[30] Meanwhile, Annie has been left a female fraction, "Minus passing-magistrate / Minus passing-lofty light / Minus passing-stars for night" (88)—in short, an other without a one.

Just as the ballad of Fine Prince rescuing White Maid from Dark Villain betrayed those who got cast in it, so Annie's dream of boy meets girl has betrayed her. But Brooks did more than deconstruct the dangerous story of Annie Allen. Instead of leaving Annie disillusioned but as powerless as ever, Brooks used the final sequence of *Annie Allen,* the fifteen poems entitled "The Womanhood," to relocate Annie in Bronzeville reality. There Annie slowly recovers from the ravages of romance until in the final poem (*WGB* 123–24), she is able to rally other Bronzevilleans to unite and meet the demands of their daily lives without expecting leadership to come from some magical, romantic otherworld:

> . . . Rise.
> Let us combine. There are no magics or elves
> Or timely godmothers to guide us. We are lost, must
> Wizard a track through our own screaming weed.
>
> (124)

Annie Allen no longer trusts heroics. In that sense, she is an anti-heroic figure. But unlike the enervated or hapless misfits of familiar modernist tradition, Brooks's Annie Allen retains faith in an ideal of empowerment based on communal cooperation which specifically excludes reliance on miraculous intervention.

As a classicist and translator of Euripides, Doolittle found epic tradition congenial. In both of her book-length poems, *Helen in Egypt* and the three-poem sequence collected as *Trilogy,* she used elevated tone and mythically proportioned characters. Yet, though Doolittle's style shares features with some of Western literature's most woman-endangering stories, her epics radically revised those stories.

Doolittle conceived Helen so as to redefine both the task and the traits of traditional heroes. Helen is an anti-hero in that sense. Her revisionary task is epic in scope and requires heroic effort because it defies two deeply ingrained cultural practices—valuing physical and competitive activity at the expense of emotional and cognitive work and assuming that "opposite" sexes must oppose one another so that in all their relations, including erotic ones, one partner must always dominate while the other always submits.[31]

For her version of the Trojan War legend, Doolittle boldly abducted charming Paris and wrathful Achilles and brought them to Egypt for Helen to consider. Helen's main activity in this "meditative epic"[32] involves developing her powers of understanding so that she can accomplish a twofold cultural revision;[33] decipher her own being without regard to male-centered definitions of it and learn to imagine a suitable male partner for such a free woman.

Instead of waiting to be chosen, Helen decides what she wants in a partner and which candidate seems to offer it. With this reversal, Doolittle did more than just declare a literary leap year and let Helen play boy at some Sadie Hawkins ladies' night where males must await her whim. Doolittle created a much more radical revision: a protagonist who is woman-centered but still takes men seriously, something man-centered epics don't manage to do for women. Doolittle's anti-heroic Helen is against heroes but not against men.

It is important to notice that because she had Helen pay serious attention to Paris and Achilles, especially Achilles, Doolittle risked seeming to accept the dictates of romantic thralldom that she actually wanted to revise. Yet she gave those conventions scope precisely in order to invalidate their claims. First, Helen rejects Paris despite his charms. Though attractive, he is immature and unimaginative. He is "beautiful enchantment" (*HE* 291), but he cannot share the enlarged vision Helen is achieving (201). Paris wants to recall her to traditional domestic love based on female submissiveness, and he cannot understand why she bothers her pretty head trying to reimagine Achilles:

> why, why would you deny
> the peace, the sanctity
> of this small room . . .
>
> . . . . . . . . . . . . . . . . . .
> O Helena, tangled in thought.
> be Rhodes' Helena, *Dendritis,*
> Why remember Achilles?
>
> (142)

Of course Helen is not "tangled in thought" at all; Achilles poses a knotty problem. She is trying hard to figure out whether she can safely ally herself with so wild a man as Achilles. Paris and the male-ordered world he represents cannot see the importance of her imaginative labor. Still, his question deserves consideration. Indeed, what *is* Helen choosing when she prefers Achilles to Paris? In making Achilles's wrath more interesting than Paris's domesticity did Doolittle favor his potential for violence? Throughout the poem, Helen recalls the moment of her first physical contact with Achilles, when he, mistaking her for a witch (significantly enough), nearly strangles her. By praying "under his cloak" to Thetis, Achilles's mother and her own matriarchal guide, Helen summons the resistance to turn his stranglehold into an embrace. She transforms violence into love.[34]

Conceivably, her energetic, though meditative, move could be read either as evidence that Helen finds violence alluring or as the gesture of a True Woman taming her brutish man. The poem supports neither reading. In the first place, Helen repeatedly rebukes Achilles for his allegiance to the "iron ring" of war; she wishes nothing to do with him while he retains his warlike alliances. In the second place, Doolittle makes it clear that Helen values Achilles, not for his famous wrath, but for his other famous trait—his vulnerability.

Traditionally, Achilles's wounded heel is a defect; *Helen in Egypt* transvalues it. In Doolittle's anti-epic, his wound represents his potential for personal and social change. In the scene where Achilles first comes to Helen—drawn to her, it should be noticed, by *her* desire for him—he limps toward her. She hails him as an apparition of "the new Mortal, / shedding his glory" (10). Like Helen herself, he is shedding glory in two senses— divesting himself of the old, war-related renown and, at the same time, starting to spread a new luster. When she prefers him to Paris, she is choosing his openness. Paris likes "the lure and delight of the sheltered harbours and bays" (299), but Achilles can understand "the crash and spray of the foam, // the wind, the shoal, the broken shale, / the infinite loneliness / when one is never alone" (304).[35]

By creating a woman who desires him for his wound and refuses to honor his wrath with either fear or admiration, Doolittle transvalued both of Achilles's traditionally heroic attributes. She made Achilles's wrath repellent and his wound his saving grace. With this subversion of inherited materials, Doolittle, like Brooks, redefined the idea of heroism while refusing to discard an ideal of possible empowerment.

## Synchronicity

Like imagism, synchronicity compresses and fuses what has been held distinct; like anti-heroism, it juxtaposes contemporary plots with legendary counterparts. Usually, these synchronizing allusions make the contemporary situation look decadent or otherwise deplorable by contrast with the legendary one.

In *The Waste Land,* for example, Eliot's allusions recall a past richness so as to deplore a disorderly, futile present. In many of his satirical synchronicities, sketches of failed or unpleasant heterosexual relations indicate a general decline. When the Thames daughters at the end of "The Fire Sermon" sing a sorry little song of passionless seduction, Eliot synchronizes their song with earlier, more passionate accounts of profane love, including the *Confessions* of Saint Augustine and the beguiling songs of Wagner's Rhine maidens, in order to emphasize his point that lack of passion makes the modern seductions particularly repugnant. He uses the same synchronic technique in the famous portrait of Belladonna, the frantic woman who sits at her dressing table in the opening scene of "A Game of Chess." To underscore Belladonna's vulgarity and the emptiness of her relations with her apathetic lover, Eliot describes her dressing table as a burlesque of the barge that Shakespeare's Cleopatra sat in and he makes Belladonna herself a failed Cleopatra, emblem of a range of lost splendors, from vanished empire to degraded femininity.

Neither Doolittle nor Brooks participated in this depressive nostalgia for better days. Doolittle used synchronicity to fault the reactionary temper of nostalgia, particularly in *Trilogy,* the collection of three long antiwar poems written after her World War II years in London.[36] In each forty-three-poem section of *Trilogy,* Doolittle used historical, legendary, and biblical allusions to open new possibilities, rather than to report decline. In "The Walls Do Not Fall" (1944), she compared bomb-blitzed London to the shrines of Egypt; in "Tribute to the Angels" (1945), she juxtaposed angelology with various portraits of women to distinguish between the traditional worship of women and the new, indeed still to be mastered, kind of "tribute" that simply sees a woman as human; and in "The Flowering of the Rod" (1946), she blended biblical tales from both the beginning and the end of Christ's life into a seriocomic account of a new kind of woman, her gravely independent Mary Magdala.

For Eliot, as for most men and women writing in various Western traditions, time passes and leaves the world older and less vital than it used to be. Time takes away. For Doolittle, time was a medium of connection: "[T]he clock-hand, minute by minute, / ticks round its prescribed orbit. // but this curious mechanical perfection / should not separate but relate" (TA 24). Doolittle's palimpsests declare that the past can invigorate the present, whereas Eliot's tell readers that nothing new will occur, or, if it does, it can only defile the past, never develop its potential to a new stage. The components in Doolittle's temporal compounds enhance one another, instead of elevating one period or culture at the expense of another. The effect is to open past culture for present uses, to insist that "inspiration stalks us through gloom" (WDNF 1), waiting for us to become able to receive it.

For Doolittle, time brought clarification and fulfillment—in one word, revelation. No wonder so much of *Trilogy* alludes to the biblical Book of Revelation. Particularly in this long work, time "does not separate but relate," and synchronicity offered a technique for presenting radical reforms of consciousness, representation, and human relations. Respectively and together, the three parts of *Trilogy* urge, "Let us re-dedicate our gifts / to spiritual realism" and "in the light of what went before, // illuminate what came after," for "now is the time to re-value / our secret hoard" (WDNF 35, 36).

After she demonstrated "the need for imagistic and lexical redefinition"[37] in the first part of *Trilogy*, "The Walls Do Not Fall," Doolittle meshed new and old to accomplish two extended redefinitions of women in the second and third parts. In "Tribute to the Angels" she satirized representations of woman as other (TA 24–39). She invented a pivotal scene where an apparition of a real woman "the Lady herself" (TA 28) appears to the poem's narrator. The narrator contrasts the apparition with the many poses and fables, from picturesque to monitory, in which various cultural traditions represent women (or Woman). "Our Lady of the Goldfinch," she jeers, "Our Lady of the Candelabra, // Our Lady of the Pomegranate, / Our Lady of the Chair" (TA 29). Unlike such mistaken representations, the Lady in the apparition

> is no symbolic figure
> . . . . . . . . . . . . . . . . . . .
> of peace, charity, chastity, goodness,
> faith, hope, reward;
> . . . . . . . . . . . . . . . . . . .
> she is not Justice with eyes
> blindfolded like Love's.
>
> (TA 39)

She is herself.

In imagining "the Lady herself" as an apparition, Doolittle was clearly implying that a woman's reality as herself will remain a figment until appropriate sensibilities are formed for perceiving a woman this way, rather than as some patriarchally defined other. The "Lady herself" is newer than any of the traditional representations, not because she has never existed, but because she has not yet been recognized. *The consciousness that could comprehend her has yet to be formed.*

Throughout *Trilogy,* Doolittle dramatized the need for this imaginative reform, which she called, "spiritual realism."[38] In "The Flowering of the Rod," she created Mary Magdala and Kaspar, counterparts to the Lady and her well-intentioned but unregenerate admirer. Simply by not playing second-sex to Kaspar's first, Mary Magdala radically disorients poor Kaspar. In Doolittle's comic version, this biblical Wise Man has a lot to learn and in the end he is wise enough to learn it.

In a crucial scene, Mary Magdala refuses to let him dismiss her, staying instead to say what she had come to tell him (FR 13). Confused by even so small a demonstration of female autonomy, poor Kaspar mutters,

> *it is unseemly that a woman*
> *appear disordered, disheveled,*

> *it is unseemly that a woman*
> *appear at all.*
>
> (FR 34, 18 [without the emphasis])

As he is struggling all too manfully to make sense of Mary Magdala's independence, Kaspar experiences a sublime vision through which he receives a profound intuition of prepatriarchal civilization, "the lost centre-island, Atlantis" "before Adam" and "before Eve" (FR 31, 32).

Kaspar's enlightenment coincides with bewilderment. "What he thought was the direct contradiction / of what he apprehended" (FR 35). In synchronizing Kaspar's incredulity with his revelation Doolittle was suggesting that Kaspar is capable of changing his consciousness. He can learn. Unlike his foil, Simon, who persists in despising Mary, Kaspar, capable of change, is open enough to experience the beginnings of "spiritual realism" thanks to Mary Magdala's insistence on nothing more nor less momentous than her own independence. The story of Kaspar and Mary is Doolittle's Judeo-Christian version of the Greek-Egyptian synchronicity which she used when she restored agency to Helen of Troy as Helen in Egypt and gave Helen Achilles, rather than Paris, as her suitable partner. Both are dramas of cognition, and both require a new orientation to the old which revives a forgotten knowledge for present and future use.

Instead of revealing too much change, as it does in nostalgic poetry, synchronicity in Brooks's poems suggests that there has been too little. Using biblical parallels or abruptly elevated language, she weaves white-dominated legendary motifs through black-identified contemporary scenes to show the violence that comes from too constant a disparity of privilege and from too little movement towards egalitarian social arrangements.[39] The continuities revealed are all too consistent, as in the refrain of "The Boy Died in My Alley" where, though she neither saw nor heard the murder on her street, she wearily tells police that "The Shot that killed him yes I heard / as I heard the Thousand shots before; / careening tinnily down the nights / across my years and arteries."[40]

Actually, the most characteristic synchronicities in Brooks's poems are more spatial and cultural than temporal. In all her work before *Family Pictures* (1971),[41] and often thereafter, she revealed the diversity of black lives formed around one, ever-present irritant, whites' conscious or unconscious fear and hatred of blackness. Her modernist's love of synchronizing disparate fragments into eloquent juxtapositions found an all too apt medium in this fact of American life. Color prejudice pervades her work like the smell of "yesterday's garbage ripening in the hall" in the "Kitchenette Building" of *A Street in Bronzeville* (*WGB* 4), bringing, perforce, an ironic unity to the black diversity she celebrates.

The title poem of *In the Mecca* (1968) is a masterpiece of this more spatial kind of synchronicity, as well as of the more temporal kind. "In the Mecca" combines the patterns of a mythic quest with the daily rounds of life in a huge slum tenement. In doing so, it also meshes the human diversity of the various tenement dwellers with the uniformly oppressive conditions in the Mecca Building. The two synchronicities fuse to create the poem's astonishing satirical range and power.

Brooks's brief epic follows Mrs. Sallie Smith, a domestic worker, as she sallies forth with her eight children in a frantic search for Pepita, the youngest child of the family. Mrs. Sallie sojourns through "The Mecca," a once grand building, now a crowded tenement, questioning each of her neighbors. Not one of them has seen four- or five-year-old Pepita, whose name means seed and who is the seed of the future, the most innocent, vital one among them. As though reciting litany, each Mecca dweller gives Mrs. Sallie the same answer; it becomes the poem's refrain and theme:

> *Ain seen er I ain seen er I ain seen er*
> Ain seen er I ain seen er I ain seen er.

(WGB 386)

"In the Mecca" is a poem of voices, like Edgar Lee Masters's *Spoon River Anthology* (1914) or Ntozake Shange's *For Colored Girls Who Have Considered Suicide, When the Rainbow Is Enuf: A Choreopoem* (1977). Brooks orchestrates a medley of religious fanatics, pious quacks, love-sick lunatics, old women stuck in their youthful memories of slave times, young women steeling themselves to settle for what little male attention their dark skins can command. In all their variety, they respond to Mrs. Sallie with that one listless yet ominous, "Ain seen er." Their unanimity emphasizes how intractably common their impoverishment is, how very generally it touches their otherwise diverse individualities.

Brooks creates a counterpoint by playing the variety of their blighted histories and manifold styles of craziness against this unanimity. The counterpoint connects the corruption and promise of the poem's two main symbols, the innocent young girl-child Pepita and the Mecca Building itself. Pepita, tiny and easy to overlook, is never permitted to grow and flower because—as becomes slowly clear—she has been assaulted and murdered by "Jamaican Edward," whose name means "guardian of property"[42]; the Mecca, an inglorious monument to material opulence, has gone from showplace to slum to vacant lot in just fifty years.[43] Inhabitants of The Mecca sustain as much damage and corruption as those of Eliot's wasteland, but vitality is drained in the wasteland whereas in The Mecca it is frustrated.[44]

To convey both the vigor and the corruption of this frustrated vitality, Brooks loaded the poem's language and narrative with sexual decadence, as Eliot often does with a very different impact. Describing Pepita's pathetic death, for instance, Brooks did not spare readers the familiar repugnancies of that commonplace atrocity, children who have been assaulted sexually and murdered (usually by men); she emphasized them. She synchronized Pepita's last moments with a flashback that shows Pepita playing make-believe "at the A and P's fly-open door," and she made her readers see under Jamaican Edward's bed, where "a little woman lies in dust with roaches" (*WGB* 403). Then, as if "fly-open" and "little woman" might not sufficiently underscore the sexual violation involved in Pepita's murder, Brooks ended the entire poem with a four-line imagist vignette of the child's actual death throes (described, one is shocked to discover, from the murderer's viewpoint):

> She whose stomach fought the world
> had wriggled, like a robin!
> Odd were the little wrigglings
> and the chopped chirpings oddly rising.
>
> (*WGB* 403)

Where Eliot's sexual symbols of cultural corruption seem designed to scandalize, Brooks's equally horrifying ones often call for outrage but also for compassion. Brooks's own engagement with the "hot estrangement" identified in "In the Mecca" shows clearly in her choice of men's sexual entitlement and the corruptions and dangers it forces on women as the most apt figure for the various kinds of fury that race-ruled living has long since induced in all the Mecca dwellers. That audacious choice of metaphoric register accounts for the space she gave to misogynistic violence in the vengeful fantasy of Amos, a Mecca dweller whom Brooks presented as a sympathetic character. Envisioning all of white America as a white woman, he calls for "a long blood bath [to] wash her pure" of her racist arrogance, exploitation, and cruelty. He recommends the usual treatment—"Slap the false sweetness from that face"—complete with sadistic details from the standard repertoire: "Great-nailed boots / must kick her prostrate, heel-grind that soft breast, / . . . Let her lie there, panting and wild" and so on (*WGB* 394–95).

The poem neither endorses nor condemns Amos for his vengeful misogynistic reverie, though Brooks herself almost certainly would reject such reprisal. Still, when Brooks synchronized the clichés of pornographic violence with this portrait of a white America being taught its lesson at last and too late, she unflinchingly admitted into her already capacious poem a rage commensurate with its compassion. "These fragments I have shored against my ruins," Eliot famously chanted at the end of *The Waste Land*. The fragments of Brooks's poem are not shored against ruin; they *are* ruins. They await redefinition where possible, revenge where not.

## Obscurity

Brooks and Doolittle knew that a changed social arrangement cannot become effective without a changed mentality. Therefore, they made their most profound challenges to patriarchal privilege at the level of epistemology. Both questioned patriarchally defined boundaries of knowledge, and both called for efforts to expand cognitive capacities rather than accept principled limits to what can be known. Their struggle with the epistemological assumptions of masculinist modernism epitomizes their revisionary uses of poetic forms and suggests the most intensely revolutionary potential of modernism.

Doolittle rejected equating "real" with "physical," while Brooks rejected equating "black" with "obscure." For Doolittle, the concept "spiritual reality" was not an oxymoron. It referred to the reality of nonmaterial phenomena. "Spiritual" did not have to mean "unreal," and "reality" need not be restricted to the physical. In addition, "spiritual reality," requiring appropriately enhanced capacities to apprehend it, entailed ideas about cognitive faculties. Doolittle envisioned new *ways* of knowing, as well as new *kinds* of knowledge. Brooks's epistemological reforms aimed at dispelling every accepted definition of obscurity that equates "black" with unintelligibility and "white" with enlightenment. Moreover, she rejected the ideology that defines "black" in relation to white, but not *vice versa*.[45]

Brooks was keenly aware that the needed redefinitions entail massive transvaluation. From *In the Mecca* on, she came to endorse the creative, constructive potential of rioting:

> Fire.
> That is their way of lighting candles in the darkness.
> A White Philosopher said
> "It is better to light one candle than curse the darkness."
>            These candles curse—
> inverting the deeps of the darkness.[46]

In her midcentury poems, she demonstrated how the novelty of long-sought change can feel frightening when it finally comes. New opportunities do not automatically empower; they require changes in consciousness that themselves need political and personal supports. "And if sun comes / How shall we greet him?" she asked in "truth," a poem from the "Womanhood" section of *Annie Allen*. "Shall we not flee / Into the shelter, the dear thick shelter / Of the familiar / Propitious haze? // Sweet is it, sweet is it / To sleep in the coolness / Of snug unawareness" (*WGB* 114).

Both poets—each in her own way—fought the seductions of "snug unawareness." Both saw that ignorance easily could become the epistemological equivalent of evading responsibility. An alibi as de Beauvoir called it in *The Second Sex:*

> [T]he man who "does not understand" a woman is happy to substitute an objective resistance for a subjective deficiency of mind; instead of admitting his ignorance, he perceives the presence of a "mystery" outside himself: an alibi, indeed, that flatters laziness and vanity at once.[47]

The celebrated textual obscurity of modernism may be considered masculinist insofar as it invokes this self-indulgent alibi, flattering "laziness and vanity at once" by projecting its own ignorance as an irresolvable perplexity in what is to be known. "How can we know the dancer from the dance?" Yeats asked rhetorically. And, "Did she put on his knowledge with his power?" Such questions stop us cold, which is what they're supposed to do. Like the infamous obscurity of modern texts in general, such baffling questions are designed to make us admit how little we know, and they imply that we must learn to accept limits to what can be considered knowable.

At first glance epistemological concerns may seem to have little to do with sexual or racial politics. But when limiting the knowable is the privilege of men, whose gender has them play knower to women's unknowable, the political dimension of textual obscurity starts to emerge. The otherness assigned to women in patriarchy traditionally makes women a mystery in the sense of something irritatingly, or perhaps beguilingly, elusive. Of course, "mystery" also refers to that which always can be known more fully, rather than something that can never be known.

Keeping that more dynamic sense of "mystery" in mind, the assumption that there must be limits to knowledge begins to sound expedient, potentially oppressive, and, therefore, as much an ethical and political matter as an epistemological one. That is, someone who gets thought of as an enigma (What do women want?) or who has been assigned membership among the inscrutable exotics may prefer not to dismiss difficult mysteries as muddles or marvels. Such a person may be more inclined to try to develop new capacities for knowing than to accept principled limits to what can be known. The antipatriarchal potential of modernism extends even to how an artist construes obscurity.

Doolittle and Brooks clearly knew that a sense of being entitled to evade discomfiting knowledge operates underneath all the forms of racial and sexual arrogance they challenged. The white women of the Ladies' Betterment League in Brooks's "Lovers of the Poor," for instance, recoil from the presence of those they have come to help. Overwhelmed by guilt and disgust, they decide to look for some less disturbing place to bestow their "loathe-love largesse" (*Bean Eaters, WGB* 333). Their counterparts, the white tourists slumming in Bronzeville restaurants, "love those little booths at Benvenuti's," because, "Boothed-in, one can detect, / Dissect" (*Annie Allen,* "Womanhood" 7, *WGB* 110). Insulated by arrogance, neither group knows that it fears and despises blackness, so they either run away like the do-gooders, or feel unaccountably rejected, like the tourists who don't find the exotic behaviors they've come to ogle. In both cases, "It is the innocence that constitutes the crime."[48]

Like Brooks's tourists and do-gooders, Doolittle's conventional males illustrate the need for change at the level of epistemology itself. Her incredulous Kaspar, her mystified admirer of the Lady in "Tribute to the Angels," her slowly learning Achilles and smugly complacent Paris—all these unregenerate misunderstanders show that revised social and power relations require recognitions.

Because an epistemological complacency—de Beauvoir's "alibi"—sponsors all the other complacencies that compose oppressive privilege, an epistemological challenge is required to unsettle it. In assessing modernist obscurity for their own purposes, Doolittle and Brooks challenged, not the difficulty of knowing, but the complacency that accepts such difficulty as limiting. An ideology that sets principled limits to knowledge also limits freedom because it reifies an authority that supposedly sets these limits.[49] Accordingly, instead of accepting bafflement and exalting obscurity, Brooks and Doolittle insisted that full social reform entails reform of the theory and practice of knowledge. They challenged oppressive ideology at the level of epistemology, suggesting that the two are inextricable. They showed that "inverting the deeps of the darkness" of the most tenacious cultural institutions requires "spiritual realism," an expanded concept of reality itself. No doubt, achieving such expansion is still in the future, but these two poets use modernist techniques to point the way.

## NOTES

1. For the paradoxically integrating and disrupting drive of American Modernism, see Daniel Joseph Singal, "Towards a Defini-

tion of American Modernism," *American Quarterly* 39 (Spring 1987): 7–26.

2. Sandra M. Gilbert and Susan Gubar, *No Man's Land: The Place of the Woman Writer in the Twentieth Century, Volume I: The War of the Words* (New Haven: Yale University Press, 1987), 147 and passim. In chapters of this volume and volume 2, *Sexchanges* (1988), Gilbert and Gubar show that women writers also made direct and substantive contributions to shaping modernism.

3. Carolyn Burke, "Getting Spliced: Modernism and Sexual Difference," *American Quarterly* 39 (Spring 1987): 101; Maureen Honey, ed., *Shadowed Dreams: Women's Poetry of the Harlem Renaissance* (New Brunswick: Rutgers University Press, 1989), 1–41; Gloria Hull, *Color, Sex, and Poetry: Three Women Writers of the Harlem Renaissance* (Bloomington: Indiana University Press, 1981). For the upheaval in gender roles during the period, see Gilbert and Gubar, *Sexchanges* and Carroll Smith-Rosenberg, *Disorderly Conduct: Visions of Gender in Victorian America* (New York: Knopf, 1985), "The New Woman as Androgyne: Social Disorder and Gender Crisis, 1870–1936," pp. 245–96.

4. Simone de Beauvoir, *The Second Sex,* trans. H. M. Parshley (New York, 1974), 288; hereafter cited parenthetically.

5. Gwendolyn Brooks, *The World of Gwendolyn Brooks* (New York: Harper and Row, 1971); hereafter *WGB*.

6. Albert Gelpi, "Hilda in Egypt," *Southern Review* 18 (Spring 1982): 233–50, 234.

7. H. D., *Helen in Egypt* (New York: Grove Press, 1961); cited hereafter as *HE* plus page number.

8. The only instance I know of is Rachel Blau DuPlessis, *Writing Beyond the Ending: Narrative Strategies of Twentieth-Century Women Writers* (Bloomington, 1985), pp. 105–22; hereafter cited in the text.

9. For Doolittle's esotericism, see Susan Stanford Friedman, *Psyche Reborn: The Emergence of H.D.* (Bloomington: Indiana University Press, 1981), Part 2, "H.D. and Religious Tradition," esp. "Initiations," [157]–206. For Doolittle's political engagement, including her connections with the Harlem Renaissance, see Friedman, "Modernisms of the 'Scattered Remnant': Race and Politics in H.D.'s Development," in *Feminist Issues in Literary Scholarship,* ed. Shari Benstock (Bloomington: Indiana University Press, 1987), pp. 208–31.

10. Gwendolyn Brooks, *Report from Part One* (Detroit: Broadside, 1972), 45; hereafter *RPO*.

11. Claudia Tate, *Black Women Writers at Work* (New York: Continuum, 1983), 9.

12. Hortense J. Spillers, "Gwendolyn the Terrible: Propositions on Eleven Poems," in *Shakespeare's Sisters: Feminist Essays on Women Poets,* ed. Sandra M. Gilbert and Susan Gubar (Bloomington: Indiana University Press, 1979), 244.

13. Members of the Chicago gang Blackstone Rangers taught Brooks

about black activism while she taught them about verse-writing. See D. H. Melhem, *Gwendolyn Brooks: Poetry and the Heroic Voice* (Lexington: University Press of Kentucky, 1987), p. 154.

14. For an overview of Doolittle's style and achievement, see Alicia Ostriker, "Learning to Read H.D.," *American Poetry Review* 12 (March/April 1983): 29–38. For an overview of Brooks, see Maria K. Mootry, " 'Down the Whirlwind of Good Rage': An Introduction to Gwendolyn Brooks," in *A Life Distilled: Gwendolyn Brooks, Her Poetry and Fiction,* ed. Maria K. Mootry and Gary Smith (Urbana: University of Illinois Press, 1987), p. 1–17. For Brooks's relation to Chicago, see Kenny J. Williams, "The World of Satin-Legs, Mrs. Sallie, and the Blackstone Rangers: The Restricted Chicago of Gwendolyn Brooks," in *A Life,* ed. Mootry and Smith, 47–70.

15. For Doolittle's poetry, except *Helen in Egypt,* see Louis L. Martz, ed., *H.D.: Collected Poems, 1912–1944* (New York: New Directions, 1983); hereafter *CP.*

16. For Cousin Vit, Big Bessie, and Mrs. Sallie Smith, see, respectively, "The rites for Cousin Vit," "The Second Sermon on the Warpland," and "In the Mecca," Brooks, *WGB.* On women in Brooks's poems see Beverly Guy-Sheftall, "The Women of Bronzeville," in *A Life,* ed. Mootry and Smith, p. 151–64.

17. See Clive Scott, "Symbolism, Decadence, and Impressionism," in *Modernism: 1890–1930,* ed. Malcolm Bradbury and James McFarlane (New York, 1976), 206–27; and Natan Zach, "Imagism and Vorticism," in *Modernism: 1890–1930,* ed. Malcolm Bradbury and James McFarlane, 228–42. See also Edmund Wilson, *Axel's Castle: A Study in the Imaginative Literature of 1870–1930* (New York, 1950), esp. chaps. 1, 4, 7, 8.

18. O. W. Firkins, "The New Movement in Poetry: The Self-Exposure of a Reactionary Critic of the Imagistes," *The Nation* 101 (October 14, 1915): 458–61, 459, cited hereafter parenthetically.

19. Compare Firkins's comment to Andre Gide's similar criticism of symbolism: " 'One's great objection to the Symbolist school . . . is its lack of curiosity about life . . . [A]ll were pessimists, renunciants, resignationists . . . Poetry had become for them a refuge.' " Edmund Wilson, *Axel's Castle,* p. 257.

20. Susan Friedman, *Psyche Reborn,* p. 254–55, argues that H.D.'s Helen redefines innocence, noting that both Stesichorus and Euripides also removed Helen from Troy to Egypt, but they did it to exonerate her, not to reassess, as Doolittle did, the codes that condemned her.

21. See St. Clair Drake and Horace R. Cayton, *Black Metropolis: A Study of Negro Life in a Northern City,* 2 vols. (New York: Harper & Row 1962), 2:379–97. See also Kenny J. Williams, "The World of Satin-Legs."

22. Robert Duncan, *The H. D. Book,* quoted in Albert Gelpi, *A Coherent Splendor: The American Poetic Renaissance, 1910–1950* (Cambridge, Mass.: Cambridge Univ. Press, 1987), p. 260.

23. Ibid., p. 260.

24. Houston A. Baker in *Modernism and the Harlem Renaissance* (Chicago, 1987), p. 85 and passim., gives the sonnets of Claude McKay and the ballads of Countee Cullen as examples of the subversive "mastery of form" achieved by Afro-American modernists of the Harlem Renaissance. (Overt defiance, "the deformation of mastery," is the complement of "mastery of form.")

25. Till was a fourteen-year-old boy from Chicago. Along with his mother, he visited an uncle in Money, Mississippi in August 1955. Alleged to have whistled at a white woman, or perhaps just spoken to her, he was lynched by the woman's husband and a friend who were acquitted.

26. For a related interpretation that emphasizes narrative strategy rather than uses of imagism, see DuPlessis, *Writing Beyond the Ending*, pp. 112–15. On Brooks's uses of ballad form, see Gladys Williams, "The Ballads of Gwendolyn Brooks," in *A Life*, ed. Mootry and Smith, 205–23, which includes a discussion of "A Bronzeville Mother . . ."; also D. H. Melhem, *Poetry and the Heroic Voice*.

27. DuPlessis, "Romantic Thralldom and 'Subtle Genealogies' in H.D.," *Writing Beyond the Ending*, pp. 66–83.

28. On the mock heroic as vehicle for women's suppressed anger in "The Anniad," see Claudia Tate, "Anger So Flat: Gwendolyn Brooks's *Annie Allen*," in *A Life*, ed. Mootry and Smith, pp. 140–52.

29. *A Street in Bronzeville* (1945), *WGB*, p. 14.

30. On what he calls "the *inside* color line" (his emphasis), see Arthur P. Davis, "The Black-and-Tan Motif in the Poetry of Gwendolyn Brooks," *College Language Association Journal* 6 (December 1962): 90–97.

31. Uncovering the dynamics of oppositional pairs that are covertly hierarchical has been a crucial task of feminist criticism from *The Second Sex* on. An early example is Sherry Ortner, "Is Female to Male as Nature is to Culture?" in *Woman, Culture, and Society* (Stanford, Calif., 1974), pp. 67–87. Recent examples focusing on various areas of social life from various academic disciplines include the following: Joan W. Scott, "Deconstructing Equality-Versus-Difference: Or the Uses of Poststructuralist Theory For Feminism," *Feminist Studies* 14 (Spring 1988): 33–50; Janice Raymond, "Response" to Marilyn Friedman, "Individuality without Individualism," a review of Raymond's *A Passion for Friends, Hypatia* 3 (Summer 1988): 139–49; and Nancy Armstrong "The Gender Bind: Women and the Disciplines," *Genders* (Fall 1988): [1]–23.

32. Susan Friedman, *Psyche Reborn*, p. 69.

33. Ibid., pp. 229–72.

34. On the inclination to submission and dependency that patriarchal social arrangements can impose on women's desire, see Jessica Benjamin, "A Desire of One's Own: Psychoanalytic Feminism and Intersubjective Space" in *Feminist Studies, Critical Studies*, ed. Teresa de Lauretis (Bloomington: Indiana University Press, 1986), pp. 78–101.

35. Interestingly, Achilles's incipient capacity for paradox and inclusive, dynamic thinking makes him a kind of budding modernist. "The

Mind of the Modernist," according to James McFarlane's essay so enti-
tled, "allows workaday contraries to have at one and the same time a sepa-
rate and a shared identity, to be indifferently both 'same' and 'different' "
(*Modernism: 1890–1930*, p. 88). Certainly Doolittle herself aspired to such
a modernist mentality; it could offer significant reform to a sex-gender
system based on oppressive ideas about both sameness and difference.

36. *Trilogy* is in *Collected Poems*, ed. Louis Martz, [505]–612, here-
after in parentheses by poem number preceded by abbreviated titles for
each of the three parts, as follows: WDNF (The Walls Do Not Fall); TA
(Tribute to the Angles); FR (The Flowering of the Rod).

37. Susan Gubar, "The Echoing Spell of H.D.'s *Trilogy*," in *Shake-
speare's Sisters*, ed. Gilbert and Gubar, p. 202.

38. In addition to the Lady of TA, examples include seeing Isis as
harlot (WDNF 2) instead of as begetter of civilization (WDNF 40); under-
estimating the worm (WDNF 2 and throughout); associating Venus with
"venereal" rather than "venerate" (TA 11–12); and, in general, classifying
valuable elements of past cultures with the designation "is-not" (FR 6).

39. See, among many others, "A Lovely Love" (*WGB* 347) and
"Riot," *To Disembark* (Chicago, 1981), pp. 5–6.

40. *To Disembark*, pp. 49–55.

41. *Family Pictures* (Detroit, 1971). For Brooks's poetic development,
see George Kent, "Gwendolyn Brooks: A Developmental Survey," in
*Black Women Writers (1950–1980)*, ed. Mari Evans (Garden City, New
York: Anchor/Doubleday, 1984), pp. 88–105.

42. D. H. Melhem, *Poetry and the Heroic Voice*, p. 162. Melhem also
notes that Pepita can mean "grain of pure gold," as well as "seed."

43. D. H. Melhem, *Poetry and the Heroic Voice*, p. 158.

44. For a comparison between Brooks and Eliot which focuses on
"In the Mecca" and *The Waste Land*, see " 'Define . . . the Whirlwind':
Gwendolyn Brooks's Epic Sign for a Generation," in *Black American
Poets between Worlds, 1940–1960*, ed. R. Baxter Miller (Knoxville: Univer-
sity of Tennessee, 1986), pp. [160]–73.

45. In RPO, pp. 82–83, *q.v.*, Brooks gives a detailed comparison
between dictionary definitions of "white" and of the "world-shaking
word" "black."

46. "Riot," *To Disembark*, p. 11.

47. De Beauvoir, p. 289. See also pp. 289–91. In this connection,
recall that when Achilles and Helen first meet, he assumes she is a witch
until he finally recognizes her.

48. James Baldwin, "My Dungeon Shook: Letter to My Nephew on
the One Hundredth Anniversary of the Emancipation," *The Fire Next
Time* (New York, Dial Press, 1963), p. 20.

49. On the relation between freedom and the setting of principled lim-
its to knowledge, see Rudolf Steiner, *The Philosophy of Freedom: The Basis
for a Modern World Conception*, trans. Michael Wilson (1918; rpt, London:
Rudolf Steiner Press, 1964), Preface to the 1918 Edition and throughout.

BROOKE KENTON HORVATH

# The Satisfactions of What's Difficult
# in Gwendolyn Brooks's Poetry

Gwendolyn Brooks has been both praised and condemned for her often mandarin style. Thus David Littlejohn, writing in 1966, could acknowledge her craft—"she exercises, customarily," he wrote, "a greater degree of artistic control than any other American Negro writer"—but not, finally, the results of that craftsmanship. "In many of her early poems," Littlejohn felt,

> Mrs. Brooks appears only to pretend to talk of things and of people; her real love is words. The inlay work of words, the *précieux* sonics, the lapidary insets of jeweled images (like those of Gerard Manley Hopkins) can, in excess, squeeze out life and impact altogether, and all but give the lie to the passions professed in the verbs.[1]

For other critics, the real bone of contention has been the fact that, despite her efforts to forge a black aesthetic, Brooks has practiced a poetics indebted as much to T. S. Eliot as to Langston Hughes (though brought to bear on black subject matter). This white style/black content debate can be heard clearly in Houston A. Baker's *Singers of Daybreak*: "Mrs. Brooks," says Baker, "writes tense, complex, rhythmic verse that contains the metaphysical complexities of John Donne and the word magic of Apollinaire, Pound, and Eliot." Yet this style is employed "to explicate the condition of the black American trapped behind a veil that separates him from the white world. What one seems to have is 'white' style and 'black' content—two warring ideals in one dark body."[2]

Both of these issues are complex. Behind the former—the emotional effectiveness of the poet's meticulous "inlay work of

From *American Literature* 62 (December 1990): 606–16. Copyright © Duke University Press, 1990. Reprinted with permission of the publisher.

words"—lies in part the vexed question of modernism, which under the aegis of T. S. Eliot has been responsible, according to Christopher Clausen, for "the decline in the American poetic audience" and "the disappearance of poetry as a major cultural force."[3] Behind the latter—the problem of a "proper" aesthetic for a poet wrestling with an artistic double consciousness— stands the still-troubled assessment of, say, Phillis Wheatley and Paul Laurence Dunbar as well as more recent poets as diverse as Melvin Tolson and the Armageddon school of the 1960s.[4] In the pages that follow, I would like to add to this discussion of the appropriateness of Brooks's "tense, complex" early style as it relates to black concerns and, more centrally here, as it does or does not justify itself at its most elliptical *apart* from racial consid- erations. I intend to do this by examining in some detail one poem notable initially for its opacity: " 'do not be afraid of no,' " which constitutes section nine of the "Notes from the Childhood and the Girlhood" sequence in *Annie Allen,* Brooks's Pulitzer Prize-winning collection of 1949.[5]

A succinct example of Brooks's complexity at its most revealing/concealing, " 'do not be afraid of no' " has received little close attention. Those critics who have commented upon the poem do so only briefly and with the intention of explaining its problematic place within the larger work of which it is a part. Thus, Charles Israel suggests that the poem reveals some of the "moral and ethical lessons of Annie's youth"; D. H. Melhem offers two paragraphs arguing that the poem constitutes "An- nie's motto," her refusal "to emulate her mother's submission"; and Harry B. Shaw reads the poem as equating "the high life with death" and admonishing Annie not to choose prostitution as the only alternative to "the death of no life," a reading that finds parallels between " 'do not be afraid of no' " and other poems such as "Gang Girls" and "Big Bessie throws her son into the street."[6] If none of these readings confronts fully the interpre- tive difficulties introduced by the poem's appearance as part of *Annie Allen*—for instance, determining who is offering Annie this advice (the answer will affect one's assessment of the wis- dom of that advice and its impact upon Annie) or establishing the connection between the advice offered in the poem's opening lines and the remainder of the poem (for surely the response to this initial advice cannot be credited to even the most precocious young girl, as the poet's use of the third-person pronoun indicates)—this is not the greatest cause for disappointment.[7]

Rather, what one feels most is the lack of any extended analysis of the poem that would account not only for its "meaning" but also for the poet's stylistic choices and for the relation of both message and style to Brooks's concerns as a black female poet. I suggest that such a close reading reveals a style not merely justified by the poem's content but essential if readers are to *experience* (rather than simply be told) the truth the poem embodies.

" 'Do not be afraid of no' " begins straightforwardly enough by reiterating the advice of its title in two lines enclosed by quotation marks and concluded by a colon, which suggests that what follows will be a gloss upon this advice, the development of an argument in support of this thesis.

> "Do not be afraid of no,
> Who has so far so very far to go":

"Do not be afraid [to say] no" seems simple advice; indeed, now that "just say no" has become the lamest sort of response to social problems, Brooks's opening lines may seem not so much simple as simple-minded (they will prove to be neither). But certain problems arise even here: Who is speaking and to whom? Are these lines something the poet has been told or read (hence the quotation marks)? One can of course fall back upon the response that these lines are spoken by someone to Annie (although I don't find this wholly clarifying for reasons such as those sketched above), but here I am suggesting that for "Annie" one might—for the duration of the poem—substitute "any young (black) girl" or, more generally, "anyone"—and here it is useful to recall George Kent's observation that in *Annie Allen* one advantage of the poetic form is to "move experiences immediately into symbols broader than the person serving as subject."[8] But further, to whom or what does the "who" of line two refer: to "no," its grammatical antecedent (in which case, why "who" instead of "which"?), or to the addressee—Annie aside, the choices would seem to be the poem's readers, self-reflexively the poet, or some unknown third party—who has "so far so very far to go"? And "to go" where? In life? One can be no more precise than that for now. These questions, however, are only mildly vexing because one presumes they will be answered (they won't be) in language similarly direct (it won't be but will tend toward greater confusion before somewhat clarifying itself).

Stanza 2 acknowledges that saying "no" is never easy:

New caution to occur
To one whose inner scream set her to cede, for softer lapping and
    smooth fur!

As noted above, the opening lines appear in quotation marks possibly to suggest they contain received wisdom the perspicacity of which the poet intends to ponder. For one thing, she knows that saying "yes" means reaching agreement, solving a problem, accepting a plan, a truth, a life mate: "yes" is at least superficially positive, resolves that often unsettling uncertainty and probable antagonism "no" involves; "no" leaves one in suspense, in suspension, dissatisfied, perhaps closed off from comforts and companions. To say "no" to something is not, after all, necessarily to say "yes" to something else.

But through stanza 2 (and beyond), what exactly is at issue remains terribly amorphous. The reader, aware of who has written the poem and the historical circumstances surrounding its composition, might conclude that Brooks has something racial to denounce but is couching that denunciation in self-protectively cryptic language. But what? Is the poem an example of what Gary Smith has labeled Brooks's "remarkable consistent" identification of "white racism and its pervasive socio-economic effects" on the black community?[9] If so, how so? Or perhaps the poem is not primarily racial but speaks of some political, economic, or ideological crisis on the international scene? Or perhaps this is a prototypical instance of confessional poetry that speaks of larger concerns only as they impinge upon the private psyche? If Clara Claiborne Park is correct in reading *Annie Allen* as "a varied and inventive sequence of poems evoking a poor black woman's progress from exquisite illusion to the recognition of a harder yet more satisfying reality," and if one recalls Brooks's early poetic successes (encouraged by a mother who "intended her to be 'the *lady* Paul Laurence Dunbar' ") within the white world of poetry and subsequent break in the late 1960s with that world in favor of poetry intent on speaking to African Americans of their concerns and in their language, then the poem might well be read as offering an elliptical rejection of poetic success in white literary terms (as either the black T. S. Eliot or the "lady" Paul Laurence Dunbar).[10] Such a reading is possible, but without seeking extratextual aid one cannot say "yes" to any of these possibilities—and so the poem is already teaching the reader the wisdom of the provisional "no."

At any rate, the advice of stanza 1 is a "new caution" to one predisposed to saying "yes," a new word of warning whose wisdom has occurred to the poet. The "she" of line 4 may refer to Everywoman, but the advice is pertinent to anyone—that is, to all of us—whose heart cries out to accede, to surrender by conceding and so avoid unpleasantness and secure comfort, that "softer lapping and smooth fur!" This last phrase is a wonderfully odd and unexpected evocation of pseudo-desiderata that, in conjunction with "set her to cede" (which recalls the cliché "gone to seed"), suggests that "yes" buys the reader something that leaves her less than human. And here one recalls John Updike's remark that "a person who has what he wants"—or thinks he has—"ceases to be a person," is "just an animal with clothes on," as Brooks's images of lapping and fur imply. [11] But perhaps at this point the poem now seems more feminist than racial, the combination of the feminine pronoun and the sensual, vaguely sexual imagery suggesting that women ought not sell out by acquiescing to marriage or a subordinate position in a relationship—although this is, obviously, as conjectural as those racial/political/autobiographical concerns hypothesized earlier. Whatever surrender is to be avoided, the exclamation point registers the poet's shock that such capitulation could even be considered for the tawdry prizes it would win one.

Stanzas 3 and 4 analyze and thereby judge the kind of person who could so easily acquiesce as well as the shortsightedness of such a maneuver:

> Whose esoteric need
> Was merely to avoid the nettle, to not-bleed.
>
> Stupid, like a street
> That beats into a dead end and dies there, with nothing left to
>     reprimand or meet.

Such an individual's need is "esoteric," not in the sense of being understandable only to a few (the poet has implicitly—through her avoidance of greater specificity—acknowledged the universality of the desire to avoid pain and to seek pleasure) but in the sense of being "difficult to understand," of being "not publicly disclosed." [12] To seek merely to "not-bleed," to sell one's birthright for a mess of ease, *is* finally difficult to fathom and rarely the reason offered publicly to explain one's ceding. For instance, to return (for illustrative purposes only) to the possibility of the poem offering us a feminist commentary upon marriage: a bride's "I do" does not normally confess to a desire "merely to

avoid the nettle" but rather professes acceptance of a noble call-
ing, honorable commitments.

However, as the reader moves into stanza 4, "yes" becomes
more than demeaning; it is also "stupid": a dead end where one
dies. The "no" that typically may seem pure denial now becomes
by contrast the means of opening one to possibility, of keeping
one in motion and alive in a world where, yes, there still exists
the chance of severe censure but also of further experiences to
encounter, to undergo (for the experience "no" makes possible
never loses here its sense of trial). And beyond the multiple
apposite senses of "meet," one may also recall that "reprimand"
derives from *reprimere*, "to repress": in death those fears "yes"
repressed will indeed be at an end. In the context of the poem,
"yes" becomes a denial of life, "no" implicitly its affirmation.
Brooks is here advocating an invigorating sort of denial not
unlike that "No! in thunder" Melville spoke of and which Leslie
Fiedler has argued underlies all first-rate literature.[13] For now,
the redefinition of "yes" and "no" these lines are effecting is
perhaps best suggested by reference to Melville's famous letter to
Hawthorne in which he observes that "All men who say *yes,* lie;
and all men who say *no,*—why, they are in the happy condition
of judicious, unincumbered travellers in Europe; they cross the
frontiers into Eternity with nothing but a carpetbag—that is to
say Ego. Whereas those yes-gentry, they travel with heaps of
baggage, and damn them! they will never get through the Cus-
tom House."[14] But again, if the reader is unwilling to assent to
these remarks, she is learning Brooks's lesson.

Stanzas 5 and 6 elaborate and complicate the yea-sayer's in-
creasingly dismal situation through images and syntax them-
selves increasingly elaborate and complex.

And like a candle fixed
Against dismay and countershine of mixed

Wild moon and sun. And like
A flying furniture, or bird with lattice wing; or gaunt thing, a-
    stammer down nightmare neon peopled with condor, hawk
    and shrike.

These lines are difficult to negotiate in part because the key to
understanding Brooks's symbolic candle is buried—like the im-
plications of "yes," whose consequences now seem a nightmare
deferred—midway through a grammatical fragment (the poem's

third so far, each hinting at the level of sentence structure at the incompleteness of the yes-man or yes-woman, at his or her inability to entertain a complete thought on what consent signifies). The key is "wild" and is underscored by the "flying furniture" of line 12: in the face of present reality, "yes" is no more than a candle in the wild winds of dismay that will send one's (domestic) ease flying like tables and chairs in a tornado.

Stanza 6's imagery is apocalyptic ("countershine of mixed // Wild moon and sun"), Bosch-like ("A flying furniture, or bird with lattice wing," this last a hopeless image of impossible flight), and violent with the predatory horror or nightmarish phantasm. At this point in the poem, the reader has been sucked deep into the maelstrom of the once-benign "yes." The language has reached fever pitch with its invocation of a neon-lit landscape "peopled" by condor, hawk, and shrike (also known, tellingly, as the butcherbird) across which "stammers" a *gaunt thing*—perhaps the yes-victim, perhaps her assassin.

So that the point will not be lost, the poet recapitulates bluntly in stanza 7. Earlier, such a direct, unambiguous assertion could have passed as so much lame rhetoric, but now it strides forth as stark summation:

> To say yes is to die
> A lot or a little. The dead wear capably their wry
>
> Enameled emblems. They smell.
> But that and that they do not altogether yell is all that we know
> well.

The reader has heard before—in the final line of stanza 2—the exasperated sarcasm that reappears with "a little." This modifier is neither a crumb thrown to one's desire for mitigation nor a means of toning down the poem's rhetorical frenzy. Rather, it implies that yes-people have but a small transition to make from nominal living to quiet, smelly death, a condition they wear "capably," their headstones no doubt bearing affirmative "enameled" (protective possibly, but probably merely decorative) "emblems."

The case against "yes" complete, the poem moves explicitly into its advocacy of "no":

> It is brave to be involved,
> To be not fearful to be unresolved.

> Her new wish was to smile
> When answers took no airships, walked a while.

Nay-saying, as observed before, is not to be perceived as resolution, as a negative means (otherwise similar to "yes") of closing the books. It is instead a way of bravely remaining "involved" while vitally "unresolved." "No" engenders life and keeps that life in conceivably uncomfortable but nonetheless healthy motion. Although the specific concerns being addressed remain undefined even at poem's end, its final lines suggest that those answers to which allegiance may one day be pledged *will* come, but they must be worked for and may be some time in arriving (they walk; they do not fly). This hope, this promise of resolution has, one notices, been present throughout the poem. In line 2, for instance, the reader realizes that "so very far" was actually not a feeble attempt to intensify the initial "so far"; rather, "so far" was qualifying "so very far" in the sense of "at the moment." Thus the sense of line 2 is not primarily that "no" has "very, very far to go" but that, although it does have a long way to go, every day, every line, will find "no" closer to its goal. And after all, the poem *is* written in rhyming couplets manifesting consonance (a correspondence of sound implying agreement, harmony, accord), although line lengths and rhythm vary wildly, postponing for varying lengths of time that consonance (a consonance most readily apparent in those most regular couplets devoted to the virtues of "no"). Here, then, at the level of sound, rhythm, and structure, the poem bodies forth its message that agreement will come (though necessarily delayed) but must not be sought prematurely or expected as a matter of (strict metrical) course.

The poem's final images are clear and positive, sparkling with hope, cheer, courage, and newness (just as they introduce a new tone into the poem). They also highlight what should be obvious by now: "no" is safer than "yes" just as walking is (whatever airlines may say) safer than flying (with the walking nay-sayer contrasted with the dead yea-sayer and dead-end streets where motion comes to an end, while the airships, associated with the yea-sayer's wish for trouble-free rapid transit, recall the flying furniture of the poem's horrific sixth stanza).

The complexity of " 'do not be afraid of no' " is, then, aesthetically justified because the poem teaches at every level of itself the need to remain actively engaged (as one must be involved with it) yet wary of reaching closure (as one must be when confronted by a poem that refuses too quickly to relinquish its meaning). No image easily elicits the reader's consent, which must anyway await one's understanding of each part in relation to the whole, just as one must assess any extratextual consent in relation to its effect on one's life as a whole. Similarly, the poem's terribly precise vagueness is likewise justified insofar as it leaves the poem open to speak to anyone confronted by any situation where a preemptive assent seems the path of least resistance (a message as intensely relevant for blacks in 1949 as it ever was before or after this date). Just as does Brooks's famous sonnet "First fight. Then fiddle," " 'do not be afraid of no' " places stylistic resistance at the center of her message concerning the need for resistance at the social/political level. And if " 'do not be afraid of no' " is still worlds away from directness of, say, "We Real Cool," Brooks might be seen in this early poem to be considering already that stylistic maneuver Park discovers in the much later "In the Mecca" (1968), wherein the critic finds Brooks "los[ing] faith in the kind of music she had loved and was so well qualified to sing" but which "blacks now found unusable."[15]

At the poem's end, as I have noted, whatever it was—social issue, personal concern, aesthetic challenge—that planted the seed of the poem in Brooks's mind ("set her to cede") remains as indefinite as it was when we began. We can ask, Does she wish to urge "no" upon blacks too willing to accept token adjustments of the status quo? Or does she desire to tell women not to surrender their dreams too easily? Or to tell readers not to dismiss her work too quickly? Does she wish to say "no" to a poetic style already proving itself unsatisfactory? All would be provocative messages—and Brooks allows us to entertain each of them—but I see no special textual support for any of them.

" 'Do not be afraid of no' " works hard at keeping the reader involved with it by making her feel she has not yet fully gotten into it, leaving open a multiplicity of interpretive possibilities by neither sanctioning nor precluding any of them. And if this assessment is accurate, the poem reveals as well the wisdom of Brooks's strategy as the vehicle for black (social/political) content, for she knows, as do we all, that America will, alas, always provide situations demanding rejection but tempting us to acquiesce either because we grow exhausted and resigned or because the carrot on the stick is lusciously attractive. And beyond the circumference of these concerns, and to return to Melville by way of Fiedler, Brooks knows the aesthetic correctness of the "no! in thunder," a denial not circumscribed completely by events of the moment any more than " 'do not be afraid of no' " is delimited by its appearance originally as part of *Annie Allen*. As the engaged, topical poetry of the early Nikki Giovanni or of Don L. Lee (Haki Madhubuti) suggests, the easy "no"—to racism, poverty, whatever—can make finally for limited art.[16] Alternatively, " 'do not be afraid of no' "— which might now be seen working metapoetically—offers instead a timeless "no," a "no" applicable in any circumstance that tempts anyone with the desire to acquiesce. Thus, Brooks offers a poem that is both timely and timeless, which is, after all, one definition of a classic.

Indeed, logically, no ready consent to the poem's message is possible even after lengthy explication, for to say "yes" to " 'do not be afraid of no' " is to imply one has possibly misread it. On the other hand, to say "no" to the poem is, willy-nilly, to act upon the poem's advice, hence to concur with the wisdom of that advice, suggesting once again that the lesson has been lost upon one. In this logical conundrum the reader is left, nettled by interpretive possibilities no gloss can smooth but that serve to keep the game and so the poem alive. The poem's difficulties are, in this sense, both its content and its style, which is as it should be, for such are the ends, and the satisfactions, of Gwendolyn Brooks's craft.

## NOTES

1. *Black on White: A Critical Survey of Writing by American Negroes* (1966; reprinted New York: Viking-Compass, 1969), pp. 89, 90.

2. *Singers of Daybreak: Studies in Black American Literature* (Washington: Howard University Press, 1974), p. 43.

3. "The Decline of Anglo-American Poetry," *Virginia Quarterly* 54 (1978): 74.

4. Other issues are equally at stake, issues extending beyond poetry proper and suggested by remarks such as Littlejohn's contention that Brooks is "far more a poet than a Negro," p. 89, and Dan Jaffe's observation that "the label 'black poetry' cheapens the achievement of Gwendolyn Brooks" ("Gwendolyn Brooks: An Appreciation from the White Suburbs," in *The Black American Writer*, ed. C. W. E. Bigsby [DeLand: Everett/Edwards, 1969], vol. 2, p. 92). On Brooks's poetics and her desire to produce work espousing a black aesthetic, see Norris B. Clark, "Gwendolyn Brooks and a Black Aesthetic," in *A Life Distilled: Gwendolyn Brooks, Her Poetry and Fiction*, ed. Maria K. Mootry and Gary Smith (Urbana: University of Illinois Press, 1987), pp. 81–99; and Clara Claiborne Park, "First Fight, Then Fiddle," *The Nation*, 26 September 1987, pp. 308–12. For Brooks's comments on this matter, see Martha

H. Brown and Marilyn Zorn, "GLR Interview: Gwendolyn Brooks," *Great Lakes Review* 6, no. 1 (1979): 48–55.

5. *Annie Allen* (New York: Harper, 1949), pp. 12–13.

6. Charles Israel, "Gwendoyn Brooks," in *American Poets Since World War II, Part I: A–K (Dictionary of Literary Biography, vol. 5)*, ed. Donald J. Greiner (Detroit: Gale, 1980), p. 101; D. H. Melhem, *Gwendolyn Brooks: Poetry and the Heroic Voice* (Lexington: University Press of Kentucky, 1987), p. 60; and Harry B. Shaw, *Gwendolyn Brooks* (Boston: Twayne, 1980), pp. 71–72, 108–9.

7. As a "note" on Annie's childhood and girlhood, " 'Do Not Be Afraid of No' " is not alone in bearing a puzzling relation to the sequence and to the book as a whole; cf. " 'Pygmies Are Pygmies Still, Though Percht on Alps,' " *Annie Allen*, p. 14.

8. "Gwendolyn Brooks' Poetic Realism: A Developmental Survey," in *Black Women Writers (1950–1980): A Critical Evaluation*, ed. Mari Evans (New York: Doubleday, 1984), p. 92. Kent's observation is echoed elsewhere: see Blyden Jackson and Louis D. Rubin, Jr., *Black Poetry in America* (Baton Rouge: Louisiana State University Press, 1974), pp. 81–85; Jackson and Rubin argue, with particular reference to *Annie Allen*, that Brooks's method is constantly to subordinate matters of sex or race to universal insights.

9. "Gwendolyn Brooks's *A Street in Bronzeville*, the Harlem Renaissance and the Mythologies of Black Women," MELUS 10, no. 3 (1983): 45.

10. Park, "First Fight, Then Fiddle," *The Nation* (September 1987): 308.

11. "One Big Interview," in *Picked-Up Pieces* (Greenwich, Conn.: Fawcett, 1975), p. 485.

12. *American Heritage Dictionary,* New College Ed., 1979.

13. On the reasons why both "yes" and the easy "no" make for poor art, see Leslie Fiedler, "No! In Thunder," in *No! In Thunder* (Boston: Beacon, 1960), pp. 1–18.

14. Letter to Nathaniel Hawthorne, 16 April 1851, in *The Portable Melville,* ed. Jay Leyda (New York: Viking, 1952), p. 428.

15. "First Fight, Then Fiddle," pp. 311, 310.

16. This assessment is admittedly a matter of personal taste. Brooks herself is clearly—and particularly after 1967—not averse to writing just such poetry, as *In the Mecca* and critical favorites such as "We Real Cool" indicate. Again, I would direct the interested reader to Park, Clark, and Brown and Zorn.

BRENDA R. SIMMONS

# "Gottschalk and the
# Grande Tarantelle"

The theme of the lead poem in Gwendolyn Brooks's 1989 collection[1] is reminiscent of the meaning of the folk adage "same church, different pew." The poem, "Gottschalk and the Grande Tarantelle" comments on a well-documented pattern of cultural genocide that has plagued African Americans throughout the diaspora. The poem is named for Louis Moreau Gottschalk, an American composer and pianist, who made frequent use of African American folk songs and Creole dance tunes in his compositions. The "Grande Tarantelle" is lauded as one of the composer's virtuoso piano pieces.

Gwendolyn Brooks's poem laments how Gottschalk "stole the wealth" of African American art. The format of the poem blends with the content to dramatically demonstrate the undercurrent that exists with African Americans living in this country. As we attempt to etch out a satisfying quality of life, someone who invariably means to do harm is watching and waiting. The narrator in the first stanza immediately sends an alert to African Americans as she makes an editorial comment. The narrator replays for African Americans the recurrent scene where African American creativity, unbridled and unfettered, is displayed. The corresponding terminology captures the attitude of the African American creator, "dancing to your own music, loving your wild art." The narrator continues to characterize the art as "vertical, winnowy, willful" further delineating how much the creators wish to be left alone to create, yet there is always an impending threat. After the first six lines in the poem, the narrator's editorial points to the inevitable.

The next thirty-five lines of the poem are a downhill trek into the "all familiar" for African Americans who are cognizant of the innumerous contributions to American culture. The thirty-five lines tell the age-old story of Euro-American "discovery" and

---

Previously unpublished.

economic gain—the foundation of capitalism and imperialism. The content this time is music instead of inventions, property, language, lyrics, and labor.

The poem makes an interesting move in the last three lines. In sociological terms, if a theft takes place, a debt is owed. The debt must be paid. The narrator lodges a final insult associated with the act of thievery and the "payment" in Gottschalk's case. Readers are harkened to the "paid" debt with the line: "he inherited slaves from his father and freed them." Gottschalk is seemingly unaware of the oxymoron as he continues his wrong-doing. The poem ends with a stingingly sarcastic tone "all hail the Debt-payer."

The next poem, a tribute to Winnie Mandela, appropriately titled "Winnie," offers a longing for innocence but presents the stark reality of womanhood and personal growth. That the poet reveres Winnie Mandela is evident in how she is referred to. She is called, "the non-fiction statement," "the articulate rehearsal," "the founding mother." All of these phrases, uniquely fashioned for Winnie, point to her unmatched position in the world.

Early in the poem, the poet points to the struggle. She sets up a contrast in which nature in its vividness, sumptuousness, and warmth, all of which is generative, serves as an ointment for a gaping wound. This parallels the characterization of Winnie who "would like to be a little girl again" but is drawn into a higher calling to "direct our choir of makers and wide music."

Winnie Mandela becomes the voice of truth speaking to and speaking for the "plants and beautiful weeds in the wilderness." Winnie is there to organize the protests when justice is so unfairly and arbitrarily meted out. Winnie Mandela reinforces the "code," "the old magic," that has guaranteed survival for people of color. The poet heaps all of the nobility that corresponds with a leader upon Winnie while simultaneously showing her as "frightened," "trapped," "crippled." The striking contrasts are all brought on because of "interrupted order" and "stalled clarity," obviously referring to the police state of South Africa.

The persona introduced in the last line of the poem is Nelson Mandela. He is speaking to "the people." He manifests his great reverence for his wife with the message that although she may sometimes long for the simple and innocent life, she is a lasting agent of change in the struggle for equality borne by people of color throughout the world.

"I Nelson the Mandela tell you so."

The third poem in the volume entitled "Song of Winnie," continues and embellishes the theme of womanhood and personal growth. Gwendolyn Brooks artfully engages the persona and the poet in a dialogue. The keystone of the poem is:

> Yet I know
> that I am Poet!
> I pass you my poem.

To grasp the message of these three lines, one has to enter into the poet's world. Emma Waters Dawson, in "Vanishing Point: The Rejected Black Woman in the Poetry of Gwendolyn Brooks," speaks to Brooks's "awakening."[2] Prior to 1967, a recurrent theme in Brooks's volumes was the intimidation and rejection of the dark-skinned Black woman. Brooks internalized the saying:

> If you're white, you're right
> If you're yellow, you're mellow
> If you're brown, you can hand around
> But if you're black, stand back
>
> (Dawson 4)

As Addison Gayle puts it, much of Brooks's work before 1967 was based on the assumption not only that a Black woman's selfhood was defined by the white world (Dawson 4) concurrent with interracial rejection, but that interracial scorn is based almost solely on color.

This manner of self-searching and focusing is vital to growth. Consequently, when Brooks could get past these barriers in her personal life, her poetry reflected a similar expansion of the psyche. Brooks confirms in her autobiography her personal response to growing up in America. Along with other Black Americans, she learned to appreciate the beauty of blackness and consequently rejected the negative image as symbol in her poetry (Dawson 9). Brooks credits a Fisk University Writers' Conference as the place where she learned that "Black emphasis must be not against white but for black" (Dawson 10). Here she could distinguish the difference between being racial and racist. The racial person makes no apologies; she simply loves and takes all responsibility for being who she is. The racial response to the world reveals dominance of personhood over race, color, gender, or nationality. The steps from self-indulgence to self-esteem to self-responsibility are clearly marked in the poet's personal and professional life. These steps are evident in the dialogue in "Song of Winnie," when the poet states:

> A poem doesn't do everything for you
> you are supposed to go on with your thinking
> you are supposed to enrich
> the other person's poem with your extensions,
> your uniquely personal understandings
> thus making the poem serve you.

These lines can be tied to Brooks's sense of self-responsibility and to Winnie Mandela's struggle to achieve the same.

Brooks speaks of African Americans who have perhaps taken a rest from the struggle:

> You
> don't disorder the décor
> by looking at it too hard.

But there is yet a universal struggle that extends beyond American shores to encompass people of color everywhere. Brooks holds up for examination the daily strife in South Africa. She speaks of the pain, the anguish, the loss, and the disappointments associated with the quest to "Get you back The Land." She demonstrates that self-sacrifice and deep commitment to the cause stands as a model to emulate: "They say of me / 'Hers is a large hard beauty.' " Winnie is unselfish, for she says:

> I try to be at big remove from me; I try
> to do the good thing always because it is good.

Ever present in the quest for equality are questions and the search for answers. There is a puzzlement regarding the conditions that prevent children from experiencing childhood, that constantly pit the haves against the havenots, that cause grief and pain through death and disaster yet challenge one to be a

> "Nice Young Lady—
> and reformer/revolutionary/pioneer!"

As the poet delves into the life and times of Winnie Mandela, she compares her own development with that of Mandela. The poem reflects the poet's awakening to the human condition. Thus, she comments:

> I put my Poem, which is my life,
> into your hands, where it will
> do the best I can.
>
> I am not a tight-faced Poet

If there are to be any answers to life's questions, they are to be found in revolutionaries, be they activists or poets, who are not bound or restrained by internal or external forces.

> I am wild. I am strange. I am stiff
> and loose together

The answers are inherent in the respect for life.

> I countenance never
> the killing of Other Animals in the sacrificial splendors
> The metaphor is not to be missed, not evaded.

The answers come in personal explorations of love.

> He taught me how to love and to let go
> He taught me how to taste a darling song
> and rise from little table satisfied.

The answers are present in the exhibition of grace under pressure.

> My waiting does not whimper, does not whine.

The answers produce "Today's Woman."

> Today's Woman is not a ward nor toy nor curio game,
> nor slavery in this sun-time of the monsters
> We are hurt honey but we do retrieve
> We do not squirm, we do not squeal. We square off.
> We blue print
> not merely our survival but a flowering.

The association between self-esteem and self-responsibility is artfully present in Brooks's ballad, "Song of Winnie." The undaunted truth revealed in the poem through a commentary on the life of Winnie Mandela is a treatise to "to sense and self and mending."

The final two poems in the Gottschalk volume point to a broadened awareness of humanity. Gwendolyn Brooks shows that, ethnic origin aside, Elizabeth in "Thinking of Elizabeth Steinberg" is a young person whose untimely death is not in vain. Her death, like those of the youths in "Song of Winnie," will not go unnoticed; it will sensitize others and help to prevent man's inhumanity.

The culminating poem, "Michael, Young Russia," continues this view in looking at the condition of youth and ends the volume on a hopeful note.

> Young Russia!
> You are an affectionate spirit,
> with arms stretched out to
> life and love and truth and Celebration,
> with arms stretched out to
> what is clean and kind.

The reader, however, is left with the question, "Is Gottschalk watching?!"

## NOTES

1. Gwendolyn Brooks, *Gottschalk and the Grande Tarantelle* (Chicago: The David Company, 1988).

2. Emma Waters Dawson, "Vanishing Point: The Rejected Black Woman in the Poetry of Gwendolyn Brooks," *Obsidian II* 4 (Spring 1989): 1–11.

PART THREE    *Recent Essays*

BEVERLY GUY-SHEFTALL

# The Women of Bronzeville

An obvious difference between Gwendolyn Brooks and male writers such as Richard Wright and Ralph Ellison who have used the urban environment as the setting for their works is the greater amount of attention she devotes to the experiences of females. While women are not absent from Wright's or Ellison's ghetto worlds, they remain background figures who are of secondary importance, at best, to the central actions of their novels. Like Ann Petry, Brooks focuses on the impact of the urban experience on females as well as males. Her sexual identity as well as her racial identity has molded her vision of the city. Though this aspect of her work has been generally ignored by critics, occasionally one can find comments about the value of the insights she has gained as a result of her sex.

> . . . The life of women, particularly Negro women, and the life of Negroes, particularly those who have grown up since World War I in the North, where America's big towns are, figure prominently in Miss Brooks' poetry. Moreover, it does seem true that she is a woman writing, although not in the manner of the damned mob of scribbling women who so distressed Hawthorne—nor because of any mysterious and occult woman's intuition which seems to guide her inner labors . . . Miss Brooks is a woman, and yet not one in an ignoble way. . . . There is a general way in which women do tend to know women and also a general way in which they tend to know men, largely because our culture makes it so. Miss Brooks, whether she is talking of women or men . . . constantly speaks as a woman. . . .[1]

Though one might disagree with this assessment of her as a woman writer, it is difficult to ignore her numerous portraits of

From *Sturdy Black Bridges: Visions of Black Women in Literature*, ed. Roseann P. Bell, Betty J. Parker, and Beverly Guy-Sheftall (New York: Doubleday, 1979), 157–70. Reprinted with permission.

the women who inhabit Bronzeville,[2] the setting for much of her poetry.

Like Richard Wright, she explores the tragic aspects of black ghetto life, but she also probes beneath the surface in order to illuminate those areas of the slum dweller's life which often go unnoticed and should not be seen as ugly or horrifying. Ironically, then, her poems reveal both the destructive and the nurturing aspects of the black urban environment. Brooks's paradoxical vision is perhaps best revealed in a statement which appears in the appendix of her autobiography concerning her plans for *In the Mecca*.

> . . . I wish to present a large variety of personalities against a mosaic of daily affairs, recognizing that the *grimiest* of these is likely to have a streak or two streaks of sun.
>
> In the Mecca were murders, loves, loneliness, hates, jealousies. Hope occurred, and charity, sainthood, glory, shame, despair, fear, altruism. (189–90)

A central paradox of her composite portrait of Bronzeville is the ability of its residents to transcend, if only temporarily, the sordid conditions of their lives. They are not dehumanized or paralyzed by the poverty which engulfs them. It is against this backdrop of Brooks's overall vision of Bronzeville that her images of urban women as they appear in selected poems from *The World of Gwendolyn Brooks* will be examined. Though a discussion of the urban women in *In the Mecca, Riot,* and *Family Pictures* will not be included, it would be interesting in a more comprehensive study of Brooks's women to compare the images projected in her pre-1967 poems with these later ones.

The diverse nature of Brooks's females enables her to reveal the many facets, complexities, and paradoxes of the urban black experience. They range from the death-in-life figure of a woman in "obituary for a living lady"[3] to the life-in-death figure of a woman in "the rites for Cousin Vit." The unnamed woman in the first poem (based on a person Brooks knew well)[4] is the antithesis of Cousin Vit. Though she was a "decently wild child" and as a girl was "interested in a broach and pink powder and a curl," as a young woman she would not permit sexual contact between herself and the man with whom she had fallen in love. She continued to wait by the windows in a "gay (though white) dress," and finally decided to say "yes," though by this time it was too late because he had found a woman "who dressed in red." Though red traditionally has negative connotations where women's dress is concerned, here it is being used positively to contrast the latter woman's *joie de vivre* with the lack of it in the main character; her purity and paleness of spirit (which the white dress symbolizes) cause her to be rejected. Here Brooks has taken the conventional "scarlet woman" figure usually associated with the corrupt, sinful city and transformed her into a positive, vital force. After mourning for a long time and "wishing she were dead," the woman in white turns to religion and away from the world of the flesh.

> . . . Now she will not dance
> And she thinks not the thinnest thought of any type of romance
> And I can't get her to take or touch of the best cream
> Cologne
>
> (18–19)

Cousin Vit, on the other hand, has lived an exciting, full life and even in death refuses to be confined.

> . . . it can't hold her,
> That stuff and satin aiming to enfold her . . .
> Even now, surmise,
> She rises in the sunshine. There she goes,
> Back to the bars she knew and the repose
> In love-rooms and the things in people's eyes.
> Too vital and too squeaking.
>
> (109)

She has tasted much of life's pleasures and sorrows. Disappointments have not caused her to withdraw from life and miss out on its more pleasant aspects.

> Even now she does the snake-hips with a hiss,
> Slops the bad wine across her shantung, talks
> Of pregnancy, guitars and bridgework, walks
> In parks or alleys, comes haply on the verge
> Of happiness.
>
> (109)

She has taken chances in order to find joy. Ironically, she seems more alive in death than the living woman in the previous poem. One critic has commented on her and other women in Brooks's poems who are to be admired for attempting to get the most out of their basically narrow and drab lives.

Whatever her shortcomings, Cousin Vit has asserted her pagan self without asking questions or whining. It may be that she, Sadie, and others like them, girls who "scraped life / with a fine-tooth comb," girls who seize their love in hallways and alleys and other unconventional places—it may be that these carefree souls have a deeper understanding of the modern scene than any of their sedate sisters and friends. Perhaps they are the only ones who do understand.[5]

"Sadie and Maud" (alluded to in the previous quote) deals with two sisters whose contrasting approaches to life are somewhat analogous to the women discussed in the two previous poems. Sadie, like Cousin Vit, has gotten out of life all it has to offer, despite her limited resources.

> Sadie scraped life
> With a fine-tooth comb.
>
> She didn't leave a tangle in.
> Her comb found every strand.
> Sadie was one of the livingest chits
> In all the land.
>
> (16)

Though she bore two illegitimate daughters and shamed her family, she has left her offspring a rich heritage—her fine-tooth comb—so that they will presumably also squeeze as much joy out of life as possible. She does not have wealth to leave them but she leaves them something perhaps equally valuable. Maud, on the other hand, who followed the more conventional path and went to college, is, at the end of the poem, alone and like a "thin brown mouse." Like the unnamed woman in "obituary for a living lady," she has followed society's rules, but her life has lacked the vitality and fullness which makes one's existence meaningful.

Brooks also explores the impact of poverty on the lives of her women characters. "The mother" deals with a poor woman who has had a number of abortions and who experiences anxiety and anguish as a result of these decisions. In the appendix of her autobiography Brooks refers to her as "hardly your crowned and praised and customary Mother; but a Mother not unfamiliar, who decides that *she* rather than her World, will kill her children."[6] Accepting full responsibility for her "crime," she nevertheless remains ambivalent about her actions and exactly what she has done. Though she realizes that she has shielded her unborn babies from the harsh realities of the life they were sure to lead, she also admits having stolen from them whatever joys they might have been able to experience. She wonders if she had that right.

> . . . if I sinned, if I seized
> Your luck
> And your lives from your unfinished reach,
> If I stole your births and your names,
> Your straight baby tears and your games,
> Your stilted or lovely loves, your tumults, your marriages, aches,
>     and your deaths,
> If I poisoned the beginnings of your breaths,
> Believe that even in my deliberateness I was not deliberate.
>
> (5)

Throughout the poem, one has the feeling that if circumstances had been different, if she had been able to provide adequately for them, they would have been allowed to live. Ironically, it was her deep concern for them as well as her own situation, which caused her to have the abortions.

> Believe me, I loved you all
> Believe me, I knew you, though faintly, and I loved, I loved you
> All.
>
> (6)

She knew perfectly well what their fate would have been.

> You will never neglect or beat
> Them, or silence or buy with a sweet.
> You will never wind up the sucking-thumb
> Or scuttle off ghosts that come.
> You will never leave them, controlling your luscious sigh,
> Return for a snack of them, with gobbling mother-eye.
>
> (5)

Though George Kent criticizes the poem for failing "to convey the attitude of the author toward her subject—the several abortions of the mother,"[7] there is no question in my mind nor probably in the minds of women who have had abortions for similar or even other reasons where Brooks's sympathies lie.

"When Mrs. Martin's Booker T." contains a contrasting portrait of a mother and provides another view of the black urban resident. The code of behavior to which she adheres is more conventional. Mrs. Martin is disgraced by her son Booker T., who "ruins" Rosa Brown when he impregnates her before marriage. She is embarrassed to the point that she cannot face her community, so she moves to the other side of town and renounces her son. The intensity of her feelings is revealed in the simile "He wrung my heart like a chicken neck." The only cure for her damaged pride would be for her son to marry Rosa— "But tell me if'n he take that gal / And get her decent wed." Her strong sense of honor and decency will not permit her to condone behavior which reflects badly on the family. "Good" people marry when babies are on the way. It may also be that Mrs. Martin insists on marriage because she does not want Rosa and her illegitimate child to experience the hardships which usually befall those in their situation.

We also get glimpses into the lives of female ghetto dwellers in other poems from *A Street in Bronzeville* and *The Bean Eaters*. Though their world is drab and ordinary, and sometimes even fraught with danger, they go about their daily lives accepting their plight and somehow managing to survive. In "the battle" the persona (probably Hattie Scott, since this poem belongs to that series) would like to believe that she would have behaved differently from Moe Belle Jackson, who, after being beaten by her husband the night before because of a domestic quarrel, probably arose the next morning and continued with business as usual.

> I like to think
> Of how I'd of took a knife
> And slashed all of the quickenin'
> Out of his lowly life.
>
> But if I know Moe Belle,
> Most like, she shed a tear,
> And this mornin' it was probably,
> "More grits, dear?"
>
> (39)

In "when I die" (from the same series) there is a similar acceptance of the realities of life, no matter how unpleasant. An unnamed female, again presumably Hattie, imagines that when she dies, there will be no fanfare but simply "one lone little short man / Dressed all shabbily." Her husband or boyfriend will bring his cheap flowers—"He'll have his buck-a-dozen"—but immediately after the funeral he'll shed his mourning clothes and wipe away his tears. She also has no illusions about what will happen next—"And the girls, they will be waitin' / there's nothin' more to say." She does not romanticize him or their relationship. In "the murder"[8] a mother must face the tragic death of her barely one-year-old son which was caused by his brother, who "with a grin / Burned him up for fun." She may also have to live with a guilty conscience for the rest of her life because it might not have happened had she been there.

> No doubt, poor Percy looked around
> And wondered at the heat,
> Was worried, wanted Mother,
> Who gossiped down the street.
>
> (22)

There is no explanation for Brucie's behavior, which is even more terrifying.

> No doubt, poor shrieking Percy died
> Loving Brucie still,
> Who could, with clean and open eye,
> Thoughtfully kill.
>
> (22)

Despite their frustrations and limitations, however, happiness does penetrate the lives of the Bronzeville women, though it has to be found in small things. The woman in "patent leather" is thrilled at having a man whose hair is so slick, black, and straight that it looks like patent leather. Though the other men "don't think he's such / A much" because of his shrill voice and "pitiful" muscles (unmasculine traits as far as they are concerned), she "strokes the patent-leather hair / That makes him man enough for her" (p. 13). Similarly, the woman in "when you have forgotten Sunday: the love story" experiences extreme pleasure on Sundays when she is able to stay in bed late with her mate and forget about the cares of the week. She remembers ordinary matters such as how he reacted to interruptions during their love-making sessions, how long they stayed in bed, and what they finally had for dinner. Though their apartment is tiny and unappealing and they don't eat exotic meals, they are still able to enjoy each other on this one day of the week when their usual problems don't intrude.

> . . . we finally went in to Sunday dinner,
> That is to say, went across the front room
> floor to the ink-spotted table in
> the southwest corner
> To Sunday dinner, which was always chicken
> and noodles
> Or chicken and rice
> And salad and rye bread and tea
> And chocolate chip cookies.
>
> (20)

Though this seems to be all she has to look forward to, she's happy.

> Or me sitting on the front-room radiator in
> the limping afternoon
> Looking off down the long street
> To nowhere,
> Hugged by my plain old wrapper of no-expectation
> And nothing-I-have-to-do and I'm-happy-why?
> And if-Monday-never-had-to-come—
>
> (20)

Although life in Bronzeville is seldom without frustrations, its inhabitants do experience moments, however temporary, when they are glad to be alive.

Other urban poems reveal the plight of the dark-skinned or kinky-haired girl because of the color prejudice within the black community. Since this problem (discussed in detail in an article mentioned below) is shared by black women no matter where they live, it will not be dealt with in detail here, though a discussion of Brooks's images of women generally would include a thorough analysis of such poems as "the ballad of chocolate Mabbie," "Ballad of Pearl May Lee," "Jessie Mitchell's Mother," and selected poems from *Annie Allen*. Beauty parlors are a crucial part of the Bronzeville world as they are in other black environments, and a critic explains their significance.

> The worship of "good" hair naturally suggests the importance of beauty parlors in Bronzeville. They tend to become miracle-working shrines to which the dark girl goes in search of beauty. . . . They know that it is tough to be "cut from chocolate" and to have "boisterous hair" in a land where "white is right." To be black is to be rejected. . . .[9]

"At the hairdresser's" contains a portrait of a black girl who is almost ecstatic over the passing from vogue of long hair. Her short hair, which Madam Walker's and Poro Grower could not help, is no longer a problem now that the "upsweep" is in style. She no longer has to feel inferior to the girls with long hair.

> Gimme an upsweep, Minnie,
> With humpteen baby curls.
> 'Bout time I got some glamour.
> I'll show them girls.
>
> (37)

Brooks's urban world is also inhabited by older women who have a different kind of struggle. The persona in "A Sunset of the City" can be seen as a victim of a modern, urbanized environment, not necessarily Bronzeville, where close family ties have broken. She is resentful as she approaches middle age because of the way she is now treated by her children, husband, and lovers.

> Already I'm no longer looked at with lechery or love,
> My daughters and sons have put me away with
>         marbles and dolls,
> Are gone from the house.
> My husband and lovers are pleasant or somewhat polite
> And night is night.
>
> (337)

"Night is night" rather than a time for fun and adventure as it was when she was younger. Not only is it "summer-gone" where the seasons are concerned, but she is also approaching the winter of her own life. She is like the flowers and grass which are personified.

The sweet flowers in drying and dying down,
The grasses forgetting their blaze and consenting to brown.

(337)

She sees herself as a hopeless woman whose needs are no longer
satisfied in her cold, empty house.

> There is no warm house
> That is filled with my need.
>
> I am cold in this cold house this house
> Whose washed echoes are tremulous down lost halls.

(338)

Like old furniture, she is "dusty," and now "hurries through her
prayers," since they seem useless. She contemplates suicide as an
alternative to a numb existence where she would do nothing, feel
nothing, and desire nothing. This death-in-life quality has been
seen before in one of Brooks's women. The poem ends on a
pessimistic note with her concluding that Fate has played a cruel
joke on her. One critic sees this poem as "another indication of
the spiritual bankruptcy of our times," of "the meaninglessness
of modern living" and "our loss of faith."[10] While the poem can
be seen as having a universal theme, its central purpose should
not be overlooked—the revelation of the inner turmoil of a
woman as she faces a critical point in her life. The nature of the
frustration she feels is in many ways different from what a man
growing old would experience, yet similar.

Often Brooks's older women are seen in their relationships
with their husbands, though these portraits tend to be less
sharply focused then the ones which include a female figure only.
In "the old marrieds" she explores, among other things, the
negative impact of cramped ghetto quarters on a couple's rela-
tionship. Although the possibilities for romantic love have been
perfect on this day, they are unable to communicate with each
other because of circumstances beyond their control.

> And he had seen the lovers in the little side-streets.
> And she had heard the morning stories clogged with sweets.
> It was a quite a time for loving. It was midnight. It was May.
> But in the crowding darkness not a word did they say.

(3)

One would surmise that though it is dark, they still do not have the privacy desired for intimate contact. So, they remain silent. One might also conclude that the passage of time has caused their relationship to deteriorate to the point where it is impossible to express love.

In "The Bean Eaters," which also deals with an older married couple, Brooks explores the effect of poverty on their lives. They, like others in Bronzeville, attempt to make the most of their economic deprivation.

> They eat beans mostly, this old yellow pair.
> Dinner is a casual affair.
> Plain chipware on a plain and creaking wood,
> Tin flatware.
>
> (314)

Though they go about their daily lives in an almost mechanical manner, they refuse to give up.

> Two who are Mostly Good.
> Two who have lived their day,
> But keep on putting on their clothes
> And putting things away.
>
> (314)

Their memories, some of which are unpleasant, keep their lives from being totally meaningless.

> Remembering, with twinklings and twinges,
> As they lean over the beans in their rented back room that is full of
>     beads and receipts and dolls and cloths,
>     tobacco crumbs, vases and fringes.
>
> (314)

Though the couples in these two poems do have companionship, life seems to be just something to be endured, though the latter poem gives a more positive portrayal of the mates having endured together.

Without the perspective of the black woman writer, certain aspects of life in the urban black ghetto would possibly remain hidden. Brooks explores not only what it is like to be poor and black and male but also what it is like to be poor and black and female. She treats the relationships between males and females and the joys and frustrations which women experience in a way that is different from her male counterparts. The female images she creates reflect her personal experiences with black women, her observations of them in the community, and her general knowledge of their history in this country. These images are as varied as the human types present in any community.

Her poems present a more realistic view of the diversity and complexity of black women than the stereotypes (matriarch, whore, bitch, for example) which have persisted in other literary works by black and white artists alike. The lack of uniformity in her portraits of black women would contradict the notion that there is a monolithic black woman. There are females in her poems who commit adultery ("the vacant lot") and are sexually inhibited ("Obituary for a living lady"); they are aggressive ("Mrs. Martin's Booker T.") and passive (Maud of "Sadie and Maud"); they are extraordinary (Madam Walker of "Southeast Corner") and ordinary ("Mrs. Small"); they are exploited (unnamed women in "The Sundays of Satin-Legs Smith") and protected (young girl in "a song in the front yard"). They dream in the midst of adversity ("Callie Ford" and "hunch-back girl: she thinks of heaven") and they wallow in despair ("A Sunset of the City"). Though they share a common environment and heritage, they are still presented as individuals with different priorities and values, different levels of tolerance for misery, and different ways of dealing with problems. The major portion of Gwendolyn Brooks's work does indeed reflect, among other things, an intense awareness of our identity as black women and an unusual insight into the problems we face.

NOTES

1. Blyden Jackson and Louis D. Rubin, *Black Poetry in America: Two Essays in Historical Interpretation* (Baton Rouge: Louisiana State University Press, 1974), p. 82.

2. In a 1967 interview with Illinois historian Paul Angle, which appears in Brooks's autobiography, *Report from Part One* (Detroit: Broadside Press, 1972), pp. 160–61, she says that Bronzeville was not her own title but was "invented" many years ago by the Chicago *Defender,* a black newspaper, to refer to the black community.

3. *The World of Gwendolyn Brooks* (New York: Harper and Row, 1971), p. 18. Further references to individual poems are from this edition.

4. Gwendolyn Brooks, *Report from Part One,* p. 154.

5. Arthur P. Davis, "Gwendolyn Brooks: Poet of the Unheroic," *CLA Journal* 7 (December 1963): 118.

6. Brooks, *Report from Part One,* p. 184.

7. George Kent, "The Poetry of Gwendolyn Brooks," Part II, *Black World,* October 1971, p. 38.

8. Brooks says in *Report from Part One* that this poem was also based on a real-life situation except that the mother was really working instead of gossiping down the street. She adds, "I guess I did her an injustice there" (p. 154).

9. Arthur Davis, "The Black-and-Tan Motif in the Poetry of Gwendolyn Brooks," *CLA Journal* 6 (December 1962): 95–97.

10. Davis, "Gwendolyn Brooks: Poet of the Unheroic," p. 117.

JOYCE ANN JOYCE

# The Poetry of Gwendolyn Brooks:
# An Afrocentric Exploration

In my contribution to *Say That the River Turns: The Impact of Gwendolyn Brooks,* I introduced an idea that I would like to pursue further here. In this seventieth-birthday tribute to Brooks, I maintain,

> Having bloomed under the light of Robert Hillyer's *First Principles of Verse,* Brooks brought to modern American poetry her own peculiar sensibility which manifests at once the embodiments of both Wallace Stevens's blue guitar and the African griot's drum. Even though they have the visual and stylistic attributes of a Euro-American poetic tradition, her earlier ballads, free verse poems, and the sonnets reveal the same feelings of racial integrity and record the same malaises of racism as those poems published after 1967 when Brooks's blackness confronted her "with a shrill spelling of itself."[1]

Embedded in the above idea is the seed for detaching Gwendolyn Brooks's poetry from the branches of the Euro-American poetic tradition and planting it at the root of an Afrocentric one.

Most, if not all, literary analyses of Brooks's craft compare her to European and American poetic masters. For example, George Kent in his *A Life of Gwendolyn Brooks* states that her early poetry particularly reflects the presence of William Wordsworth, William Cullen Bryant, Henry Wadsworth Longfellow, and John Keats. He also finds strains of Lord Bryon, Sara Teasdale, and Emily Dickinson.[2] And in his essay " 'Define . . . the Whirlwind': Gwendolyn Brooks's Epic Sign for a Generation," Ron Baxter Miller argues that her compressed style resembles that of Pound, Eliot, and Thomas Gray.[3] While it is undeniably true that Brooks, as she makes clear in her autobiography,

---

From *Warriors, Conjurers, and Priests: Defining African-Centered Literary Criticism* (Chicago: Third World Press, 1994). By permission of the author.

*Report from Part One*, read voraciously the works of European and American craftsmen and adopted their poetic techniques, to continue to analyze her craft using Eurocentric hermeneutical tools illuminates both a stasis in the criticism of Brooks's poetry and a denial of the Afrocentric methodologies that emerged in the criticism of Langston Hughes and Sterling Brown, in the Negritude movement, and in the ideas of African American social scientists and philosophers since the 1960s. Despite the fact that many secondary schools in cities across the United States are embroiled in battles over the inclusion of Afrocentric courses in their curriculum, and despite the fact that this battle is so threatening to the Eurocentric hegemony that it appears on the pages of the *New York Times* and *Newsweek,* African American literary scholars are still held hostage to literary analyses firmly rooted in a Eurocentric literary tradition.

Yet, in the analysis of even the works of an African American writer like Gwendolyn Brooks, whose works exemplify a strong affinity with a Eurocentric literary tradition, a severe contradiction exists between the application of Eurocentric literary tools and Gwendolyn Brooks's artistic sensibility. In her interview with Haki Madhubuti [Don L. Lee] in the premiere issue of *Words Work,* she restates her position that a racial element has always been present in her poetry and that that element underwent a change. She says,

> . . . our people have been looked upon as curios, something to look at and be amazed by—something other than ordinarily human. And of course I can't accept that. I happen to know myself and I know that inside myself, I am not a curio. I am perfectly human and certainly capable of at least as much warmth as any white that was ever created. I've fought that idea, a little less (in the late '60s and thereon) than formerly because I used to feel it was my DUTY to change everybody's ideas about Blacks! Now I don't feel that that is my duty. It is my duty to express what I feel, to say certain things to Blacks that others are not going to say to them, and who want to read the results of this intense commitment and involvement are perfectly welcome, whatever their orientation. But I don't sit down now and write, hoping that I can change the hearts of white people.[4]

Although traditional Euro-American aesthetic tools are not equipped to handle Brooks's aesthetic requirement of "intense commitment" and "involvement," these criteria lie at the heart of ideas of Afrocentric philosophers and scholars such as Maulana Karenga, Fred Hord, and Molefi Asante. These scholars implicitly provide the answers as to why we need to reclaim Gwendolyn Brooks and as to how we can foreground her art at the center of an Afrocentric literary tradition. In his *Reconstructing Memory: Black Literary Criticism,* Fred Hord discusses the need for African American literary scholars to address the needs of their students who are characterized by materialistic values and identity ambivalence. He says, "the vast majority of more than five hundred students he has taught at Howard University seem confused—though concerned—about who they are and the propriety of an extreme individualistic/materialistic value system. What is more, they do not appear to understand the implications of identity ambivalence, much less the limited practicability and unlimited danger of their projected attempts to operationalize that value system."[5] Hord's explanation of the role literature can play in liberating Black students echoes Gwendolyn Brooks's criteria of "intense commitment" and "involvement": "Cognizant that all education is political, the increasingly insistent question has become not how one can assume that teaching will insure strong black student consciousness—or even have a predictable impact upon that consciousness—but rather how can it best relate to that consciousness by relating to their concerns. The writer's opinion is that literature can be useful in helping black students to clarify their relationship to the past and thus in making them informed mediators of present issues of racial pride and values."[6]

Thus it is the scholar/teacher's responsibility to serve as mediator between the creative writer and the student. So far a serious gap exists between the political involvement and commitment Brooks aims at in her poetry and the literary analyses of that poetry. Rather than following the hermeneutical lead of the hegemony, African American literary scholars must come to understand the urgency of Maulana Karenga's sixth goal of Black Studies, which he sees as the need for the "creation of a body of conscious, capable and committed Black intellectuals who self-consciously chose to use their knowledge and skills in the service of the Black community and by consequence and extension, in the interest of a new and better society and world."[7] Perhaps, the first step in the African American scholar's contribution to servicing the Black community and developing a liberating worldview is that of using our own historians, social scientists, and philosophers as the touchstone and foundation for critical analyses.

It is liberating for the African American student and scholar/ teacher alike to see ourselves and our art in new ways, to critique African American literature from the perspectives of Afrocentric thinkers rather than Eurocentric ones. In his latest book *Kemet, Afrocentricity and Knowledge,* Molefi Asante lists Kariamu Welsh-Asante's aesthetic characteristics of African dance: polyrhythm, polycentrism, dimensional, repetition, curvilinear, epic memory, and wholism.[8] Though Welsh-Asante applies her aesthetic criteria basically to African dance, these same attributes work equally as well when applied to African American literature, especially poetry, which can be defined as the dance of language. Looked at from the perspective of the components of this African aesthetic, Gwendolyn Brooks's poetry emerges as Afrocentric in its persistent placement of Blacks as subjects rather than as objects, in its emphasis on communal human values, and in its emphasis on the integrity of form.

Although many of Brooks's poems satisfy simultaneously several of Welsh-Asante's aesthetic senses, some poems do tend to have strong characteristics that make them more suitable for one category than another. However, rather than being sacrosanct, the following categorization is instead an exploration. Brooks's "The Mother," "When You Have Forgotten Sunday: The Love Story," "Ballad of Pearl May Lee," "To Those of My Sisters Who Kept Their Naturals," "Horses Graze," "Infirm," and "The Near-Johannesburg Boy" all satisfy Asante's criteria for polyrhythm, defined as "the simultaneous occurrence of several major rhythms."[9] Because of its high rhythmical quality and because this rhythm directly parallels the message in the poem, "Infirm" emerges as one of Brooks's strongest manifestations of polyrhythm. This sixteen-line, eighty-syllable poem levels all humanity as the first two lines tells us "Everybody here is infirm." Five lines in the poem contain only three syllables; five lines have six syllables; the eighth line and last line have four syllables; line thirteen has seven syllables; line fourteen has eight syllables. The ninth line which is halfway through the poem is the longest line with ten syllables. For this line marks the turning point in the poem where the poet avers that we are all beautiful in our imperfections, in our infirmities. Finally, the effect of the rhythm corresponds to the jocular, agile mood of the poem, which parallels the poet's message, but which contrasts with our typical notions of infirmities.

Although Brooks's oral presentation of all her poetry is unique and quite difficult to imitate, her reading of "Infirm" and "The Life of Lincoln West" emerge as particular examples of what Welsh-Asante refers to as polycentricism, "the presence of several colors in a painting or several movements on a dancer's body occurring in the context of a presentation of art."[10] Brooks's affected hoarse voice and the manner in which she extends the words *in firm* and *beau ti ful* give the poem "Infirm" a contrapuntal effect achieved in painting by the mixture of colors and in dance by the dancer's body. She begins her reading of "The Life of Lincoln West" by using her voice to extend the first word *ug li est* beyond the usual time range of its three syllables. Similarly, the emphasis she places on the words *Black, ugly,* and *odd* in describing Lincoln has the same effect as the contrasting movements of a dancer's body. For the way in which she uses her voice forces the listener to denounce society's condemnation of Lincoln's distinctively Black features and simultaneously confront his or her role in the propagation of that condemnation.

In her autobiography *Report from Part One,* Brooks explains that it was her mother who taught her in her preschool years the value of reading with expression. At the ages of four and five, Brooks, coached by her mother, "spent much time rehearsing . . . in the delivery of recitations for various programs."[11] Not only did Brooks quite early in her life learn to master the art of recitation, she also, according to George Kent in his *A Life of Gwendolyn Brooks,* at age fourteen had a sense of form and engaged in self-criticism.[12] Brooks's mastery of that sense of form and the discipline of self-criticism is evident in the typography of her poetry. Typography in poetry corresponds to Welsh-Asante's definition of the dimensional in African dance. The dimensional, according to Welsh-Asante, "is spatial relationships and shows depth and energy, the awareness of vital force."[13] While Brooks's typographical virtuosity deserves an in-depth study, two poems that are immediately and strikingly different in appearance, "We Real Cool" and "The Wall," demonstrate her ability to use the arrangement of the words on the page to illuminate her message. Whereas the spatial relationships of the words in "We Real Cool" satirize the jocund mood of the young pool players wasting their lives, the typography of "The Wall" formally celebrates the seriousness of the occasion of the poem: the dedication of the Wall of Respect, a mural with images of Black leading figures such as W. E. B. DuBois, Thelonius Monk, Wilt Chamberlain, Dr. Martin Luther King, Jr., and Gwendolyn Brooks herself.

As challenging as the diverse typography of Brooks's ballads, sonnets, the altered rime royal of "The Anniad," and her free verse forms is her mastery of what Welsh-Asante defines as the curvilinear, which "means that the lines are curved in the art, dance, music, or poetry—this is normally called indirection in the spoken or written forms."[14] Indirection, the ability to force the reader to see familiar words in a new context and to deduce the poet's meaning from analogy, imagery, symbolism, short lines contrasting with long ones, comparisons and contrasts in descriptions, characterizes most, if not all, of Brooks's poetry from *A Street in Bronzeville* (1945) to her most recent chapbooks entitled *Gottschalk and the Grande Tarantelle* and *Winnie,* both published in 1988.

Though much has been made of the change in Brooks's consciousness that occurred in 1967 when she met and began to work with the Blackstone Rangers, a young gang in Chicago, full of creative talent, her use of Black subjects and concern for Black people permeate her entire canon as much as her mastery of indirection. Discussing the way in which Brooks incorporates Black subjects into her poetry before 1967, George Kent explains that some of her poems "evoke identification of poetic style with Blackness, often by a single word or phrase or through voice tones and familiar images which would be seen as involving Blacks."[15]

Brooks's continuous use of Black subjects and her emphasis on Blacks as her audience parallel Welsh-Asante's description of repetition and epic memory in African dance. Welsh-Asante defines repetition as "the recurring theme in a presentation of art. The recurrence is not necessarily an exact one but the theme or concept is presented as central to the work of art"[16] and epic memory "carries with it the idea that the art contains the historic memory that allows the artist and audience to participate in the same celebration or pathos."[17] Repetition and epic memory conjoin in Brooks's poetry. While poems throughout her canon, such as "Negro Hero," "The Ballad of Chocolate Mabbie," "Of DeWitt Williams on his way to Lincoln Cemetery," "At the Hairdresser's," "Queen of the Blues," "A Black Wedding Song," "A Bronzeville Mother Loiters in Mississippi. Meanwhile, a Mississippi Mother Burns Bacon," "The Lover's of the Poor," "The Ballad of Rudolph Reed," "Bronzeville Woman in a Red Hat," "Winnie," and "Gottschalk and the Grande Tarantelle," and many others, especially those set in the Black community of Bronzeville, demonstrate how the recurrent or repetitive themes of Black alienation, white racism, exploitation, intraracial conflicts make up Gwendolyn Brooks's historic memory and bond her relationship to a Black audience.

In her interview with George Stavros, which she includes in *Report from Part One,* Brooks, addressing her need to connect with her audience, says, "I don't want to stop a concern with words doing good jobs, which has always been a concern of mine, but I want to write poems that will be meaningful to those people I described a while ago [Black people], things that will touch them."[18] Yet, having understood the importance of mastering form since age fourteen, Brooks has never compromised the complexity of her craft. Her virtuosic skill at integrating form and content suggests Welsh-Asante's final characterization of African dance—wholism, which she defines as "the unity of the collective parts of the art work despite the various unique aspects of the art."[19]

And like a true African griot, Brooks herself in *Report from Part One* implicitly makes the connection between African dance and the art of writing poetry. She says, "So much is involved in the writing of poetry—and sometimes, although I don't like suggesting it is a magic process, it seems you really do have to go into a *bit* of trance, self-cast trance, because 'brainwork' seems unable to do it all, to do the whole job. The self-cast trance is possible when you are *importantly* excited about an idea, or surmise, or emotion."[20]

NOTES

1. Joyce Ann Joyce, "Gwendolyn Brooks: Jean Toomer's November Cotton Flower," *Say That the River Turns,* ed. Haki Madhubuti. (Chicago: Third World Press, 1987), p. 82.

2. George Kent. *A Life of Gwendolyn Brooks* (Lexington: University Press of Kentucky, 1990), p. 7.

3. R. Baxter Miller, " 'Define . . . the Whirlwind': Gwendolyn Brooks's Epic Sign for a Generation," *Black American Poets Between Worlds, 1940–1960,* ed. R. Baxter Miller (Knoxville: University of Tennessee Press, 1986), p. 164.

4. Haki Madhubuti, "Gwendolyn Brooks." *Black Books Bulletin: Words Work* 1, no. 1 (July/August 1991): 3–4.

5. Fred Hord, *Reconstructing Memory: Black Literary Criticism* (Chicago: Third World Press, 1991), pp. iii–iv.

6. Hord, p. v.

7. Maulana Karenga, *Introduction to Black Studies* (Los Angeles: University of Sankore Press, 1982), p. 372.

8. Molefi Asante, *Kemet, Afrocentricity, and Knowledge* (Trenton, N.J.: Africa World, 1990), p. 11.

9. Asante, p. 11.

10. Asante, p. 11.

11. Gwendolyn Brooks, *Report from Part One* (Detroit: Broadside Press, 1972), p. 49.

12. Kent, p. 15.

13. Kariamu Welsh-Asante, "Commonalities in African Dance: An Aesthetic Foundation for African Dance," in *African Culture: The Rhythms of Unity,* ed. Molefi Asante and Kariamu Welsh-Asante (Westport: Greenwood Press, 1985), p. 11.

14. Welsh-Asante, pp. 11–12.

15. George Kent, "Aesthetic Values in the Poetry of Gwendolyn Brooks," in *Black American Literature and Humanism,* ed. R. Baxter Miller (Lexington: University Press of Kentucky, 1981), p. 82.

16. Welsh-Asante, p. 11.

17. Welsh-Asante, p. 12.

18. Brooks, *Report from Part One,* p. 152.

19. Welsh-Asante, p. 12.

20. Brooks, *Report from Part One,* p. 183.

HENRY TAYLOR

# Gwendolyn Brooks:
# An Essential Sanity

Gwendolyn Brooks's emergence as an important poet has been
less schematic, but not less impressive, than commentary upon it
has suggested. It is difficult to isolate the poems themselves from
the variety of reactions to them; these have been governed as
much by prevailing or individual attitudes toward issues of race,
class, and gender, as by serious attempts at dispassionate exami-
nation and evaluation. Furthermore, Brooks's activities in behalf
of younger writers have demonstrated her generosity and large-
ness of spirit, and wide recognition of these qualities has led
some critics away from the controlled but genuine anger in
many of the poems. Brooks has contributed to this process; in
interviews and in her autobiographical *Report from Part One*
(1972), she speaks engagingly and with apparent authority about
her own work, and many of her judgments have become part of
the majority view of her career. Nevertheless, it is worthwhile to
consider whether there might be more unity in the body of her
work than conventional divisions of her career suggest.

Brooks herself, as William H. Hansell has noted, indicated the
divisions when, "in a 1976 interview at the University of
Wisconsin-La Crosse, [she] said that her work falls into three
periods that correspond to 'changes' in her perspective." Hansell's
note: "Works of the first period are *A Street in Bronzeville* (1945),
*Annie Allen* (1949), and *The Bean Eaters* (1960). The second period
is represented by the "New Poems" section of *Selected Poems*
(1963) and by two uncollected poems, "The Sight of the Horizon"
(1963) and "In the Time of Detachment, in the Time of Cold"
(1965). The third phase of her development is marked by her most
recent collections: *In the Mecca* (1969) [1968], *Riot* (1969), *Family
Pictures* (1970), and *Beckonings* (1975)."[1]

This essay, first published in *Kenyon Review*—N. S., 8, no. 4 (Fall 1991), copy-
right © 1991 by Kenyon College, is reprinted by permission of Louisiana State
University Press from *Compulsory Figures: Essays on Recent American Poets* by
Henry Taylor. Copyright © 1992 by Louisiana State University Press.

Whether a writer's development involves improvement is highly questionable, but writers often think they are improving because they are usually more interested in work in progress than they are in work long since completed. Since the mid-1960s, Brooks has revealed these attitudes in numerous comments on her awakening to the situation of the Black writer in America. On the other hand, when she ended her association with Harper and Row, and began to place her work with Black publishers, she retained the rights in her early work, and reprinted the bulk of it in a collected volume entitled *Blacks*.[2] The stark inclusiveness of that one-word title suggests that Brooks perceives unity as well as variety in the range of her concerns and voices.

*Report from Part One* and, more recently, the late George Kent's *A Life of Gwendolyn Brooks*[3] provide generous insight into the origins of Brooks's art. Her own work provides a livelier evocation of her early years than Kent manages in his first two chapters, but he has made a thorough examination of the young girl's notebooks, which she kept industriously. The child appears to have taken seriously her mother's prediction that she would grow up to be the "lady Paul Laurence Dunbar." Kent finds that she was a victim of an intraracial prejudice which put very dark girls at a social disadvantage among Black people of her age. (This theme recurs in Brooks's poetry through *In the Mecca*.) The energy which might have gone into a more active social life was instead poured into poems and stories which show promise more in their profusion than in their accomplishment.

Though she had been publishing poems in the *Chicago Defender* since her high school days, she was twenty-eight when *A Street in Bronzeville* (poems, 1945) appeared. Concerning what was "new" about it, Kent writes:

> The poet had rejected the exotic vein of the Harlem Renaissance—the celebration of unique racial values, such as defiance of social proscription through emphasis upon joy and soul. A few poems in *A Street* work close to this vein, allowing the reader the enjoyment of the old colorful images, but use one device or another to bring them to the court of critical intelligence. Thus "patent leather" and other poems devalue the "hipness" that the Harlem Renaissance would have celebrated.[4]

As have all American poets, Brooks inherited the old problem of language, which in the nineteenth century divided poets into rebels and loyalists—those who knew that the central problem was to establish independence in the language of the colonizing country, and those who were content with the poetic tradition of the colonizers. This dilemma is exponentially more difficult for a Black woman; a term like "the lady Paul laurence Dunbar" hardly needs comment on the forms of oppression it implies and, implicitly, accepts.

Still, Brooks had applied herself assiduously to the absorption of a largely white male tradition, in the apparent belief that all great poetry in English had something of value to teach her. *A Street in Bronzeville* introduced a poet of more technical accomplishment than was usual even in the mid-1940s. Forty-five years later, the variety of forms and tones in the collection remains impressive; Donne, Robinson, Frost, Dickinson, and even Ogden Nash seem to have left occasional marks, as well as Hughes and the blues.

But what strikes most forcibly now is the sophistication, and the Dickinsonian way in which sophistication sometimes becomes a shield, from behind which almost invisible darts fly often and accurately. Throughout Brooks's poetry, delicate satire regularly breaks through a surface which is pretending in some way to be well behaved.

In twelve lines, for example, "The Vacant Lot" provides a richly populated scene, in tones modulating from apparent nostalgia and regret through sarcasm to controlled, satiric flatness:

> Mrs. Coley's three-flat brick
> Isn't here any more.
> All done with seeing her fat little form
> Burst out of the basement door;
> And with seeing her African son-in-law
> (Rightful heir to the throne)
> With his great white strong cold squares of teeth
> And his little eyes of stone;
> And with seeing the squat fat daughter
> Letting in the men
> When majesty has gone for the day—
> And letting them out again.

(41)

Throughout *A Street,* individual poems have lowercase titles when they are grouped under a larger heading. Despite this consistency, however, the device occasionally creates a local effect; here the suggested insignificance of the lot is emphasized by an immediate and energetic portrayal of what is not there. Among the departures is the mysterious African son-in-law, who briefly dominates the poem, his teeth packing the seventh line with stressed monosyllables, but whose "majesty," by the end of the poem, is cruelly diminished.

The gulf between imagined majesty and hard reality is a frequent theme in *A Street*. Its most ambitious treatment is "The Sundays of Satin-Legs Smith," a narrative of just over 150 lines in which satire is deepened by compassion. The ironic contrasts begin with the title; the protagonist's name yokes the exotic and the ordinary. The polysyllabic opening introduces a narrator whose self-consciously elegant language is mock-heroic:

> Inamoratas, with an approbation,
> Bestowed his title. Blessed his inclination.
>
> He wakes, unwinds, elaborately: a cat
> Tawny, reluctant, royal. He is fat
> And fine this morning. Definite. Reimbursed.
>
> (42)

As Satin-Legs commences his morning ablutions, the speaker becomes an ironically patient lecturer, addressing a "you" who is presumed innocent of the life being unfolded here, and who may therefore be taken as white. In the following excerpt, the sentence "Maybe so" ends a passage of fourteen lines, concerning the appropriateness of Satin-Legs's choice of scents and oils, which both recalls and quietly subverts the sonnet tradition:

> . . . might his happiest
> Alternative (you muse) be, after all,
> A bit of gentle garden in the best
> Of taste and straight tradition? Maybe so.
> But you forget, or did you ever know,
> His heritage of cabbage and pigtails,
> Old intimacy with alleys, garbage pails,
> Down in the deep (but always beautiful) South
> Where roses blush their blithest (it is said)
> And sweet magnolias put Chanel to shame.
>
> (42–43)

Satin-Legs has only an artificial flower, made of feathers, for his lapel; in the first of two brief asides, the speaker says, "Ah, there is little hope." Satin-Legs will have "his lotion, lavender and oil."

> Unless you care to set the world a-boil
> And do a lot of equalizing things,
> Remove a little ermine, say, from kings,
> Shake hands with paupers and appoint them men
>
> (43)

But the speaker decisively returns to an inspection of "The innards of this closet." More strongly than "Maybe so" above, "innards" underscores the speaker's dualistic sense of language and class; if Satin-Legs is being satirized, so is the addressee, whose ignorance is more broadly satirized in such later poems as "I love those little booths at Benvenuti's," "The Lovers of the Poor," and "Bronzeville Woman in a Red Hat."

The closet contains the gaudy accoutrements of such a dandy as Satin-Legs is or aspires to be; colors are "sarcastic," tailoring is "cocky," ties are "hysterical." Following this exposition of his tastes, two lines in a second brief aside hover between solemnity and humor:

> People are so in need, in need of help.
> People want so much that they do not know.
>
> (44)

True enough; but the idea is complicated by its placement, which suggests that Satin-Legs needs advice from a refined haberdasher. Creating himself "is all his sculpture and his art." However, after he enters the street, halfway through the poem, there is no further description of his appearance; instead, we see how things appear to him. Through the narrator, we experience his surroundings more vividly than he does. "He hears and does not hear" an alarm clock, children, a plane, voices, and the elevated train. "He sees and does not see" broken windows patched with newspaper, children in worn but decently patched clothes, and

> men estranged
> From music and from wonder and from joy

But far familiar with the guiding awe
Of foodlessness.

(45)

The music he hears is popular blues; the narrator notes the absence of strains by Saint-Saëns, Grieg, Tschaikovsky, Brahms, and questions whether he could love them if they were audible; one brings to music what one is:

The pasts of his ancestors lean against
Him. Crowd him. Fog out his identity.
Hundreds of hungers mingle with his own

(46)

From a movie, where he is reminded that "it is sin / For his eye to eat of" the heroine's "ivory and yellow," he proceeds toward the goal of all his efforts. In a line that tumbles anticlimactically from faint echoes of the courtly tradition to a place where main courses are served on meat platters, he "Squires his lady to dinner at Joe's Eats" (46). The "lady" is different every Sunday, but there are constant characteristics, most of them supplied by the overstated dress and makeup that Satin-Legs could be expected to admire. The ending of the poem subtly suggests that this is a kind of death-in-life. Remarking that the food is plentiful at Joe's Eats, the narrator interjects: "(The end is—isn't it?—all that really matters.)" The poem concludes with the achievement of Satin-Legs's objective:

*Her body is like new brown bread*
*Under the Woolworth mignonette.*
*Her body is a honey bowl*
*Whose waiting honey is deep and hot.*
*Her body is like summer earth,*
*Receptive, soft, and absolute . . .*

(47)

The slant rhymes undercut the directness of the statements, and draw attention to the "absolute" nature of receptive earth, where, in the old courtly usage, Satin-Legs Smith is about to die. Unlike the pool players in "We Real Cool," who "die soon" in many senses, Satin-Legs will survive; this Don Juan's version of Hell is to repeat this cycle indefinitely, with "little hope" of redemption. The ignorant white observer is presumed to accept this ending as all that really matters.

Brooks wrote this accomplished poem toward the end of her work on *A Street,* probably in response to Richard Wright's evaluation of the manuscript she had sent to Harper and Brothers; he praised her skill and genuineness, but added that "most volumes of poems usually have one really long fine poem around which shorter ones are added or grouped."[5]

*A Street* concludes with a sequence of twelve sonnets, "Gay Chaps at the Bar," which is close enough to what Wright was asking for. "Gay Chaps" is among the stronger poetic responses we have to World War II and deserves inclusion in anthologies devoted to that subject, along with "Negro Hero," the monologue of a Black mess attendant who took up a machine gun and used it effectively when his ship was attacked at Pearl Harbor, despite regulations of the strictly segregated Navy of that era, in which Black personnel did not handle firearms.

Brooks adopts several points of view throughout "Gay Chaps at the Bar"—omniscient, first person singular, first person plural—and her speakers demonstrate that Black soldiers suffered the same terrors and hopes as any other soldiers. But she is equally concerned to present the injustices of the Black warriors' situation, and reasonable doubts about what they might have been fighting for. The sonnets submit to convention in several ways, but Brooks uses slant rhyme in them more often than she had earlier; they extend the range of sonic choices and help to emphasize the paradox that these men were fighting for a country which in many ways refused to claim them.

Brooks's interest in traditional technical virtuosity reaches an apex in *Annie Allen,* the collection for which she received the 1950 Pulitzer Prize. The book is arranged in three sections: "Notes from the Childhood and the Girlhood," "The Anniad" (which includes the long poem of that title and two short pieces as "Appendix to The Anniad"), and "The Womanhood." The eleven short poems in the first section establish Annie as a daydreamer, resentful of restrictions imposed by her parents and society, hopeful of some idealized rescuer.

"The Anniad" is a technical tour de force: 301 lines in forty-three seven-line stanzas, employing thirty different rhyme schemes, a compelling meter (trochaic tetrameter catalectic), and a diction that is elaborate, dense, and compressed. Paraphrase is often difficult, and it is also difficult to resist being carried along on the sound waves, heedless of incomprehen-

sion. There is a definite narrative; some of the details are ob-
scure, though the poems in the first section of *Annie Allen*
provide background for the entrance to the poem:

> Think of sweet and chocolate,
> Left to folly or to fate,
> Whom the higher gods forgot,
> Whom the lower gods berate;
> Physical and underfed
> Fancying on the featherbed
> What was never and is not.
>
> What is ever and is not.
> Pretty tatters blue and red,
> Buxom berries beyond rot,
> Western clouds and quarter-stars,
> Fairy-sweet of old guitars
> Littering the little head
> Light upon the featherbed.
> . . . . . . . . . . . . . . . .
> Watching for the paladin
> Which no woman ever had,
> Paradisiacal and sad
> With a dimple in his chin
> And the mountains in the mind;
> Ruralist and rather bad,
> Cosmopolitan and kind.

(99–100)

The imperative of the first line, repeated six more times
throughout the poem, implies a reader or listener. This strategy,
not as fully developed as in "The Sundays of Satin-Legs Smith,"
still gives the speaker awareness of an audience, and an inclina-
tion to perform. In various tones—affectionate tolerance, adult
amusement, or sadness and anger—the speaker shows us the
impossible romantic aspirations that fill Annie's "light" and "lit-
tle" head. The paladin's virtues are impossibly contradictory;
that he is not a person but an imaginary being is obvious enough,
but emphasis is provided in the relative pronoun: "Which no
woman ever had."

As she grows older, a "man of tan" courts Annie, and his
qualities and her predilections arouse her:

What a hot theopathy
Roisters through her, gnaws the walls,
And consumes her where she falls
In her gilt humility.

(100)

They move to a "lowly room" which she tries to transform into a lovely love nest. There follows a passage which has been subject to more than one critical bias:

Doomer, though, crescendo-comes
Prophesying hecatombs.
Surrealist and cynical.
Garrulous and guttural.
Spits upon the silver leaves.
Denigrates the dainty eves
Dear dexterity achieves.

Names him. Tames him. Takes him off,
Throws to columns row on row.
Where he makes the rifles cough,
Stutter. Where the reveille
Is staccato majesty.
Then to marches. Then to know
The hunched hells across the sea.

Vaunting hands are now devoid.
Hieroglyphics of her eyes
Blink upon a paradise
Paralyzed and paranoid.
But idea and body too
Clamor "Skirmishes can do.
Then he will come back to you."

(101–2)

To the reader biased toward a belief in the occasional usefulness of paraphrase, "Doomer" presents difficulties; but the second of these three stanzas helps to identify it as a power suggestive of Uncle Sam, the draft, and the intrusion of war. Noisily, prophesying slaughter, speaking almost bestially, it attacks the little home-life Annie has, with difficulty, achieved. It calls "tan man's" name, inducts him into armed service, sets him to drill with guns, reveille, and marches, and ships him overseas. Annie, bereft, looks blankly on her altered life, but wants to believe he will not be killed.

Hortense J. Spillers, on the other hand, offers a feminist reading of the passage in "Gwendolyn the Terrible: Propositions on Eleven Poems": "As it turns out, he is not the hot lover 'theopathy' would make him out to be, but Annie denies it, fearing that to say so would be to evoke an already imminent betrayal: [quotes first and third of above stanzas]. This scene of 'ruin,' brought on by sexual impotence, gains a dimension of pathos because it anticipates the woman's ultimate loneliness, but this judgment is undercut by the caricature of the male."[6]

This may constitute misreading for the sake of an overriding theme, but Spillers characterizes, with justice and unintended irony, the poem's "specific end: to expose the sadness and comedy of self-delusion in an equally deluded world."[7]

Upon his return, troubled by conflicting recollections of horror and of power and by predilections imposed on him in a white-dominated society, "tan man" finds a mistress whose color is more honey than chocolate. The twenty-third stanza begins by repeating the first line of the poem and launches an account of Annie's life alone, from winter through the following fall; she attempts social gaiety, esoteric learning, the high life, and then tries to settle toward her husband's return. The speaker turns to "tan man" and chastises him:

> Hence from scenic bacchanal,
> Preshrunk and droll prodigal!
> Smallness that you had to spend,
> Spent. Wench, whiskey and tail-end
> Of your overseas disease
> Rot and rout you by degrees.

> (107)

At home again, he wastes away, and at last leaves the world, and the two women, who are contrasted harshly in successive stanzas:

> Leaves his mistress to dismiss
> Memories of his kick and kiss,
> Grant her lips another smear,
> Adjust the posies at her ear,
> Quaff an extra pint of beer,

Cross her legs upon the stool,
Slit her eyes and find her fool.

Leaves his devotee to bear
Weight of passing by his chair
And his tavern. Telephone
Hoists her stomach to the air.
Who is starch or who is stone
Washes coffee-cups and hair,
Sweeps, determines what to wear.

(108–9)

The second of these stanzas, the fortieth in the poem, reflects Annie's static helplessness; it is the only one with two rhymes instead of three. She becomes the victim of nightmares and a harried resignation, but the final stanza mutes the verbal flash:

Think of almost thoroughly
Derelict and dim and done.
Stroking swallows from the sweat.
Fingering faint violet.
Hugging old and Sunday sun.
Kissing in her kitchenette
The minuets of memory.

(109)

Though much of the satire in this poem seems to be directed at Annie's innocent romanticism and at the circumstances which have nourished it, the tone of the last stanza turns toward sympathy. Annie's pathetic stillness, the amatory participles describing small aimless gestures, are mitigated by the "almost" in the first line and by the iambic fullness of the last. Annie is now twenty-four, and has endured a series of disillusionments and bereavements. If she is to blame for some of them, so is the world.

Whereas the poems of the first two sections of *Annie Allen* speak of Annie in the third person, the third section opens with a sequence of five sonnets, "the children of the poor," in which the mother speaks in the first person. The sequence quickly ranges over several questions arising from the profoundly mixed blessings and curses of disadvantaged parenthood—how to protect children, teach them, prepare them for the fact of death. The fourth sonnet is a complex variation on the persistent American theme that art could not flourish in the period when people of ability were occupied with settling the country. Its punctilious adherence to Petrarchan conventions of structure momentarily withholds the sarcasm that bursts through in the sestet. It begins with two short sentences occupying exactly half a line: "First Fight. Then fiddle." The remainder of the octave describes the fiddling, fraught with "feathery sorcery" and "silks and honey," yet covertly rebellious:

> muzzle the note
> With hurting love; the music that they wrote
> Bewitch, bewilder.

The sestet returns to the fighting:

> But first to arms, to armor. Carry hate
> In front of you and harmony behind.
> Be deaf to music and to beauty blind.
> Win war. Rise bloody, maybe not too late
> For having first to civilize a space
> Wherein to play your violin with grace.
>
> (118)

Enjambment and shifting caesuras lend energy to much of the poem, but in the final couplet the energy is "civilized" to excessive tameness, reinforcing the "maybe" in the preceding line. The poem hovers between satire and direct polemic, both attacking and appropriating the notion behind it.

The inclusive vision that results in such a poem finds a variety of more single-minded expressions in the remainder of the book; this section of *Annie Allen* contains a few underachieved poems, but on the whole it is a sustained illustration of Brooks's many virtues. There are straight-forwardly affectionate sketches, satiric portrayals of Black characters and of ignorant or sheltered whites, seized moments in the manner of Emily Dickinson, love poems, polemical addresses. The book concludes with an untitled poem of considerable power, addressing "Men of careful turns, haters of forks in the road," and declaring the speaker's full humanity. Its characterization of establishment caution is icily exact:

> "What
> We are to hope is that intelligence
> Can sugar up our prejudice with politeness.

Politeness will take care of what needs caring.
For the line is there.
And has a meaning. So our fathers said—
And they were wise—we think—At any rate,
They were older than ourselves. And the report is
What's old is wise. At any rate, the line is
Long and electric. Lean beyond and nod.
Be sprightly. Wave. Extend your hand and teeth.
But never forget it stretches there beneath."

(140)

The poem ends with a chilling recognition that things will not soon change, especially if polite requests are depended on. The last line memorably combines determination and pessimism:

Let us combine. There are no magics or elves
Or timely godmothers to guide us. We are lost, must
Wizard a track through our own screaming weed.

(140)

If there are sharp divisions in Brooks's career, one of them comes at this point. As George Kent puts it, "For both whites and Blacks, Gwendolyn would from now on be tagged 'the first Negro to win a Pulitzer Prize,' and with that label would come the roles of spokeswoman and arbiter in the upper realms of her city's and her nation's cultural affairs" (Kent 102). We may be able to see whether Brooks's work changed noticeably after this, but the question is obfuscated by the churning assortment of critical responses to her new status. The problem of Brooks's place in a white literary establishment had in fact been thrown into relief by Paul Engle's August 26, 1945, review in the *Chicago Tribune*, of *A Street in Bronzeville*. Especially in the 1940s, trying to declare Brooks's transcendence of racial differences was to fall into the nearly inescapable trap of simultaneously affirming and denying the importance of race in her work: "Miss Brooks is the first Negro poet to write wholly out of a deep and imaginative talent, without relying on the fact of color to draw sympathy and interest. . . . The finest praise that can be given to the book is that it would be a superb volume of poetry in any year by a person of any color."[8]

There is no reason to doubt Engle's sincere admiration of Brooks's work or the honesty of his conviction that race should not be the issue that it is, but it is hard to get away from the hint of exclusiveness, the suggestion that Brooks is a fine poet, not regardless of her color, but despite it. In later years, increasing numbers of Black writers would question the extent of Brooks's commitment to Blackness; but there were confusing earlier questions by less militant writers. J. Saunders Redding, for example in a generally favorable review of *Annie Allen* in the *Saturday Review,* found references to intraracial color preferences too esoteric: "Who but another Negro can get the intimate feeling, the racially-particular acceptance and rejection, and the oblique bitterness of this? . . . The question is . . . whether it is not this penchant for coterie stuff—the special allusions, the highly special feeling derived from an even more special experience—that has brought poetry from the most highly regarded form of communication to the least regarded."9

Redding and Engle were saying remarkably similar things, and missing an important element of Brooks's art. She sought to maker her Black characters as rounded as poetry permits; this necessarily involved treating aspects of the Black experience which are imposed by white society. Through her first two books, her anger at injustice is comparatively restrained, but several poems in *The Bean Eaters* greatly increase the pressure of rage against the control of mature technique.

In one or two instances, the pressure overcomes control. "A Bronzeville Mother Loiters in Mississippi. Meanwhile, a Mississippi Mother Burns Bacon" is a daring response to the murder of Emmett Till, a Chicago teenager who was beaten and killed in 1955, during a visit to Mississippi. Brooks adopts the point of view of the young white woman who accused the youth of making sexual advances toward her. The sympathetic portrayal of the woman is striking; the husband, however, is a flat symbol of murderous white male oppression. He deserves that status, but in the poem he fails to earn it; instead of a plausible and therefore frightening and disgusting human, we have something too much like a cartoonist's drawing of Bull Connor. On the other hand, the woman's romantic vision of southern womanhood collapses convincingly before her growing knowledge of the Dark Villain's innocent youth:

Had *she* been worth the blood, the cramped cries, the little stuttering bravado,
    The gradual dulling of those Negro eyes,
    The sudden, overwhelming *little-boyness* in that barn?

                                        (336)

Flat portrayal of white characters is more effective in such satirical poems as "The Lovers of the Poor" and "Bronzeville Woman in a Red Hat," where reduction of characters to cartoons serves a dual function: it permits broad sarcasm and indulgence in playful diction, and it invites the white reader to feel excluded from the portrait until it is too late to escape inclusion in it. Both poems portray whites in the act of dehumanizing Blacks, though "Bronzeville Woman" is heavy-handed in this respect. A rich and overbearing woman has had to replace her Irish housemaid, and the agency has sent a Black woman, whom the employer calls "it" throughout the poem. The portrayal becomes more effective, if nearly sentimental, in contrasting the reactions of the employer and the employer's child, "Not wise enough to freeze or be afraid" (370).

The other major treatment of racial violence is "The Ballad of Rudolph Reed," a fiercely ironic narrative of the violence that follows a Black family's purchase of a house in a white neighborhood. Traditional ballad meter and language give the poem a strange atmosphere of remoteness:

> Rudolph Reed was oaken.
> His wife was oaken too.
> And his two good girls and his good little man
> Oakened as they grew.
>
> (376)

Contemporary racist brutality breaks with great force into such a setting, but the poem is strong enough to contain the atrocity of Reed's death, which comes as he is defending his house against rock-throwers who have wounded one of his daughters. The end of the poem is a powerful tableau of grief and strength:

> By the time he had hurt his fourth white man
> Rudolph Reed was dead.
> His neighbors gathered and kicked his corpse.
> "Nigger—" his neighbors said.
>
> Small Mabel whimpered all night long,
> For calling herself the cause.
> Her oak-eyed mother did no thing
> But change the bloody gauze.
>
> (378)

These somewhat extended poems concerned with racial injustice, white insensitivity, and violence, are scattered through an unusually varied collection of shorter poems, from the brilliant miniature "We Real Cool" to such humorous pieces as "On the Occasion of the Open-Air Formation of the Olde Tymer's Walking and Nature Club." It is this mixture, perhaps, more than the presence of the longer poems, which led some readers to regret the increased emphasis on social issues in *The Bean Eaters*—as if social issues were making their first appearance in Brooks's work. It is true that these longer poems are more explicit and reveal anger more openly than do most of Brooks's earlier poems, but most of the shorter poems aroused regret that Brooks could not be consistently polite.

The new poems in *Selected Poems* (1963) did little to change these impressions; "Riders to the Blood-Red Wrath," with its evocations of African majesty, the squalor of slave ships, and the commitment of Freedom Riders, both extends and rejects the polemical manner. Its content is occasion for celebration and exhortation, but in style it reverts to a density Brooks had not used at length since "The Anniad." It crams a racial history into a single consciousness, which ranges without transition between individual and collective recollection, and gathers momentum toward the polemical ending: "To fail, to flourish, to wither or to win. / We lurch, distribute, we extend, begin" (392).

On the other hand, a number of the new poems are brief character sketches; these presage the ambitious and thickly populated *In the Mecca* (1968), the book which has been said to initiate the third period in Brooks's career. If it does mark a significant shift in Brooks's way of writing and of thinking about what she is doing, this is more evident in the shorter poems that follow the title poem. "In the Mecca" is, at just over 800 lines, Brooks's most ambitious single poem; but in strategy and style it is an extension, not a repudiation, of her earlier excellences.

Epigraphs provide the information that the Mecca building, an extravagant apartment complex erected in Chicago in 1891, degenerated into an overcrowded tenement. Kenny J. Williams adds the important fact that the building was razed in 1952.[10]

In bare outline, the narrative is grim: Mrs. Sallie Smith returns to her apartment from hard domestic labor and begins to prepare dinner for her family of nine children; she notices suddenly that the youngest, Pepita, is missing. There is a fruitless search, police are called, and at last the child is found murdered.

The poem begins with a single line on a page by itself: "Now

the way of the Mecca was on this wise." It remains for the poet
to unfold the wrathful irony in this echo of Matthew 1:18 ("Now
the birth of Jesus Christ was on this wise"). The rest of the poem
is based in the present tense; Mrs. Smith encounters four neigh-
bors on the way to her apartment, and each is sketched briefly;
Alfred, an English teacher and untalented would-be writer,
comes to act as a choral commentator as the poem develops. The
children have their distinctive ways of trying to defend them-
selves against the reality of their lives; Melodie Mary, for exam-
ple, "like roaches, / and pities the gray rat." She is dimly aware
of headlines announcing strife and suffering in China, but

> What if they drop like the tumbling tears
> of the old and intelligent sky?
> Where are the frantic bulletins
> when other importances die?
> Trapped in his privacy of pain
> the worried rat expires,
> and smashed in the grind of a rapid heel
> last night's roaches lie.
>
> (412)

When the family goes in search of Pepita, they inquire of
several neighbors, each of whom is given several lines of charac-
terization. Great-great Gram, who recalls her childhood in slav-
ery, reverts to childhood as she recalls popping little creatures
that "creebled" in the dirt of the cabin floor, thus inverting
Melodie Mary's treatment of the same subject. Aunt Dill, revel-
ing in her report of a child's rape and murder the previous week,
is a gruesome parody of unfeeling self-satisfaction.

Toward the end of this section, there are three portraits with-
out reference to Pepita or her whereabouts. The first, concerning
Don Lee, is similar to several other poems Brooks has written
about notable Blacks; even in the context of this poem, it appears
to portray the poet and activist now named Haki R. Madhubuti.
Along with Alfred's references to Léopold Sédar Senghor, "Poet,
and muller, and President of Senegal," this constitutes unobtru-
sive anachronism. "In the Mecca" contains few references which
can be dated precisely, but some of them, such as Senghor's
presidency of Senegal (1960–1980), convey the impression that
the Mecca existed in the 1960s. This effect is only slightly compli-
cated for the reader in possession of such arcana as the year of its
demolition; the building itself may have been infamous, but its

destruction did not significantly change the lives with which the poem is concerned. Brooks's Mecca outlives its namesake and becomes a perceptible metaphor as well as a symbol.

The increasing desperation of the search for Pepita is reflected in the rapidity with which new characters are introduced from this point on. In the whole poem, over fifty people are mentioned by name or characteristic label; more than half of them appear in the last 200 lines. Because this large cast moves in quickly, sometimes at the rate of four people per line, there is room near the end of the poem for four strophes of between a dozen and two dozen lines each, the first two introducing new characters, the third and fourth returning to Aunt Dill and Alfred, respectively. The two new characters reinforce the balanced vision of the whole poem: Way-out Morgan is collecting guns, imagining "Death-to-the-Hordes-of-the-White-Men!" (430); Marian is ironing, wishing for some disaster to befall her so she may be noticeable. Absorbed in their visions, they have no time to wonder where Pepita is. Aunt Dill reappears in a gooey cloud of self-satisfaction; the narrator calls her

> the kind of woman you
> peek at in passing and thank your God or zodiac you
> may never have to know

(432)

In this welter of selfishness, Alfred makes a final appearance, allowing Brooks a sly reference to the temporal limbo in which she has erected this cosmos:

> I hate it.
> Yet, murmurs Alfred—
> who is lean at the balcony, leaning—
> something, something in Mecca
> continues to call! Substanceless; yet like mountains,
> like rivers and oceans too; and like trees
> with wind whistling through them. And steadily
> an essential sanity, black and electric,
> builds to a reportage and redemption.
>     A hot estrangement
>     A material collapse
> that is Construction.

(433)

The next strophe begins with two lines that look back toward this reverie, and forward to the discovery of Pepita's body:

> Hateful things sometimes befall the hateful
> but the hateful are not rendered lovable thereby.
> The murder of Pepita
> looks at the Law unlovably.
>
> (433)

Beneath Jamaican Edward's bed lies the body of Pepita, who "never learned that black is not beloved." Remembering a rhyme the child once made with "rose," her mother decides to "try for roses." The final four lines of the poem revert to what only Jamaican Edward could have seen, but the powerful image of horror is rendered in a style that can only be the narrator's:

> She whose little stomach fought the world had
> wriggled, like a robin!
> Odd were the little wrigglings
> and the chopped chirpings oddly rising.
>
> (433)

"In the Mecca" is a large and largely successful poem, a benchmark in Brooks's career. The poem draws its strength both from her increasing interest in the possibilities for polemic in poetry and from her broad and deep familiarity with poetry's technical resources. Except in scope and achievement, it is not a radical departure from the work which preceded it. However, it was completed during a time of upheaval in Brooks's sense of herself as a poet, and the shorter poems collected with it are evidence of a major division in Brooks's career.

Much has already been made of the external forces that wrought important changes in Brooks's thinking about her life and work. At the Fisk University Writers' Conference in 1967, she encountered, more forcibly than she had before, the power of young Black writers committed to making a literature for Black people, and to liberating themselves and their people from white oppression. The experience energized her in new ways. She also worked briefly with the Blackstone Rangers, a street gang whose younger mentors, especially Walter Bradford and Don L. Lee, provided encouragement as she sought her "newish voice"[11] (Kent 180ff.).

"After Mecca" is a coherent sequence of separate poems; it

gathers force by proceeding from individual portraits, through two "public occasion" poems and the three-part "Blackstone Rangers," to "The Sermon on the Warpland" and "The Second Sermon on the Warpland." As the field of vision expands from one poem to the next, the formal scope extends from brief and nearly metrical to more widely various free verse lines. The direction, however, remains characteristically Brooksian, as in this conclusion to "The Leaders," the second part of "The Blackstone Rangers":

> The Blackstone bitter bureaus
> (bureaucracy is footloose) edit, fuse
> unfashionable damnations and descent;
> and exulting, monstrous hand on monstrous hand,
> construct, strangely, a monstrous pearl or grace.

(448)

But along with certainty that she had much to learn from younger Black writers, there came a desire to reach audiences unaccustomed to hearing or reading poetry. This arose partly from increasing doubt about dependence on the Eurocentric tradition she had so thoroughly commanded for most of her career; at this point, the language problem referred to early in this essay becomes extremely difficult, despite Anglo-American's flexibility and relative openness to other traditions. With a few notable exceptions such as "We Real Cool," Brooks's poetry has depended not only on fresh and unusual language, but on the varying degrees of surface difficulty that such wordplay often creates. Her attempts at a more accessible style have sometimes resulted in oversimplified moralizing and in indecision about which poems or versions of poems to reprint.

Of the roughly fifty poems Brooks published between 1968 and 1987, a few have appeared only in periodicals, and only nineteen are collected in *Blacks*. A white reader might be tempted to think that some of this indecision arises from Brooks's having accepted, in 1985, her second major accolade from the literary establishment, when she became Poetry Consultant to the Library of Congress; but in interviews over the past twenty years, and in her tireless work for Black writers during her tenure at the Library, she has demonstrated unwavering commitment to the cause of freedom for oppressed people.

Brooks's wavering over certain poems is evidence of crisis, but it is important to remember that crisis is usually much more rewarding for artists than for politicians. In adjusting her accustomed tools to her new tasks, she has taken some directions which she seems later to have reconsidered, but occasional frustrations have not sent her back to techniques in which she has long been adept. Her most recent collection, *Gottschalk and the Grande Tarantelle* (Chicago: The David Company, 1988), is cause for gratitude that she has not retreated from trying to perfect her new ways of working.

This handsome chapbook contains only four poems, but one of them is "Winnie," some 375 lines spoken by Winnie Mandela. The character is, of course, a literary creation, partaking of what Brooks knows of Mrs. Mandela, and of what she knows of herself and the world. There are passages where one might wish that more memorable language has been found for the urgent messages:

> we are all vulnerable—
> the midget, the Mighty,
> the richest, the poor.
>
> (18)

But Brooks has hold of something here. In her early work, personal history (not necessarily her own) was a dependable provider of material. She began to merge social and political history with that strain in poems like "The Ballad of Rudolph Reed" and "A Bronzeville Mother Loiters," and perfected that merging in "In the Mecca." Now, she is after larger historical scope and appears to be on the brink of finding the means to achieve it without surrendering particularity. As she has Winnie Mandela say,

> This is the time for Big Poems,
> roaring up out of sleaze,
> poems from ice, from vomit, and from tainted blood.
>
> (19)

## NOTES

1. Maria K. Mootry and Gary Smith, "The Poet-Militant and Foreshadowing of a Black Mystique: Poems in the Second Period of Gwendolyn Brooks," *A Life Distilled: Gwendolyn Brooks, Her Poetry and Fiction* (University of Illinois Press, 1987), p. 71 and p. 80n. Hereafter referred to as Mootry and Smith.

2. *Blacks* (Chicago: The David Company, 1987). Page references following quotations are to this volume unless otherwise specified.

3. George Kent, *A Life of Gwendolyn Brooks* (University Press of Kentucky, 1990). Hereafter referred to as Kent.

4. Kent, p. 66.

5. Kent, p. 63.

6. Mootry and Smith, p. 230.

7. Ibid., p. 231.

8. Quoted in Kent, pp. 74–75.

9. Ibid., p. 79.

10. Mootry and Smith, p. 60.

11. Kent, pg. 180ff.

ANGELA JACKSON

# In Memoriam: Gwendolyn Brooks

Who will herald the passage of a Poet among poets but a myriad of poets singing with gifted tongues? Who will pick up pens and go against the swords and slay them in a kind kill as she did? Who will study war no more but the blessings of the spirit evoked in the world as did Gwendolyn Brooks, whose word was poetry itself and whose being was African and American and mighty?

Gwendolyn Brooks, poet, novelist, memoirist, poet laureate, was the author of more than twenty volumes of poetry, among them *Blacks, In Birmingham, Annie Allen, A Street in Bronzeville, Selected Poems, The Near Johannesburg Boy and Other Poems;* author of the novel *Maud Martha;* memoirs *Reports from Part One* and *Two;* and children's books *The Tiger Who Wore White Gloves, Aloneness,* and *Children Coming Home.* Brooks was the first African American to be awarded a Pulitzer Prize, in any literary genre; she served as poetry consultant to the Library of Congress (the U.S. poet laureate) in 1985–86 and as Illinois poet laureate from 1968 to 2000. In 1994 she was awarded the Medal of Art by President William Jefferson Clinton. She was the recipient of the Frost Medal from the Poetry Society of America and was awarded ninety honorary degrees.

Gwendolyn Brooks, born in Topeka, Kansas, was the devoted daughter of David and Keziah Brooks; the family moved to Chicago shortly after her birth. She was the loving wife of the late Henry Blakely, poet and author of *Windy Place,* and mother of Henry and Nora Blakely, digital artist, and playwright and founder/ director of Chocolate Chips Theater Company, respectively.

Were there no honors garlanding her name, Gwendolyn Brooks's work would remain as evidence of a gifted spirit and a unique presence that amplified us all. And her work would ennoble us as it does now as we honor her still. Yet her rather early assumption into literary legend status, at the age of thirty-two, as a result of the groundbreaking Pulitzer, did not cloister her from the injuries inflicted by racism, sexism, colorism, classism, or humankind's personal injuries. Nor save her from the foibles and faults of humanity

From *Callaloo* 23, no. 4 © 2000, Johns Hopkins University Press.

as she herself cautioned in a salute to Lerone Bennett and Hoyt Fuller; elevating certain others to godhood must not be our way of alleviating ourselves of responsibility for ourselves and each other. She celebrated the wondrous complexity of humanity, and she exalted us.

Perhaps one of her sweetest poems, a lyric with a lovely lilt, the upturned cry in mid-poem sounding the spirituals, concludes *Blacks*.

Infirm

Everybody here
is infirm.

Everybody here is infirm.
Oh. Mend me. Mend me. Lord.

Today I
say to them

say to them
say to them, Lord:

look! I am beautiful, beautiful with
my wing that is wounded
my eye that is bonded
or my car not funded
or my walk all a wobble.
I'm enough to be beautiful.

You are
beautiful too.

The intense humanism of Gwendolyn Brooks's identity as poet and person is distilled into these few lines. Direct, graceful, and vivid in their depiction of a humanity of imperfection and blessedness.

The *Chicago Sun-Times* described Gwendolyn Brooks as opposed to force or agitation, which may belie her militancy and support for African and African-American freedom and well-being and undying support for full equality among Americans. She cared that the Mrs. Smalls, Malcolm Littles, Xs, Martin Luther Kings, and "the children of the poor" all flourish in a land that learns to love its own diversity, its heterogeneity. Of racists and racism she said, "They do not love us." Her understatement, as often was the case, spoke volumes that could fill the Report of the Kerner Commission, the governor who first installed her as poet laureate of Illinois.

The veiled civility of some of her early work gave way to a stark simplicity that nevertheless lent to itself an air of mystery. Her work itself continued to be characterized by oxymorons, replete with vital, complementary contradictions. Whether richly ornamented or deceptively plain speech, Brooks's trademark is the nobility of language that signals great poetry. The nobility of her language ennobles her readers as well. We are enchanted by the sound and deep sense of it. Illuminated by its epiphanies. Fired by its sweet or dry passion. And clarified by its detached intellectuality.

THE SIGHT OF HORIZON

We seek no clue of green
We seek a garden; trees,
The light, the cry,
The conscience of the grass
In this most social of all
Centuries
We seek informal sun,
A harvest of hurrah.
We seek our center and our
Radius
Profound redemption
And America

Heightened language, though spare, is meaning-rich. "The conscience of the grass" offers a subtle, fluid commentary on humanity. Do we have the clear conscience of grass? We think of Whitman's *Leaves of Grass,* but not too much. Her most economical poems resonate as richly as the ornate, lavish "Sundays of Satin Legs Smith":

Inamoratas, with an approbation,
Bestowed his title. Blessed his inclination

He wakes, unwinds, elaborately: a cat
Tawny, reluctant, royal. He is fat
And fine this morning. Definite. Reimbursed.

He waits a moment, he designs his reign,
That no performance may be plain or vain.
Then rises in a clear delirium.

. . . . . . . . . . . . . . . . . . . . . . . . .

     Here are hats
Like bright umbrellas and hysterical ties
Like narrow banners for some gathering war.


People are so in need, in need of help.
People want so much that they do not know.


While much of her earlier work has been favorably compared to Emily Dickinson, Gwendolyn Brooks's work continued to move out of the private, privileged realm inhabited by Dickinson and to resound in the public arena. Gwendolyn Brooks herself was an amazing amalgam of the sublime artiste and the people's poet. In this sense she was an essentially African-American poet. In the footsteps of the poets of the Harlem Renaissance (most notably Langston Hughes) Gwen's poetry depicted the Black poor and working class in full humanity with nuances of the heroic, the tragic, and the comic. In the tradition of the Moderns she firmly eschewed any easy sentimentality or the slightest semblance thereof. Hers was the sharp, clear eye. Yet her rhythms as sensuous and intelligent as jazz, Black Classical Music, our noble sound. Just as her friend the late critic George Kent said, Gwendolyn Brooks achieved universality by being faithful to the specific. And her specific was not only her private experience but the experiences of African America. And as Wynton Marsalis described Black Classical Music—hers was "the nobility of the race."

The intense, ornamented language of the epic mystery *In the Mecca* gathers inside itself a clamorous, insulted populace, tenants of a large and legendary apartment building on the Southside, and marked a milestone for Gwendolyn. Rekindled by the poets of the 1960s, burned to the core in her baptism by the fires of the 1960s, after *In the Mecca* all but the essentials of her voice remained. She stripped herself down to the most necessary elements in language— eschewing the artifice of forms in which she had excelled. Her sonnets of Annie Allen are some of the greatest sonnets of the twentieth or any other century.

The opening lines of *In the Mecca* inform us that Gwendolyn Brooks has taken on the role of tribal storyteller, griot:

Now the way of the Mecca was on this wise.

Sit where the light corrupts your face.
Mics Van der Rohe retires from grace.
And the fair fable falls.

She establishes a fireside, campfire, homefire, a setting around which many are gathered—or only one reader and the poet. We sit inside a circle of intimate events and diverse characters that are heroic and tragic. She displays an arsenal of weapons that redeem memory and authenticity at the heart of our experience. Irony is a weapon, and Gwendolyn Brooks wielded it well, along with a keen sense of the absurd, dispassionate passion, and a dry, stern empathy and compassion. In another sense *In the Mecca* is a collage of figures, some distorted, in vivid and varying colors, its composition comparable to that of her peer, the great Romare Bearden. In any case it is tribal art, and with it Gwendolyn Brooks established herself as chief griot of the tribe of African America.

Gwendolyn Brooks served as Illinois poet laureate from 1968 to 2000, thirty-two years in which she gave significance and vitality to what had been initially an honorary title that came with no salary because her duties were expected to be minimal. It would seem that Gwendolyn Brooks created a role model of the poet laureate as vigorous advocate for the expressions of young people and as bearer of poetry to the people in all walks of life. She established a yearly Young Poets Poet Laureate contest for elementary and high school students and funded it out of pocket. It is difficult to know just how extensive Gwen's financial support of young people was because giving was a habit of hers. She supported the endeavors of any number of students and extended her gift giving to adult poets as well. She herself said that her husband had chided her that she would have been a millionaire if not for her generosity.

I think a wellspring of her generosity was her own humanistic vision and the prosperity of the spirit that art and religion render to believers, practitioners, acolytes. It also may be sprung from Miss Brooks's own regality, an appreciation of noblesse oblige, an acknowledgment that she knew herself to be a gifted person who worked attentively at her craft and was rewarded with not only the expansion of her gift but the highest reward for an artist—great work, which was in turn appreciated as great work by many. Many are called, but few are chosen. One chosen, Gwendolyn Brooks chose others, especially young people in need. Offering monetary support to many and the gift of individual attention, responsiveness, and criticism to countless writers and students, hopefuls, and admirers who sent her poems and letters. At her annual Young Poets Poet Laureate Awards ceremonies she honored students of all colors and backgrounds; she encouraged each of them with a special word. For adult poets she established the Significant Illinois Poet Award, and on her seventieth birthday, in 1987, honored seventy of her fellow Illinois poets. She continued these awards as well.

Gwendolyn Brooks herself told the story of how, when she received news of her Pulitzer, the lights were off in the Blakely household. The memory of early financial difficulties is for many a cause for tightfistedness. For Gwen it was the incentive for public generosity, an incentive to others to give.

I am sure that Gwendolyn Brooks knew she was embraced by many because of her achievements who might just as easily have looked down on her because of her color. The problem of intra-racial "racism" is a recurring theme in her work. And she attacked the issue with forthrightness and a vengeance. And, in the case of "The Lives of Lincoln West," with kindness and humor. Gwen Brooks's words were balm to feelings of loneliness, rejection, and low self-esteem, especially in work addressed to children: *Bronzeville Boys and Girls, Aloneness, The Tiger Who Wore White Gloves,* and *Children Coming Home.*

Unostentatious in dress, her easy, elegant simplicity drew her audience to the gifts she gave from the inside out; a far cry from this age of celebrity, glittering, bodacious "packages," empty inside. Her style was not confined to literary fashion. She was not a confessional poet in the heyday of the confessionals. Nor was she a new Black revolutionary poet, but an avid admirer of them. She did not return to formal poetry as it became fashionable again, to re-prove her mastery and artistic supremacy. Her association with words remained constant. She, as she described Malcolm X in a one-word opening line, was "Original." She put words together that did not belong together until her, and their insight gained new meaning by not only the surprise of juxtaposition but the rightness of it. There is always a tension between words and sounds in Gwen's lines, alliterative and assonant; there is an energy. Her hallmark was not only the heightened language of all good poetry but her own distinguished use of language, created distinguished language, making use of African-American idiom yet distinctly "Gwendolynian." We will miss her precise genius.

Gwendolyn Brooks is described mainly as a poet, yet she was a significant fictionist as well. Her novel, *Maud Martha,* is a minor classic, a lovely perennial with deeply rooted insights into the interior and daily life of a young African-American woman growing into early adulthood. It stands alongside Cyrus Colter's also underappreciated classic *The Beach Umbrella and Other Stories* in its empathetic depiction of the unseen and unpublicized frustrated beauty and ambitions of everyday and middle-class Black people. As a traditional novel, it presages the early work of Toni Morrison and in its own time was a companion voice to the openly militant voice of Lorraine Hansberry. Gwendolyn Brooks's voice reflected African-American double consciousness, and *Maud Martha* is the backstory to Gwen's own transformation from alert, life-studious, self-conscious, and optimistic Negro to the same wise, ironic, woman in a fiercer, more confident Blackness.

She said:

> This is the urgency: Live!
> And have your blooming in the noise of the whirlwind.

And we fell in love with her and followed her command. She directed us to be brave, but she had always been brave. Her work always exhibited bravery of topics, oft forbidden topics for poetry, from abortion in "The Mother" to bodily affliction in "Hunchback Girl: She Thinks of Heaven" to the lecherous preacher in "Obituary for a Living Lady" to the deadly perils of interracial romance in "Ballad of Pearlie May Lee," all from *A Street in Bronzeville,* her first book, through *The Bean Eaters* and *Selected Poems.* "We Real Cool" was banned by a school district. Yet her witness was ostensibly uncensored; she pressed through the veil of civility, social conventions.

Out of the 1967 Fisk University Writers Conference and Gwen Brooks Writers Workshop with the Blackstones Rangers (with Walter Bradford) developed a circle of young revolutionary Black poets who would form the first ranks of the magic circle that enjoyed intimacy with and a loyalty to Gwendolyn Brooks. They met regularly at Gwen and Henry's—Haki Madhubuti, Carolyn Rodgers, Sharon Scott, Willie Keoropetse Kgotsitsile, Sterling Plumpp; add to these Sonia Sanchez, Mari Evans, Nikki Giovanni, Amiri Baraka; and so many others, the best and brightest of the Black Arts Movement, Lerone Bennett, Val and Francis Ward, Hoyt W. Fuller, Ann Smith, Jeff Donaldson, Abena Joan Brown, Roy Lewis, and her first independent Black publisher, Dudley Randall of Broadside Press, who preceded her in death by only a few months. Margaret Burroughs remained her oldest friend and comrade from their days together in the Inez Starks Boulton Writers Workshop with Richard Wright and Margaret Walker, among others, at the Southside Community Arts Center in the 1930s. It was Margaret Burroughs, artist and poet, who "introduced" Gwendolyn to her future husband and fellow poet, Henry Blakely.

A favorite subject of Gwen's poetry is her literary and "adopted" son Haki Madhubuti, who first appeared as Don L. Lee in *In the Mecca*, again in *Family Pictures* in "To Don at Salaam," and finally in *The Near Johannesburg Boy and Other Poems* as "The Good Man" whom she counseled, "In the time of detachment, in the time of cold, in this time / tutor our difficult sunlight." Their relationship remains the stuff of literary legend, reciprocal and encouraging. He and Walter Bradford enjoyed some of the deep maternal feeling and care that Brooks gave to her children Henry and Nora, who was her mainstay, legacy, bodyguard, representative, ombudsman, administrator, friend, confidante, and devoted daughter. Her children, especially Nora and Henry Blakely, she encouraged in "Speech to the Young, Speech to the Progress Toward" to "Live not for the battles won, / Live not for the end-of-the-song. / Live in the along."

Within days of being diagnosed with cancer, her body disabled by a sudden stroke, Gwendolyn Brooks lay in her own bed in her own home surrounded by family and friends. They read to her. She leaves this question, this eloquent challenge, from *In the Mecca*, hanging in the air—"What else is there to say but everything?" But she herself said so much and said it so exquisitely that her words still make us ache, nourish, strengthen, embolden us, and urge us forward into a new century.

> In the wild weed
> She is a citizen,
> And is a moment of highest quality, admirable.

> It is lonesome, yes. For we are the last of the loud.
> Nevertheless, live.

> Conduct your blooming in the noise and whip of the
>         Whirlwind.

# Selected Bibliography

## Works by Gwendolyn Brooks

### Poetry
*A Street in Bronzeville*. New York: Harper and Brothers, 1945.
*Annie Allen*. New York: Harper and Brothers, 1949.
*Bronzeville Boys and Girls*. New York: Harper and Brothers, 1956.
*The Bean Eaters*. New York: Harper and Row, 1960.
*Selected Poems*. New York: Harper and Row, 1963.
*In the Mecca*. New York: Harper and Row, 1968.
*Riot*. Detroit: Broadside Press, 1969.
*Aloneness*. Detroit: Broadside Press, 1971.
*Family Pictures*. Detroit: Broadside Press, 1970.
*The World of Gwendolyn Brooks*. New York: Harper and Row, 1971.
*The Tiger Who Wore White Gloves, or What You Really Are, You Really Are.* Chicago: Third World Press, 1974.
*Beckonings*. Chicago: Third World Press, 1975.
*Primer for Blacks*. Chicago: Brooks Press, 1980.
*To Disembark*. Chicago: Third World Press, 1981.
*Mayor Harold Washington and Chicago, the I Will City*. Chicago: Brooks Press, 1983.
*Very Young Poets*. Chicago: Brooks Press, 1983.
*Blacks*. Chicago: The David Company, 1987.
*Gottschalk and the Grande Tarantelle*. Chicago: The David Company, 1988.
*Winnie*. Chicago: The David Company, 1988.
*Children Coming Home*. Chicago: The David Company, 1991.

### Prose
*Maud Martha*. New York: Harper and Brothers, 1953. (Novel)
*Report from Part One*. Detroit: Broadside Press, 1975. (Autobiography)

### Other Publications
"Poets Who Are Negroes." *Phylon* 2 (December 1950): 312.
"Why Negro Women Leave Home." *Negro Digest,* March 1951, pp. 26–28.
"Foreword," *New Negro Poets: USA*. Ed. Langston Hughes. Bloomington: Indiana University Press, 1964.
"We're the Only Colored People Here." *The Best Short Stories by Negro Writers: An Anthology from 1899 to the Present*. Ed. Langston Hughes. Boston: Little, Brown, 1967.
*A Broadside Treasury*. Detroit: Broadside Press, 1971.
*Jump Bad: A New Chicago Anthology*. Detroit: Broadside Press, 1971.
"Introduction." *The Poetry of Black America: Anthology of the Twentieth Century*. Ed. Arnold Adoff. New York: Harper and Row, 1973.

*A Capsule Course in Black Poetry Writing.* Ed. with Keorapetse Kgositile, Haki R. Madhubuti, and Dudley Randall. Detroit: Broadside Press, 1975.

## Works about the Author

Brown, Patricia L., Don L. Lee, and Francis Ward, eds. *To Gwen, with Love.* Chicago: Johnson, 1971.

*Colorado Review* (Special Issue) n. s. 16, no. 1 (Spring/Summer 1989).

Kent, George E. *A Life of Gwendolyn Brooks.* Lexington: University Press of Kentucky, 1990.

Kufrin, Joan. "Gwendolyn Brooks." In *Uncommon Women,* 35–51. Piscataway, N.J.: New Century Publishers, 1981.

Loff, Jon N. "Gwendolyn Brooks: A Bibliography." *College Language Association Journal* 17 (September 1973): 21–32.

Madhubuti, Haki R., ed. *Say That the River Turns: The Impact of Gwendolyn Brooks.* Chicago: Third World Press, 1987.

Melhem, D. H. *Gwendolyn Brooks: Poetry and the Heroic Voice.* Lexington: University Press of Kentucky, 1987.

———. "Gwendolyn Brooks: Humanism and Heroism." In *Heroism in the New Black Poetry: Interviews and Interviews,* 11–38. Lexington: University Press of Kentucky, 1990.

Mootry, Maria K., and Gary Smith. *A Life Distilled: Gwendolyn Brooks, Her Poetry and Fiction.* Urbana: University of Illinois Press, 1987.

Shaw, Harry B. *Gwendolyn Brooks.* Boston: Twayne, 1980.

Wright, Stephen Caldwell. *The Chicago Collective: Poems for and Inspired by Gwendolyn Brooks.* Sanford, Florida: Christopherr-Burghardt, 1990.